GERSHWIN
IN HIS TIME

GERSHWIN IN HIS TIME

A BIOGRAPHICAL SCRAPBOOK, 1919-1937

Edited, with an Introduction, by
Gregory R. Suriano

Foreword by
Marvin Hamlisch

GRAMERCY BOOKS

New York

This edition is published by Gramercy Books,
a division of Random House Value Publishing, Inc.,
201 East 50th Street, New York, New York 10022.

Gramercy Books® and design are registered trademarks of
Random House Value Publishing, Inc.

Random House
New York • Toronto • London • Sydney • Auckland
http://www.randomhouse.com/

Printed and bound in Singapore

Library of Congress Cataloging-in-Publication Data
Gershwin in his time: a biographical scrapbook, 1919–1937/
edited, with an introduction, by Gregory R. Suriano;
foreword by Marvin Hamlisch.
p.   cm.
Includes index.
ISBN 0-517-20198-4
1. Gershwin, George, 1898-1937—Criticism and interpretation.
I. Suriano, Gregory R., 1951–
ML410.G288G48   1998
780′.92—dc21   98-3055   CIP
MN

8 7 6 5 4 3 2 1

Book design by Gregory R. Suriano
Electronic publishing consultant: Frank J. Finamore

*Permissions, photo credits, and additional copyright information appear
on pages 133 and 134.*

CONTENTS

ACKNOWLEDGMENTS

The editor wishes to acknowledge and thank all those who helped to assemble the photographs and art, granted reprint permissions for the text, and otherwise aided in the research for this book: Sam Daniel, at the Library of Congress Prints and Photographs Division, and Raymond White, at the Music Division; Marty Jacobs and Marguerite Lavin, at the Museum of the City of New York; Mary Corliss and Terry Geesken, at the Museum of Modern Art Film Stills Archive; Annette Marotta, Vivian González, and the librarians at the Billy Rose Theatre Collection of the New York Public Library for the Performing Arts; consummate sheet music collector and Gershwin enthusiast Sandy Marrone; Archive Photos; Rose Cervino, at the New York Times; Theresa Lynch, at the Putnam Publishing Group; Janet Glass, at Eric Glass, Ltd.; Lisa Diaz, at The Condé Nast Publications; Natira McDermott, at Brandt & Brandt Literary Agents; Debra Cohen, at Time, Inc.; and Carole A. Bell, at the Library of Congress U.S. Copyright Office. Acknowledgment of the debt owed to previous Gershwin biographers is also gratefully given: for their brilliant and affectionate work, innumerable readers and music lovers must thank Isaac Goldberg, Merle Armitage, David Ewen, Charles Schwartz, Deena Rosenberg, Hollis Alpert, Robert Kimball, Alfred Simon, Lawrence D. Stewart, Edward Jablonski (the dean of them all), and of course, Ira Gershwin. Foremost thanks is extended to Marvin Hamlisch, for his warm and wonderful tone-setting Foreword.

This book is dedicated to my son Daniel, an eager, curious, and music-loving little boy.

FOREWORD

Marvin Hamlisch

Even with both my beloved parents deceased, I can still hear the voice of my father—looking down at me from some celestial plane, with the music of Mozart in the background—saying, "What's the matter, Marvin? By the time Gershwin was your age, he was gone. And, he'd written a concerto."

Gershwin died at the age of thirty-eight. But by then, he had a long list of hit songs, hit shows, Hollywood pictures, a concerto, a rhapsody, and the first great American opera. He was, it seems, in a very big hurry.

Did he think that he might die young, and therefore he set about to compose all of his music as fast as possible?

No, I think Gershwin was in a hurry because everyone was in a hurry. New, syncopated rhythms, "fascinating rhythms," seemed to beckon him. Their pulse was his pulse.

The stock market may have died in the late 1920s, but the Jazz Age had not. Gershwin continued to fuse its optimistic point of view, its pulse, its charm, with his gift for melodies, some haunting, some humorous, some serious.

As a composer myself, I can just imagine the many musical sides of Gershwin doing battle. How could he reconcile his serious musical abilities with popular tastes? How could he sit down and write an opera if his songs were being performed at the *Scandals*? The answer was remarkably simple: he'd do it all!

And that's probably why he was in such a rush.

Gershwin's immigrant parents had great respect for European music and traditions. Brought up in this environment, Gershwin had a love for "serious" music that was intense, and his musical knowledge was extensive. He loved all kinds of music, and did not forsake his popular fare when creating his immortal works. Indeed, Gershwin was writing *Rhapsody in Blue* in the same month his show *Sweet Little Devil* opened in New York; *An American in Paris* was completed in the same year that "The Man I Love" achieved its wide popularity.

I believe that Gershwin the songwriter fully realized his ambition of fusing his popular style with the classical compositional style. In other words, he took the European tradition bequeathed to all composers and poured his American, jazzy soul into it. This unique fusion is simply called: Gershwin.

My piano teacher once told me that talent is like a well-water pump. The more you use it, the colder

Sweet Little Devil, *1924, sheet music.*

and fresher the water will be as it surfaces.

Gershwin went to the well every day. Every hour. Every minute. All he ever seemed to want to do was be at a piano.

Groucho Marx once threw an "A" party for the who's who of Hollywood. Everyone was invited. *Except* George Gershwin. The night before the party, George phoned Groucho.

"Groucho," George began, "you probably made a mistake. I was visiting Ira today, and he asked me if I was going to your party. I told him I hadn't received the invitation. So, what gives?"

Groucho, slowly, began his explanation. "Look, George, I didn't invite you."

George became furious. "Why not?" he yelled.

"Well, let's face it. Every time anyone invites you to a party, you come in, drop your coat, run to the piano, and play for four hours. Well, I'm not going to do that. I'm not gonna be one of those people who takes advantage of you. As far as I'm concerned, it's better if I just don't invite you."

The next day, Groucho's party began at 8:00 p.m. George crashed the party at 8:15, and played till around 1:00 a.m. This was exactly what Groucho had wanted all along.

Years ago, I was a guest on a television show. The host thought it would be nice to invite my mother on the show. Since she had never been on TV, he decided to ask her an easy question.

"So, Mrs. Hamlisch, tell me, who's your favorite composer?"

Without any hesitation, my mother looked at me, smiled, turned to the host, and said, "George Gershwin."

From me, she gets no argument.

Marvin Hamlisch has written the music for the Broadway shows A Chorus Line *and* They're Playing Our Song *and the motion picture* The Way We Were. *He conducts and performs as soloist with major orchestras worldwide, and he is music director for both the Baltimore and the Pittsburgh Symphony Pops orchestras. Mr. Hamlisch is a graduate of the Juilliard School of Music.*

A Damsel in Distress, *1937, movie theater ad.*

INTRODUCTION

Gregory R. Suriano

This is a book about the tragically short creative career of arguably America's greatest composer.

Many superb biographies of George Gershwin have appeared in the years since his untimely death in 1937, but not until now has there been an opportunity to experience the Gershwin era from virtually the composer's own perspective. *Gershwin in His Time* is essentially a "scrapbook" of articles, reviews, photographs, sheet music, posters, and other ephemera, such as Gershwin himself might have kept. There are no posthumous reassessments or academic critiques. This journey through Gershwin's career chronicles the contemporary reactions to his works, from "Swanee" of 1919 to his 1935 operatic masterpiece *Porgy and Bess* and beyond. And for the first time, most of Gershwin's own writings are collected together, exactly as they appeared during the 1920s and 1930s.

If there is a theme to this scrapbook, it is the constant struggle to evaluate the merits of American popular culture, which at the time was creating new art forms that in some quarters seemed to merit serious consideration. The essays in this book show that there was both an appreciation of what Gershwin represented and a critical division about whether he was succeeding in doing the seemingly impossible—marrying high and low art. The critics constantly brought the subject up and assessed Gershwin's work based upon their own inclinations, or lack thereof, to accept the basic premise that the two worlds could be combined. Gershwin mere-

"Swanee," The Capitol Revue, *1919, record label.*

ly represented the most important figure doing the combining.

The essays in this book, assembled from newspapers, magazines, and books of the period, are on-the-spot examinations of the musical phenomenon known as Gershwin. He was a star. His work was debated in serious magazines, and his glamorous life was spotlighted in the popular media. He was a man of the people, a symbol of his time, and everyone could understand and appreciate his joyous music. This collection covers nearly all of the composer's musical creations—from songs to symphonic works—in chronological order, as his career unfolded, as a scrapbook would be filled.

The players in the drama of George Gershwin's musical life—those who knew him well or merely interviewed him—bring to this book their firsthand accounts of the era. Paul Whiteman tells how the "Experiment in Modern Music" concert at Aeolian Hall came about, giving birth to the *Rhapsody in Blue*; Gilbert Seldes's program notes for the concert's booklet are also included. Alexander Woollcott, the acerbic critic and Algonquin Round Table denizen, offers his observations in several next-day reviews of Gershwin musicals. Playwright S. N. Behrman paints an intimate picture of Gershwin and his family and friends in their daily lives. Hyman Sandow's sketch of the composer's working methods and compositional concerns was written as Gershwin was completing *An American in Paris,* a work that is further explored in Deems

Taylor's famous "scenario" from the 1928 pre-miere's program notes.

There are three magazine articles by Isaac Goldberg, a friend and confidant of the composer who wrote the first Gershwin biography in 1931. Carl Van Vechten writes approvingly (in a 1925 article) of the composer's earliest contributions to American music and also provides two character-revealing, moodily artful photographs of Gershwin. Olin Downes, the legendary music crit-ic of the *New York Times* (for more than thirty years, beginning in 1924), offers his reservedly appreciative reviews of the *Rhapsody in Blue*, the *Second Rhapsody,* and *Porgy and Bess*—originally printed within hours of their New York premieres. And DuBose Heyward, the librettist of *Porgy and Bess,* gives the entire genesis of the opera, from the composer's first reading of Heyward's novel *Porgy* in 1926 to the rehearsals on the eve of its opening.

Several articles trace Gershwin's family back-ground and career. Writing in May 1930 in the New York *World*, Arthur Kober is particularly generous with anecdotes about the composer's personality and habits. Perhaps the most intimate sketch of all is provided by Ira Gershwin, who with characteristic humor and insight discusses (in a 1930 *New York Times* article) the art of lyric writing and his collaboration with his brother.

While some of the biographical information that ends up in these articles may occasionally be regarded with healthy skepticism, the portrait of the composer's character, which seems fairly con-sistent from writer to writer, is accurate, and has been upheld by Gershwin biographers in the ensu-ing years. Plainly, George Gershwin was a boy who never grew up: the adjective most often used to describe him is *ingenuous.* He honestly was awestruck by his own talents, and reveled in hear-ing his music played (especially by himself at social gatherings, at which his piano playing was notably ubiquitous). It was difficult for him to believe any of his friends or relations could not be more inter-ested in *his* work than in anything else in their lives. Yet, it was usually acknowledged that this was not conceit; on the contrary, he was seen as straight-forward, and despite his delight in material suc-cess, he avoided ostentation. It seems he was

unequivocally generous, and since he was so con-fident and secure in his own abilities, he was happy to give encouragement and even money to help other composers. Considered quite easygo-ing (even regarding close-to-the-heart musical matters), he rarely had anything mean or sniping to say about events and people. He was described by all who knew him intimately or met him briefly as warm, gregarious, charismatic, and absolutely brimming with vitality.

George Gershwin is represented in this collec-tion by almost all of his published writings, whose very style conveys much about the man and his music. These essays reveal someone sure of his place in musical history, and intelligent and knowl-edgeable, yet not quite a master of the written word. Often Gershwin's language is awkwardly colloquial, and the words used do not seem to be exactly right for the purposes at hand; there is an

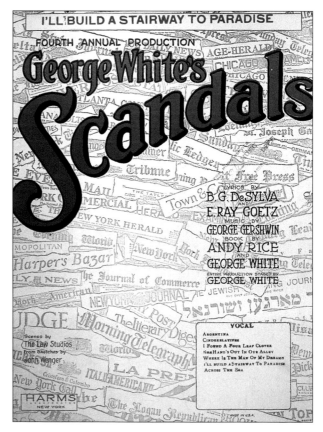

"I'll Build a Stairway to Paradise," George White's **Scandals of 1922,** *sheet music.*

endearing touch of the Yogi Berra/Casey Stengel non sequitur in these passages.

For Gershwin and these other writers on the popular arts, it was an era when ethnic and racial characterizations were broad, yet obviously well intentioned. In one of the articles reprinted in this book, "American Operetta Comes of Age," Isaac Goldberg's running theme is a play on his subject's *Of Thee I Sing* political slogan, "Loves the Irish and the Jews." But Goldberg's treatment

here of "Jewish" and "Irish" elements in the theater (he brings in Eugene O'Neill), and his serious examination, in many of his writings, of the Jewish elements in Gershwin's music, make it clear what his sympathetic concerns are. Similarly, when the authors of these articles speak of "jazz"—and this includes Gershwin himself—not nearly enough attention is paid to the great contemporary black jazz musicians who were creating the most authentic exam-

George Gershwin, on board ship, c. 1923–1924.

ples of this art. Yet there is always a significant appreciation—albeit somewhat paternalistic—of the African-American contribution to "modern" music. For Gershwin and many others, jazz *was* modern American music, as was anything serious or popular that took elements of jazz and created something that differed from the musicals of Victor Herbert or the symphonic compositions of Edward MacDowell. Therefore, these writers should not be judged too harshly when they insist on considering Paul Whiteman's syncopated band arrangements the highest form of jazz.

In this newly assembled scrapbook, George Gershwin's fascinating career unfolds with each succeeding essay and pictorial souvenir of his works. Before stepping into the pages of the past, however, a brief introduction to the composer's most important musical creations is essential.

George Gershwin, born of Russian immigrant parents (with the family name of Gershovitz) in Brooklyn on September 26, 1898, was undoubtedly a piano prodigy; there was money for local music lessons, but for the teen-aged Gershwin neither college nor music school—nor graduation from high school—was in the cards. Nevertheless he was, from the beginning, a serious musician brimming with ideas, who chose to enter his profession by the most obvious and accessible route available to him—popular-song accompanying, plugging (playing the hits of the day for clients at a Tin Pan Alley music publisher), and writing.

The young Gershwin's talent was natural and flowed like a waterfall; at the same time, he knew he needed classical training in order to expand his musical ideas in the most creative ways. So while he plugged songs at Remick's, he studied piano

with Charles Hambitzer. When "Swanee" became his first big hit, among his existing compositions was *Lullaby,* a string quartet composed for his harmony/theory teacher, Edward Kilenyi. And as his early show tunes—"Nobody but You," "Do It Again," "I'll Build a Stairway to Paradise"—captured the public's imagination, he had already begun thinking in grand terms, composing a short opera called *Blue Monday* for *George White's Scandals of 1922,* which featured Paul Whiteman's jazzy orchestra. It was this strange work (totally inappropriate for the *Scandals* and dropped immediately) that Whiteman remembered when it was time to coordinate the program for his "Experiment in Modern Music" at New York's Aeolian Hall in 1924: he asked Gershwin to compose a new American rhapsody.

Like *Blue Monday,* the *Rhapsody in Blue* was not orchestrated by Gershwin. Completion of the *Rhapsody* was on such a tight schedule that Gershwin didn't even have time to write out his own solo piano passages and left the instrumentation to Whiteman's brilliant arranger, Ferde Grofé (later well known for his *Grand Canyon Suite*).

Following the incredible success and fame of the *Rhapsody,* Gershwin broke musical-comedy custom and orchestrated three numbers for a London show, *Primrose*—and then wrote and orchestrated his piano concerto: the Concerto in F premiered in December 1925. But throughout the 1920s he continued to study—under Rubin Goldmark, Wallingford Riegger, and Henry Cowell—and he was still a student (of the revolutionary musical theorist Joseph Schillinger) even as he composed *Porgy and Bess* in the 1930s.

"The Life of a Rose," **George White's Scandals of 1923,** *sheet music.*

"Somebody Loves Me," **George White's Scandals of 1924,** *sheet music.*

As Gershwin piled up one hit show after another—*Lady, Be Good!* in 1924, *Tip-Toes* in 1925, *Funny Face* in 1927, *Strike Up the Band* and *Girl Crazy* in 1930—he continued to expand both his serious output and the form of the American musical and its individual songs. He followed the Concerto in F with, in 1928, *An American in Paris*—which, after the *Rhapsody,* has become his most popular orchestral composition; it may well be his best.

George Gershwin, c. 1925.

While the *Rhapsody* is original, innovative, and brilliantly melodic, it is nevertheless a flawed signature piece—repetitive and structurally unimaginative, with the orchestration left in other hands. The piano concerto—hailed, at the time, by British conductor Albert Coates as among the fifty best musical compositions of the modern era—is a sublime and serious work: here, on a majestic scale, are the qualities that make George Gershwin a great composer on the world scene, not just a fine representative of the "symphonic jazz" style. The Concerto in F, together with *An American in Paris,* the *Cuban Overture, Porgy and Bess,* and most of his songs, are musical works of impeccable balance—alternately poignant and jubilant, pensive and danceable, songful and rhythm-driven.

The inherent drama in all of Gershwin's music is created by these contrasts and also resides within smaller units of themes and melodies. Individual songs, and passages in the "serious" compositions, abound in the tension generated by blue notes, by the interplay of major and minor. Harmonies and melodies together (they are inseparable in Gershwin's music) participate in the game of anticipation-and-resolution, which is intensified by the notes' roller-coaster climbs and descents and dramatic leaps of wide intervals—and by the frequently used techniques ("'S Wonderful," "They Can't Take That Away from Me," "Fascinating Rhythm") of successively repeating notes or note groups and emphasizing insistent rhythms.

All of these elements are combined with total originality of melody and harmonic treatment, innovations in rhythm and orchestration (by the time of *Porgy and Bess,* Gershwin's orchestration was approaching that of Maurice Ravel), and an organizational technique that allows not only the musicologist but the average listener to ascertain the thematic links, repetitions, transformations, and parallels.

While some critics have pointed to a lack of formulaic sophistication and true "classical" development in Gershwin's larger compositions, this is not —with the exception of the *Rhapsody*—an accurate characterization of these works. In his 1926 book, *So This Is Jazz,* Henry Osgood devoted a number of pages solely to a technical examination of the Concerto in F, going beyond the usual superficial "making a lady out of jazz" commentary and providing intellectually sound reasons for admiring the work as a superb serious composition; his essay is included in this collection.

There is an additional organizational quality in this music that is a distinct Gershwin touch: the myriad minor musical ideas themselves are the bonds that link major themes and passages. Tiny one- or two-bar sections—which with other composers would be inconsequential, uninspired con-

"Do Do Do," Oh, Kay!, *1926, record label.*

necting tissue to variations and developments of a few main ideas—become in Gershwin's music memorable elements in themselves. Each of these, always relating in some way to the principal themes, can be likened to an insignificant shadow in a great Impressionist painting: it takes on an interesting shape of its own and contains many of the colors from throughout the work. Gershwin's large compositions—and his best musicals and songs—succeed as art because of his commanding sense of drama and balance. His works are never overblown, and within them there is rarely a passage, no matter how insignificant, that is throwaway or does not contain an original idea. *Porgy and Bess* may be the only opera from which the average listener can walk away humming part of a recitative or a minor orchestral bridge.

One of Gershwin's symphonic works, the

Second Rhapsody, is an expanded version of an eight-minute orchestral passage in the 1931 film *Delicious,* underlying a nightmarish trek by a young immigrant (Janet Gaynor) through the streets of New York. This fairly forgettable movie features George Gershwin's first original film score; it also has an operettalike dream sequence ("Welcome to the Melting Pot"). Here, on a small (and unsuccessful) scale, is a summation of all of Gershwin's musical concerns of the period: popular song, serious symphonic composition, and operetta.

Operetta is how many critics refer to the outstanding and innovative works that George Gershwin and his lyricist brother Ira created for Broadway in the 1930s. Gershwin musicals, from the very beginning, usually included scenes with choral-dance numbers and musical underpinnings of the dialogue. By the time of *Strike Up the Band* in 1927, the Gershwin style of operetta that revolutionized American musical theater was blooming. After the success of that show's revised 1930 version, the Broadway stage would no longer be limited to revues with chorus girls or collections of snappy tunes and dance numbers superimposed upon flimsy mistaken-identity comedic love stories. With the help of dramatic satirists George S. Kaufman and Morrie Ryskind, the Gershwin brothers from 1927 to 1933 created satiric musicals in which the major songs reflect the elements of the story and music propels complete scenes, many of them with sung dialogue. The first *Strike Up the Band*'s sendup on war-makers and big corporations did not meet with public approval in 1927. In its revamped form, with partially new music and slightly less biting satire, the musical was a success in 1930; the Depression had apparently intervened to create a more accepting audience for such intelligent shows.

The Gershwins' greatest Broadway triumph was their penultimate operetta, *Of Thee I Sing.* It became a huge success and won the 1932 Pulitzer Prize for drama. Boasting only a few "hits" ("Love Is Sweeping the Country," "Of Thee I Sing," "Who Cares?"), the numerous other songs in the score are all part of long, flowing scenes of music, interwoven themes, and recitative. As in George Gershwin's larger compositions, even small connecting passages in *Of Thee I Sing* are memorable and formally innovative. Its 1933 sequel, *Let 'Em Eat Cake,* has still greater musical ambitions. Gershwin commented that he was proud of the contrapuntal elements in this score; there is more music in it than in its predecessor (although "Mine" was its only "song-chart" hit), all of which moves the story forward in a completely musical way. Compared with *Of Thee I Sing,* the satire in *Let 'Em Eat Cake* is a little more strident and off-putting (two revolutions and some executions!), but many of the scenes could easily find their way into any critically acclaimed opera.

The genesis of George Gershwin's only real opera—and greatest accomplishment—is a tale worth telling, the story of a mature artist creating a timeless, unique work that is both musically and socially significant.

After Gershwin read DuBose Heyward's year-old novel *Porgy* in 1926, he contacted Heyward about doing an opera. That tantalizing possibility was postponed, however, due to the impending dramatic production of *Porgy* by the Theatre Guild in

George Gershwin, c. 1930.

New York—and by the composer's acknowledgment that he was not yet fully prepared to write an opera. The Theatre Guild's 1927 *Porgy* was a groundbreaking piece of theater—with its African-American cast, soul-stirring spirituals, and dynamic staging by Rouben Mamoulian (who was to become a major Hollywood director).

Gershwin contacted Heyward again about an operatic *Porgy* in 1932, but regretted that he wouldn't be able to start work on it for a while. Later in the year Heyward revealed that he had been approached by Al Jolson, who wished to star in a new production of the play, possibly adding music by Jerome Kern and Oscar Hammerstein II. Fortunately for posterity, Kern and Hammerstein decided against it, and Jolson gave up his plans.

In 1933 Gershwin and Heyward finally agreed to go full steam ahead on the opera; they would once again entrust Heyward's story to the Theatre Guild, with which they signed a contract in October 1933. Gershwin was adamant that a serious opera about the people of Catfish Row be authentic. He chose the Theatre Guild over the opera house because of its previous experience with *Porgy* and because of the greater number of performances possible on a Broadway stage. But he also realized that his desire to handpick a cast of well-trained African-American singers would probably have been unattainable if he had accepted an offer from the Metropolitan Opera to produce the work.

After a short visit to Heyward's home in

Charleston, South Carolina, Gershwin spent December 1933 in Palm Springs, Florida, where he wrote a showy orchestral piece, the *Variations on "I Got Rhythm."* He wanted something new to program on his upcoming month-long concert tour (a celebration of the tenth anniversary of the *Rhapsody in Blue*) with the popular Leo Reisman band. After the tour, he began a stint as a radio host, the star of his own series, *Music by Gershwin.* This unique 1934 program lasted two seasons. The announcer was Don Wilson, later known for his work on the Jack Benny radio and television shows; among the arrangers was Morton Gould, who was soon to become one of the great American composers and conductors; the orchestra included master jazz musicians Tommy and Jimmy Dorsey; and in addition to playing his own music, Gershwin featured as guests such established and up-and-coming composers as Irving Berlin, Cole Porter, Richard Rodgers, Vernon Duke, Harold Arlen, Arthur Schwartz, Rube Bloom, and Dana Suesse.

Gershwin and Heyward began their long-distance working relationship in earnest in early 1934. In June, Gershwin went to Charleston to confer with Heyward and immerse himself in the atmosphere of the work's actual setting. He stayed for about six weeks in a beachfront cottage on Folly Island. Nearby James Island had a large population of Gullahs, the people upon whom *Porgy* was based. Gershwin visited, and played piano at, local schools and churches with Heyward.

It was at this time that Gershwin encountered a number of the authentic musical experiences that he would use to make *Porgy and Bess* a true folk opera. On one island, he attended a prayer meeting, joining in with the "shouting"—singing accompanied by a primitive yet complex rhythmic pattern. At another religious service, Gershwin become entranced by the intense and sophisticated singing of a chorus of celebrants, with many different prayers voiced simultaneously; it was upon this real African-American religious expression that he based perhaps the most powerful passage in the opera, the six-part aleatory prayer ("Oh, Heav'nly Father") in the hurricane scene.

Gershwin completed the opera's orchestration in September 1935. During the previous year he

had taken a hand in all facets of the production, which was to be directed by Rouben Mamoulian, with Alexander Smallens conducting and the Eva Jessye Choir as the Catfish Row residents. He personally auditioned and chose much of the cast, almost all of them classically trained African-American singers: Todd Duncan (as Porgy), a Howard University graduate who was not a big fan of jazz; J. Rosamond Johnson (as the lawyer Frazier), the famed arranger and black-music historian, who also helped cast many of the singers; Anne Wiggins Brown (as Bess) and Ruby Elzy (as Serena), both from New York's Juilliard School of Music; Abbie Mitchell (as Clara), the wife of black composer Will Marion Cook; and Edward Matthews (as Jake), from the 1934 Virgil Thomson–Gertrude Stein opera *Four Saints in Three Acts.* John W. Bubbles, the famous vaudeville performer, and the main actor from the popular stage, was troublesome, unreliable, musically unsophisticated—and ultimately brilliant as Sportin' Life once the curtain went up.

Porgy and Bess opened in Boston on September 30, 1935, to glowing notices extolling its merits as a serious opera and deeming it a significant contribution to American music. For the New York staging at the Alvin Theatre, which premiered on October 10, 1935, Gershwin agreed to some cuts (including the stirring "Buzzard Song" and the opening honky-tonk piano solo music) to shorten the excessive length and add better flow to the action.

The critical reaction to the New York production was mixed. While most writers—particularly the theater critics—were captivated by the beauty, power, and inventiveness of the opera, many music commentators (such as fellow composer Virgil Thomson) were condescending—or merely uncomfortable with the work's juxtaposition of Broadway and opera-house elements.

An irony of the contemporary reaction to *Porgy and Bess* is that one review that came close to understanding its true strengths, in very specific detail, was written by the same man who in 1926 contributed an article to *Singing* magazine criticizing Gershwin's essay ("Does Jazz Belong to Art?") in a previous issue. Both A. Walter Kramer's opera review in *Musical America* and Gershwin's *Singing* article—and subsequently published response to Kramer's criticism—are included in this book.

Porgy and Bess ran for 124 performances at the Alvin Theatre: hardly a success by Broadway standards—but an amazing phenomenon by opera-house practices. After the closing, the Theatre Guild took the opera on a multicity tour. To promote interest at the first stop, Philadelphia, in late January 1936 Gershwin appeared there in concert, playing his Concerto in F, with Alexander Smallens conducting. For this occasion he prepared his Suite from *Porgy and Bess* (later called *Catfish Row*), a rousing and atmospheric piece that outlines the opera's story in, basically, its correct scene sequence and recreates large sections of orchestral and choral music; this is the antithesis of the hodgepodge of strung-together songs from the opera assembled by Robert Russell Bennett in his 1943 work, *A Symphonic Picture*.

If *Porgy and Bess* was the climax of his short life, Gershwin's last year in Hollywood (beginning in August 1936) was the denouement, filled with the creation of some of his and his brother's most enduring songs: "They All Laughed," "Let's Call the Whole Thing Off," "They Can't Take That Away from Me," "A Foggy Day," "Nice Work If You Can Get It," "Love Walked In," and "Love Is Here to Stay." These were written for three films, *Shall We Dance*, *A Damsel in Distress*, and *The Goldwyn Follies*. Before Gershwin was able to complete the ballet music for George Balanchine in the *Goldwyn* movie, the headaches that had been plaguing him for months

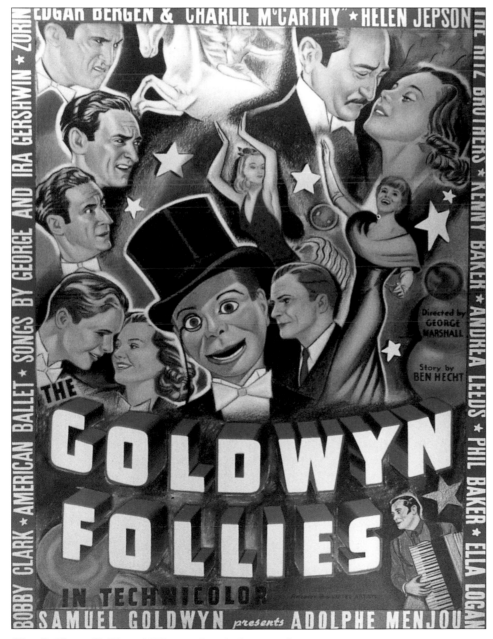

The Goldwyn Follies, *1938, movie window card.*

had worsened to the point of his complete incapacitation. An emergency operation for a brain tumor was unsuccessful; George Gershwin died on July 11, 1937, at age thirty-eight.

When readers—and writers—arrive at this point in the Gershwin story, there is often a terrible, engulfing sadness. Even in retrospect, it is hard to believe: following the short two-decade career of this energetic, vital young man from triumph to triumph and through successively finer and ever-unique musical compositions—and then it all abruptly ends. The tragedy is further compounded by the realization of how much more music the world might have received from George Gershwin—a man who once showed little regret at losing a valuable notebook filled with ideas because he knew very well that within him was a fountain of music ready to overflow on cue. The story, even in printed form, is over too soon.

Fortunately, readers of this book need only to turn the page to begin again—to watch the theatrical-musical world of the 1920s and 1930s unfold in colorful detail, to experience once more the exuberant life and creative brilliance of an American genius.

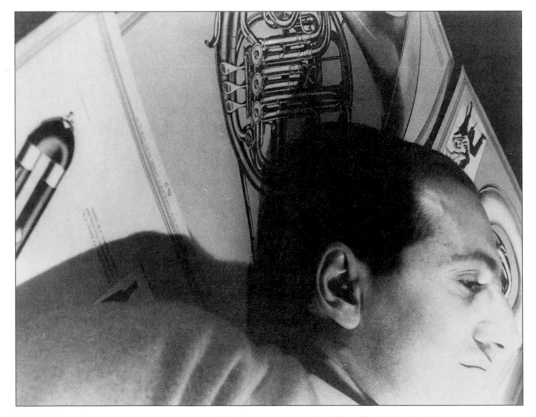

George Gershwin, c. 1933, as photographed by Carl Van Vechten.

A BIOGRAPHICAL SCRAPBOOK

1919-1937

EDITORIAL PREFACE

The accessible organization of the material in this book has been a prime concern. The essays are in (roughly) chronological order, by date of their original publications—subject to the (again, roughly) chronologically arranged list of works, whose titles act as encyclopedic subject headings for every page. In the interest of providing a complete biographical picture of George Gershwin, the detailed explanatory captions can be read continuously as a narrative of the life and works of the composer. The essays appear as they did when first published; due to space limitations, however, exceptionally long articles and book chapters have been abbreviated slightly. The language of the writers remains as written, with only a few deletions of inappropriate phrases and of passages that make little sense out of context, plus some insertions in brackets to clarify phrases, correct spelling, and adjust titles; where words, titles, and statements are clearly incorrect, [sic] has been inserted. Punctuation, capitalization, and spelling in general have been modernized and made consistent for all essays. In some instances of inconsistent or incorrect spelling, especially of titles, a priority has been to maintain uniform treatments. Similarly, personal names and titles of works have been carefully checked for most common treatment, usually based upon such primary sources as song sheets, theatrical programs, and film materials. Regarding the art, an attempt has been made to provide a collection of illustrations that, for the most part, have not appeared in previous Gershwin biographies; their reproduction in color is another unique feature of this book. Following the Epilogue is a list of George Gershwin's works; the guiding principle here is to offer a handy and uncluttered catalogue of all the musical shows, concert works, operas, and individual songs that were performed or published during the composer's lifetime, and of all the films with original scores. This is followed by a detailed list of permissions and art sources. Finally, it cannot be stressed enough that this book does not replicate any existing or actual scrapbook that George Gershwin or members of his family created or kept; rather, its purpose is to provide a biography of Gershwin from the perspective of a newly compiled "scrapbook" of material such as any composer might have assembled during his career.

PROLOGUE

George Gershwin left high school in 1914—at age fifteen—for a job as a piano pounder, or song plugger, at Jerome H. Remick & Company, in the heart of Tin Pan Alley in New York City (West Twenty-eighth Street between Fifth and Sixth avenues). While there he began a secondary "career"—which would last about ten years—as a performer for piano rolls. In 1916, the Harry Von Tilzer Music Publishing Company issued Gershwin's first song, "When You Want 'Em You Can't Get 'Em, When You've Got 'Em You Don't Want 'Em," which Gershwin cut for a roll, the first of his own composition; he also cut his "Rialto Ripples," written with Will Donaldson, which was published by Remick the following year.

Gershwin quit Remick in March 1917 and began getting jobs as a rehearsal pianist for a number of Broadway shows. When Vivienne Segal, the star of one of these shows, Jerome Kern's Miss 1917, added a few of Gershwin's own compositions to a series of Sunday night concerts at the Century Theatre, a scout for the eminent music-publishing firm T. B. Harms was in the audience. Gershwin soon met with the company's Max Dreyfus, who saw the young man's potential and offered him, at the age of nineteen, the prestigious position of staff composer. Gershwin joined Harms in February 1918. One of the Vivienne Segal songs, "You-oo, Just You," was his first to be interpolated into a show, Hitchy-Koo of 1918. Soon thereafter, Gershwin's initial Harms-published piece, "Some Wonderful Sort of Someone," was taken by popular vaudeville performer Nora Bayes for her show Ladies First. But the first Gershwin song to gain a measure of popular approval was "I Was So Young (You Were So Beautiful)," inserted into Good Morning, Judge, which opened in February 1919.

'LA LA LUCILLE' A LIVELY AND AMUSING FARCE COMEDY SET TO MUSIC

New York *Evening Mail,* May 27, 1919

BURNS MANTLE

Not the least interesting of theater-going diversions is that of trying to fit the title of the play to the action or the character thereof.

Take, as an example, the case of *La La Lucille* at the Henry Miller Theatre last night. We had not the least difficulty in locating Lucille. But the "La La" escaped us entirely. It probably was slipped in while we were inattentive. It is so hard to concentrate in May.

Of the recent musical plays, *La La Lucille* is much the best. It combines the bedroom with the co-respondent school of farce comedy set to tunes, and boasts a snappiness of dialogue that few musical-comedy set books are able to boast these days. A bit broad for mother and the girls, but neither father nor the boys will object to it.

The score, too, embraces one or two dance numbers that are both spirited and original—one bearing the classic and self-explanatory title of "Tee-Oodle-Um-Bum-Bo" that threatens to rival the long-popular "Tickle-Toe," which came in with *Going Up.*

In addition to these virtues, the story has a reasonable farcical basis. The hero and heroine are happily married, but awfully poor in the first act. They have spent their last thousand on a brightly colored and most attractive apartment and a handsome set of costumes for the chorus, and they are being hounded by scores of creditors.

Then they learn that the hero's aunt has died and left him a couple million—if he will immediately divorce the heroine. She was a stage beauty before he married her, and Auntie never could stand actresses.

At first they insist that their love is worth much more than money, but, living in New York, they soon conclude that if, by being divorced, they can get the money and later remarry, they will be able to go on living in the same flat, take ice, and indulge all the minor luxuries. Hence the engaging of a professional co-respondent.

Instead of employing the usual cabaret dancer, however, they finally agree upon the wife of the janitor, a frowzy female, but pure. With her in tow the hero seeks out one of those John Smith hotels familiar to farces, and there the complications become riotous.

There is also an unusual turn at the finish, but it always spoils a problem play to tell too much of the plot, so we leave that as a surprise.

The cast is exceptionally talented. John Hazzard is the comedian, and John has an original way with

him that is a great help to farce. The heroine is Janet Velie, a stranger to us, but an attractive young woman who, we hear, played the lead in *Going Up* near the end of that play's run at the Liberty—and did it very successfully, which is easy to believe.

The others include a graceful dancing pair, Marjorie Bentley and John Lowe, who are certain soon to be in demand at the ballroom cabarets if, indeed, they are not already engaged. They were big favorites with last night's audience, and deserved to be.

Assisting are Helen Clark, a dainty and pleasing ingenue, Lorin Baker, Eleanor Daniels, Clarence Harvey, Cordelia McDonald, Alfred Hall, George Callahan, M. Rale, Stanley Forde, and Estar Banks.

Alfred Aarons is the producer, the chorus is young, pretty, and well drilled, the costumes fresh and handsome, and the setting in excellent taste.

Fred Jackson wrote the book and George Gershwin the music. The very good lyrics were contributed by Arthur Jackson and B. G. DeSylva.

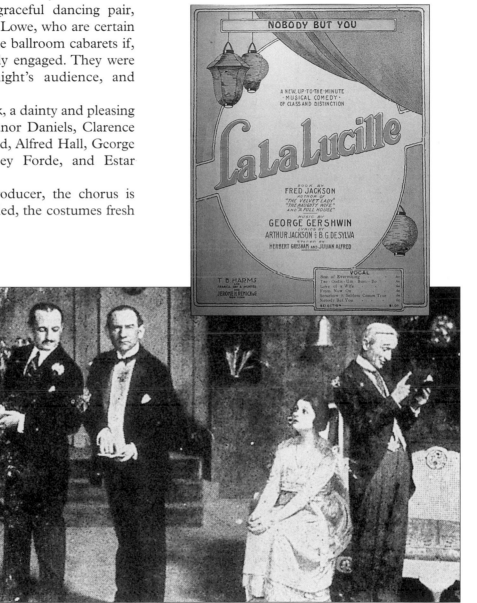

La La Lucille opened at Henry Miller's Theatre on May 26, 1919. It was the first Broadway show for which George Gershwin created the entire score, and it was a major success. The lyrics were written by Arthur Jackson and Buddy DeSylva. Although the reviews were uniformly positive, the show's composer was mentioned only peripherally. The jovial permutations in La La Lucille of the tried-but-true "bedroom farce," with the added benefits of a musical score, seemed to delight its audiences as well as the critics. A consistent favorite of the composer over the ensuing years, and perhaps the first song to reveal the unique Gershwin musical personality, "Nobody but You" was one of the two big hits from La La Lucille. The other, a "show-stopper" according to most of the reviews, was "Tee-Oodle-Um-Bum-Bo."

'LA LA LUCILLE,' NEW BROAD FARCE, IS WELL PLAYED

New York Herald, May 27, 1919

Oh, La La Lucille! Oh, what will Henry Miller say when he finds they have put a boisterous boudoir farce with jazzy musical accompaniments into his theater? If pictures could blush, the graceful panel of John Philip Kemble as Hamlet, which looks down from a side wall, would turn hunter's pink.

La La Lucille is that kind of a musical comedy. There are three acts and all save the first pass in bedrooms in the Hotel Philadelphia and concern the frantic efforts of one John Smith, played by John E. Hazzard, to get a divorce from his wife to comply with the terms of his late aunt's will. The aunt had lived in Boston, which may explain the whys and wherefores of the risqué scenes.

John Smith, dentist, happily married to pretty Mrs. John Smith, falls heir to a fortune of $2 million by the terms of Fred Jackson's book if he will consent to be divorced by his wife. To outwit the will the young couple arrange to bring about a divorce and then remarry. The chief accomplice is a janitress, more hideous than a Chinese idol, to whom the husband is to make love ostentatiously in the boudoirs aforementioned.

Second only to the hilarious troubles of Mr. Hazzard in a continuous state of embarrassment were the amusing antics of Miss Eleanor Daniels, as Fanny, the prim little janitress, who stripped to her

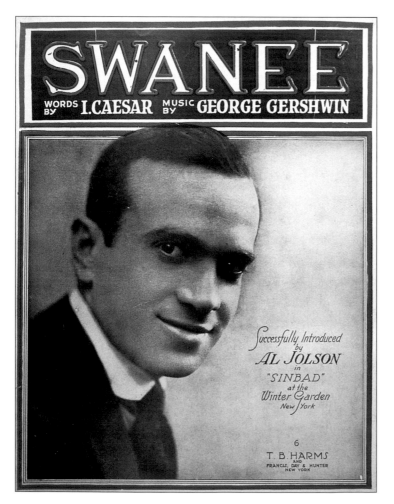

The story is that George Gershwin and Irving Caesar, a savvy Tin Pan Alley lyricist of the period (the deceptively simple lyric for Vincent Youmans's "Tea for Two," from No, No, Nanette, *is also Caesar's), wrote "Swanee" lock, stock, and barrel in fifteen minutes one day in 1918. Caesar presented the song to Ned Wayburn, the director of* Ziegfeld Follies of 1918, *for which Gershwin was the rehearsal pianist. Wayburn was impressed, and took it (along with Gershwin's "Come to the Moon") for the opening of the Capitol Theatre in October 1919. But it was only after Gershwin played the song for Broadway star Al Jolson at a party late in 1919 that "Swanee" took on epic popularity. Jolson grabbed it for his touring show,* Sinbad, *and recorded it on January 8, 1920. The Jolson sheet music and record sold in the millions; it was the beginning of Gershwin's worldwide fame as a songwriter.*

"woolen unders" with a desperate determination to make a divorce between Mr. and Mrs. Smith possible.

She played the part of the grimly humorous woman with heroic consistency. It was a rough but faithful character study, and there has been nothing funnier in broad comedy since Miss Maude Eburne's debut several years ago in *A Pair of Sixes*.

After Mr. Hazzard and Miss Daniels came a brilliant performance with Miss Helen Clark as a bride from Georgia, who with her affectionate husband chanced to have the room adjoining that taken by John and Fanny. All were soon compro-

mised in the statutory complications of the second and third acts, the surprise which closed the performance being the sudden appearance of the supposedly late aunt from Boston, who had arranged the will and the joke to test her nephew's affections. The song which pleased the audience most was "Tee-Oodle-Um-Bum-Bo," which Miss Janet Velie and an intelligent chorus sang with lively charm, Miss Marjorie Bentley contributing dances to the ensemble effect. Lorin Baker was an amusing bridegroom from Georgia, and the cast was excellent throughout.

For boisterous and exceedingly broad nonsense, *Oh, La La Lucille* hits on all eight cylinders. . . .

Dancer-impresario George White often joined the chorines of his **Scandals.** *When Gershwin was still relatively unknown (albeit with "Swanee" behind him), White gave him the opportunity to write the music for his entire revue. This series of lavish spectacle-and-dance-oriented* **Scandals** *under White's name was mounted in rivalry to Florenz Ziegfeld's sensational* **Follies.** *Gershwin wrote the scores for five successive* **Scandals,** *starting in 1920.*

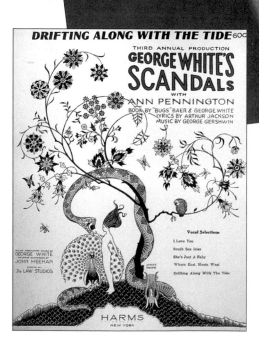

Ann Pennington had danced with George White in the Ziegfeld Follies *before becoming one of the featured attractions in White's* Scandals, *beginning with the first, in 1919. "Drifting Along with the Tide," with lyrics by Arthur Jackson, is a lively tune (recorded by Gershwin for a piano roll) from* George White's Scandals of 1921.

A DANCER'S REVUE: 'GEORGE WHITE'S SCANDALS OF 1922'

New York Times, **August 30, 1922**

ALEXANDER WOOLLCOTT

For the fourth time in as many years that feather-footed graduate of the two-a-day, George White, came to town last evening at the head of his own revue, a multicolored, eye-disturbing, ear-filling musical show that took over the Globe Theatre for the last weeks of the warm weather. It is the custom, of course, to hold up each new revue beside the *Follies* and see which reaches further. It may be said of the new *Scandals* that they are nowhere near so fair to look upon as Mr. Ziegfeld's show but, being less majestical and less concerned with piling beauty on beauty, are, all told, a little more entertaining. Also that being less a matter of habit, less routined, less rut-worn, there is here and there in them the stir and flutter of some new ideas.

It is, first and last, a dancer's idea of an entertainment, this current hubbub at the Globe. Besides Mr. White himself, who obliges with a few enthralling steps in his own manner, there are several others who foot it featly throughout the evening. There is, for instance, a minute and immensely comic dancer named Lester Allen, who is most entertaining, and there are two described as the Argentinas who dance a singularly venomous Apache dance, or whatever they call that dance down in Buenos Aires.

It was during the 1922 edition of **George White's Scandals** *when Gershwin began his association with Paul Whiteman, who led his Palais Royal orchestra for the show. "I'll Build a Stairway to Paradise" was the much-talked-about spectacular number that enchanted critics and the public alike—all seemingly in awe of the new jazzy sounds coming from the orchestra pit of a Broadway show. Opening night also offered the only* **Scandals** *performance of Gershwin and DeSylva's operatic sketch,* **Blue Monday,** *later revived by Whiteman for a 1925 Carnegie Hall concert.*

Mr. White may be fooled into engaging a singer or two with rather painful voices, and he is still in that stage of revue-making where he would feel it a matter of duty not to let the Argentinas dance without first having a Jack McGowan come on in a sailor's uniform and sing a dull song about going to the Argentine. But he knows dancers when he sees them, and he knows dance music when he hears it. Wherefore he engaged Paul Whiteman's extraordinary orchestra from the Palais Royal and gave his stage over for a little while to such a festival of jazz as sets the audience to swaying like a wheat field touched by the wind. Here is jazz teased and coaxed to the nth degree, and last night's assemblage was supremely happy about it. It does begin to look as though the "National Anthem" had been written in vain—and after all the trouble Laurette Taylor went to in playing and lecturing about it, too.

It might be mentioned that one stray from the *Follies*—W. C. Fields—bobs up in the *Scandals.* He bobs up several times—notably with some of his old juggling and with a rather hilarious slapstick travesty on the radio passion of the moment. Indeed, he bobs up once too often in a stupid baseball sketch. The program accuses him of having written this little interlude, but that is libelous. Mr. Fields will hardly admit having written the story which is the climax of the sketch—for it has been circulating in this town these many weary years.

However, authorship of a revue is always a bit mixed. You find yourself wondering how one and the same man could plan and approve both the incredibly flat number called "Just a Tiny Cup of Tea," which clogs the second act, and yet have the ingenuity to stage that smart and spectacular finale, "I'll Build a Stairway to Paradise"—which brings down the curtain at the end of part one.

All the good music in the *Scandals* was written for something else—some of it before young Mr. White was born. But some of this has been well chosen, and there should certainly be honorable mention awarded whichever one of the twelve authors thought of the proper musical setting for the Garden of Eden scene, which as a tribute to "Back to Methuselah," opens the show. There are Eve and Adam in the costumes of the period, and the orchestra plays " 'Neath the Shade of the Old Apple Tree."

Originally sung by Irene Bordoni in 1922's **The French Doll,** *"Do It Again" was presented as an encore at Eva Gauthier's Aeolian Hall recital on November 1, 1923. The concert highlighted classical songs by, among others, Bellini, Milhaud, and Bartók, as well as popular American songs, including three by George Gershwin, "Innocent Ingenue Baby," "I'll Build a Stairway to Paradise," and "Swanee." The event marked Gershwin's first professional performance in a concert hall and received accolades as a significant musical event from such critics as Deems Taylor and Carl Van Vechten. "The Yankee Doodle Blues" was interpolated into the score of* **Spice of 1922.**

George and Ira Gershwin (as Arthur Francis) wrote "The Sunshine Trail" as a theme song for Associated First National's 1923 silent film of the same name. This unusual comedy-western is set in the present (like the brothers' later Broadway "western" hit, **Girl Crazy**) and features a sequence wherein the stars, reliving their childhoods, romp in kids' clothes in a roomful of over-sized furniture. It was the first association of the Gershwins with the movies—a medium that would provide both creative opportunities and frustration for the brothers in the coming four-teen years.

In addition to his fourth, and fairly lackluster, score for the **Scandals**, Gershwin in 1923 wrote a few tunes that were interpolated into other shows. "I Won't Say I Will" was performed in **Little Miss Bluebeard** by Irene Bordoni, whose suggestive delivery in the recording echoes a simi-lar successful approach with her rendition of Gershwin's "Do It Again." "Nashville Nightingale," from **Nifties of 1923**, was a popular favorite, and one of the early Gershwin pieces that contemporary critics pointed to when extolling the virtues of "jazz."

'A RHAPSODY IN BLUE'

Concert Program, "An Experiment in Modern Music," Aeolian Hall, New York City, February 12, 1924

GILBERT SELDES

Mr. Gershwin has written a *Rhapsody in Blue,* which he has consented to play, accompanied by the orchestra. He is capable of everything, from "Swanee" to "[I'll Build a] Stairway to Paradise," from "[Innocent] Ingenue Baby" and "Virginia" to "Do It Again." Delicacy, even dreaminess, is a quality he alone brings into jazz music. Gershwin's sense of variation in rhythm, of shifting accents, of emphasis and color is faultless. He has, moreover, an insatiable curiosity about everything connected with his work and, for that matter, with music in general. He is learning and he is not forgetting, and being one of the youngest of the composers he is actually one of the brightest hopes of our popular music.

This is the first rhapsody written for solo instrument and modern orchestra. Prophecy being not the function of an annotator, it may be said that the importance of the *Rhapsody,* quite apart from its own value, must depend to an extent upon it being kept alive in a repertoire—and there is no organization to do this unless the present concert is, as its conductor hopes, only the beginning of a series.

Gershwin is a close student of music and a listener; yet there is not a derivative phrase in his work. He has composed a rhapsody and has chosen to build it out of materials known to him: the rhythms of popular American music, the harmonies pro-duced by American jazz bands. None of the thematic material has been used before; the *Rhapsody* is not a pastiche. The structure is simple, and it resembles concertos written by pianists in what seems, at first, the predominance of the single instrument. Mr. Gershwin's manuscript is complete for the piano. The orchestral treatment was developed by Mr. Grofé.

The *Rhapsody* is a free development of almost all of Gershwin's qualities alluded to . . . [above]. It has a little more crispness, a shade more of jazz, and a shade less of gentleness, than some of his compositions; there is more of "Stairway to Paradise" than of "Do It Again"; and this is natural in a composition intended specifically for jazz orchestra.

Those who care for jazz will naturally be grateful to Mr. Whiteman for urging Mr. Gershwin to compose this rhapsody. He had had it in mind for some time but had no intention of going to work upon it until the announcement was made that the *Rhapsody* would be played at this concert. For those who remain skeptical, another test case may be provided. It is not inconceivable that an intelligent conductor of a symphony orchestra may want to play the *Rhapsody*; it would probably need rescoring, but the saxophone, which has been used ever since Meyerbeer in serious music, need not be exiled.

Gershwin claimed he had gotten the ideas for the "plot" of the Rhapsody in Blue *on a train—with its noises and rhythms—on his way to attend the Boston tryout premiere of* Sweet Little Devil. *As he put the finishing touches on that musical in January 1924, he was beginning work on the* Rhapsody.

A CONCERT OF JAZZ

New York Times, February 13, 1924

OLIN DOWNES

A concert of popular American music was given yesterday afternoon in Aeolian Hall by Paul Whiteman and his orchestra of the Palais Royal. The stage setting was as unconventional as the program. Pianos in various stages of dishabille stood about, amid a litter of every imaginable contraption of wind and percussion instruments. Two Chinese mandarins, surmounting pillars, looked down upon a scene that would have curdled the blood of a Stokowski or a Mengelberg. The golden sheen of brass instruments of lesser and greater dimensions was caught up by a gleaming gong and carried out by bright patches of an oriental backdrop. There were also, lying or hanging about, frying pans, large tin utensils, and a speaking-trumpet, later stuck into the end of a trombone—and what a silky, silky tone came from that accommodating instrument! The singular assemblage of things was more than once, in some strange way, to combine to evoke uncommon and fascinating sonorities.

There were verbal as well as programmatic explanations. The concert was referred to as "educational," to show the development of this type of music. Thus, the "Livery Stable Blues" was introduced apologetically as an example of the depraved past from which modern jazz has risen. The apology is herewith indignantly rejected, for this is a gorgeous piece of impudence, much better in its unbuttoned jocosity and Rabelaisian laughter than other and more polite compositions that came later.

The pianist gathered about him some five fellow performers. The man with the clarinet wore a battered top hat that had ostensibly seen better days.

Sometimes he wore it, and sometimes played into it. The man with the trombone played it as is, but also, on occasion, picked up a bathtub or something of the kind from the floor and blew into that. The instruments made odd, unseemly, bushman sounds. The instrumentalists rocked about. Jests permissible in musical terms but otherwise not

Bandleader Paul Whiteman and Gershwin had discussed the idea for a jazz concert and a large work for orchestra in 1923. Gershwin began composing in earnest only when he was surprised by a notice in the **New York Tribune** *of January 4, 1924, announcing a Whiteman concert scheduled for February 12—and indicating that Gershwin himself was "at work on a jazz concerto."*

printable were passed between these friends of music. The laughter of the music and its interpreters was tornadic. It was—should we blush to say it?—a phase of America. It reminded the writer of someone's remark that an Englishman entered a place as if he were its master, whereas an American entered as if he didn't care who in blazes the master might be. Something like that was in this music.

There were later remarkably beautiful examples of scoring for a few instruments; scoring of singular economy, balance, color, and effectiveness; music at times vulgar, cheap, in poor taste, elsewhere of irresistible swing and insouciance and recklessness and life; music played as only such players as these can play it. They have a technique of their own. They play with an abandon e q u a l e d

only by that race of born musicians—the American Negro, who has surely contributed fundamentally to this art which can neither be frowned nor sneered away. They did not play like an army going through ordered maneuvers, but like the melomaniacs they are, bitten by rhythms that would have twiddled the toes of St. Anthony. They beat time with their feet—lèse-majesté in a symphony orchestra. They fidgeted uncomfortably when for a moment they had to

stop playing. And there were the incredible gyrations of that virtuoso and imp of the perverse, Ross Gorman. And then there was Mr. Whiteman. He does not conduct. He trembles, wabbles, quivers—a piece of jazz jelly, conducting the orchestra with the back of the trouser of the right leg, and the face of a mandarin the while.

There was an ovation for Victor Herbert, that master of instrumentation, when his four *Serenades* composed for this occasion were played, and Mr. Herbert acknowledged the applause from the gallery. Then stepped upon the stage, sheepishly, a lank and dark young man— George Gershwin. He was to play the piano part in the first public performance of his *Rhapsody in Blue* for piano and orchestra. This composition shows extraordinary talent, just as it also shows a young composer with aims that go far beyond those of his ilk, struggling with a form of which he is far from being master. It is important to bear both these facts in mind in estimating the composition. Often Mr. Gershwin's purpose is defeated by technical immaturity, but in spite of that technical immaturity, a lack of knowledge of how to write effectively for piano alone or in combination with orchestra, an unconscious attempt to rhapsodize in the manner of Franz Liszt, a naiveté which at times stresses something unimportant while something of value and effectiveness goes by so quickly that it is lost—in spite of all this, he has expressed himself in a significant and, on the whole, highly original manner.

His first theme alone, with its caprice, humor, and exotic outline, would show a talent to be reckoned with. It starts with an outrageous cadenza of the clarinet. It has subsidiary phrases, logically growing out of it, and integral to the thought. The original phrase and subsidiaries are often ingeniously metamorphosed by devices of rhythm and instrumentation. There is an oriental twist to the whole business that is not hackneyed or superficial. And—what is important—this is no mere dance tune set for piano and other instruments. It is an idea, or several ideas correlated and combined, in varying and well-contrasted rhythms that immediately intrigue the hearer. This, in essence, is fresh and new and full of future promise.

The second theme, with a lovely sentimental line, is more after the manner of some of Mr. Gershwin's colleagues. Tuttis are too long, cadenzas are too long, the peroration at the end loses a large measure of wildness and magnificence it could easily have if it were more broadly prepared, and, for all that, the audience was stirred and many a hardened concertgoer excited with the sensation of a new talent finding its voice and likely to say something personally and racially important to the world. A talent and an idiom also rich in possibilities for that generally exhausted and outworn form of the classic piano concerto.

Mr. Gershwin's *Rhapsody* also stands out as counteracting, quite unconsciously, a weakness of the program—that is, a tendency to sameness of rhythm and sentiment in the music. When a program consists almost entirely of modern dance music, that is naturally a danger, since American dances of today do not boast great variety of step or character; but it should be possible for Mr. Whiteman to remedy this in a second program, which he will give later in the season. There was tumultuous applause for Mr. Gershwin's composition. There was realization of the irresistible vitality and genuineness of much of the music heard on this occasion, as opposed to the pitiful sterility of the average production of the "serious" American composer. The audience packed a house that could have been sold out twice over.

Gershwin completed the score of the **Rhapsody** *in roughly two and a half hectic weeks in January 1924. Because of the impossible time constraints, the piece was orchestrated by Ferde Grofé, the Whiteman band's exceptional composer/ arranger (who would later become famous in his own right as the creator of such Gershwin-style pieces as the* **Grand Canyon Suite** *and* **Mississippi Suite***); Grofé was able to quickly assign the instrumentation based on his familiarity with the particular players of the band. Gershwin provided a two-piano score of the* **Rhapsody** *(subsequently published by Harms); the manuscript's second-piano part was for the orchestra and included instrumental suggestions. Whiteman's second recording of the* **Rhapsody** *with Gershwin at the piano (the first was in June 1924) was made in 1927, and is notable not only for its pianist but for the other great jazz players in the band: Jimmy and Tommy Dorsey and Bix Beiderbecke.*

AN EXPERIMENT

from *Jazz* (1926)

PAUL WHITEMAN AND MARY MARGARET McBRIDE

Visions of playing a jazz concert in what a critic has called the "perfumed purlieus" of Aeolian Hall used to rouse me up at night in a cold perspiration. Sometimes a nightmare depicted me being borne out of the place on a rail, and again I dreamed the doors were all but clattering down with the applause.

That's the way I lived during waking hours, too, all the time I was planning the Aeolian Hall experiment—alternating between extremes of dire fear and exultant confidence.

We began to rehearse for the concert as soon as we came back from England. The idea struck nearly everybody as preposterous at the start. Some hold to the same opinion still. But the list of pessimists was a little shorter, I believe, when at half-past five, on the afternoon of February 12, 1924, we took our fifth curtain call. . . .

If I'd been willing to to wait a few centuries for a verdict on my work, I wouldn't have been so wrought up over the Aeolian Hall concert. But here I saw the common people of America taking all the jazz they could get and mad to get more, yet not having the courage to admit that they took it seriously. I believed that jazz was beginning a new movement in the world's art of music. I wanted it to be recognized as such. I knew it never would be in my lifetime until the recognized authorities on music gave it their approval.

My idea for the concert was to show these skeptical people the advance which had been made in popular music from the day of discordant early jazz to the melodious form of the present. I believed that most of them had grown so accustomed to condemning the "Livery Stable Blues" sort of thing that they went on flaying modern jazz without realizing that it was different from the crude early attempts—that it had taken a turn for the better.

My task was to reveal the change and try to show that jazz had come to stay and deserved recognition. It was not a light undertaking, but setting Aeolian Hall as the stage of the experiment was probably a wise move. It started the talk going, at least, and aroused curiosity. "Jazz in Aeolian Hall!" the conservatives cried incredulously. "What is the world coming to?" . . .

I trembled at our temerity when we made out the lists of patrons and patronesses for the concert. But in a few days, I exulted at our daring, for the acceptances began to come in—from Damrosch, Godowsky, Heifetz, Kreisler, McCormack, Rachmaninoff, Rosenthal, Stokowski, Stransky. We had kindly response, too, from Alda, Galli-Curci, Garden, Gluck, and Jeanne Gordon. Otto Kahn and Jules Glaenzer agreed to represent the patrons of art on our roster and the prominent writers we asked were equally obliging. These included: Fannie Hurst, Heywood Broun, Frank Crowninshield, S. Jay Kaufman, Karl Kitchin, Leonard Liebling, O. O. McIntyre, Pitts Sanborn, Gilbert Seldes, Deems Taylor, and Carl Van Vechten. . . .

That concert cost $11,000. I lost about $7,000 on it. The program alone, together with the explanatory notes, cost $900. We rehearsed for many weeks and since it was outside our regular work, every rehearsal meant extra pay for the men. Nine musicians were added for the occasion and their salaries also piled up the total.

I didn't care. It would have been worth it to me at any price. But never in my life had I such stage fright as that day. I had no doubt of the orchestra. But how would people take it? Would we be the laughingstock of the town when we woke the "morning after"? Would the critics decide I was trying to be smart and succeeding in being only smart-alecky? Or might I be able to convince the crowd that I was engaged in a sincere experiment, designed to exhibit what had been accomplished in the past few years with respect to scoring and arranging music for the popular band—that we

Paul Whiteman's concert at Aeolian Hall on February 12, 1924, attracted luminaries from the media and music circles, from Jascha Heifetz and Sergei Rachmaninoff to Walter Damrosch and Leopold Stokowski. The critical attention and acclaim for the concert labeled "An Experiment in Modern Music" added to Whiteman's fame, and almost overnight the **Rhapsody** *and its composer became phenomena of the music world.*

were making a bona fide attempt to arouse an interest in popular music rhythm for purposes of advancing serious musical composition?

Fifteen minutes before the concert was to begin, I yielded to a nervous longing to see for myself what was happening out front, and putting an overcoat over my concert clothes, I slipped around to the entrance of Aeolian Hall.

There I gazed upon a picture that should have imparted new vigor to my wilting confidence. It was snowing, but men and women were fighting to get into the door, pulling and mauling each other as they do sometimes at a baseball game, or a prize fight, or in the subway. Such was my state of mind by this time that I wondered if I had come to the

right entrance. And then I saw Victor Herbert going in. It was the right entrance, sure enough, and the next day the ticket-office people said they could have sold out the house ten times over.

I went backstage again, more scared than ever. Black fear simply possessed me. I paced the floor, gnawed my thumbs, and vowed I'd give five thousand dollars if we could stop right then and there. Now that the audience had come, perhaps I had really nothing to offer after all. I even made excuses to keep the curtain from rising on schedule. But finally there was no longer any way of postponing the evil moment. The curtain went up and before I could dash forth, as I was tempted to do, and announce that there wouldn't be any concert, we were in the midst of it.

It was a strange audience out in front. Vaudevillians, concert managers come to have a look at the novelty, Tin Pan Alleyites, composers, symphony and opera stars, flappers, cake eaters, all mixed up higgledy-piggledy.

Beginning with the earliest jazz composition, "Livery Stable Blues," we played twenty-six selections designed to exhibit legitimate scoring as contrasted with the former hit-and-miss effects which were also called jazz. At that time I argued that all was not jazz that was so called. I still believe that "Livery Stable Blues" and *A Rhapsody in Blue*, played at the concert by its talented composer, George Gershwin, are so many millions of miles apart that to speak of them both as jazz needlessly confuses the person who is trying to understand modern American music. At the same time, in the course of a recent tour of the United States, I have become convinced that people as a whole like the word *jazz*. At least they will have none of the numerous substitutes that smart wordologists are continually offering. So I say, let's call the new music jazz.

This, then, is the jazz program we played that day:

True Form of Jazz
   a. Ten Years Ago —"Livery Stable Blues"
   b. With Modern Embellishment — "Mama Loves Papa" (Baer)

Comedy Selections
   a. Origin of "Yes, We Have No Bananas" (Silver)

b. Instrumental Comedy—"So This Is Venice" (Thomas) (Adapted from *The Carnival of Venice*)

Contrast—Legitimate Scoring vs. Jazzing
   a. Selection in True Form—"Whispering" (Schonberger)
   b. Same Selection with Jazz Treatment

Recent Compositions with Modern Score
   a. "Limehouse Blues" (Braham)
   b. "I Love You" (Archer)
   c. "Raggedy Ann" (Kern)

An Experiment

Zez Confrey (Piano—Accompanied by the Orchestra)
   a. Medley Popular Airs
   b. "Kitten on the Keys" (Confrey)
   c. "Ice Cream and Art"
   d. "Nickel in the Slot" (Confrey)

Flavoring a Selection with Borrowed Themes
   "Russian Rose" (Grofé) (Based on the "Volga Boat Song")

Semisymphonic Arrangement of Popular Melodies
   Consisting of:
   a. "Alexander's Ragtime Band" (Berlin)
   b. "A Pretty Girl Is Like a Melody" (Berlin)
   c. "Orange Blossoms in California" (Berlin)

A Suite of Serenades (Herbert)
   a. Spanish
   b. Chinese
   c. Cuban
   d. Oriental

Adaptation of Standard Selections to Dance Rhythm
   a. "Pale Moon" (Logan)
   b. "To a Wild Rose" (MacDowell)
   c. "Chansonette" (Friml)

George Gershwin (Piano—Accompanied by the Orchestra)
   A Rhapsody in Blue (Gershwin)

In the Field of Classics
   "Pomp and Circumstance" (Elgar)

I was very proud of the suite the late Victor Herbert wrote especially for that occasion. He was a great-souled, wonderful musician and my loved friend. His encouragement during the weeks we were rehearsing meant a great deal to all of us. I asked him to conduct the *Suite,* and after he had watched me do it, he almost consented to take my place, because he thought I wasn't getting the most out of his music.

"But I'll wait," he said, his eyes twinkling. "I'll wait, Paul, until you've tried it a little longer and then if I say to you, 'Yes, I'll be pleased to conduct the *Suite,*' you'll know what I mean."

Evidently my conducting improved, for he told me at last that I did very well.

"I guess I won't take the stick, Paul," he decided. "There would always be some fool critic to say that I was better than you or you were better than me—and it might cause hard feeling."

He was joking, of course, for it would have been nearly impossible for me to have felt hard toward a genius like him and my friend as well. I relied upon his judgment always and his approval, when it came, was priceless, because it was so sincere. I am glad that he was alive to sit in a box at the first performance and bow to the cheers that greeted the playing of his *Suite.* Writing for a jazz orchestra was new to him, and he complained a little about the doubling, which he said hampered him when he wanted an oboe, say, and found the gentleman who should play the oboe busy with the bass clarinet.

"But I respected the rules of the game," he boasted, "and I might even say of this suite, in the words of the seventh-century nun, that even if other people do not like it, it pleases me because it is I who did it."

A Rhapsody in Blue was regarded by critics as the most significant number of the program. It was the first rhapsody written for a solo instrument and a jazz orchestra. The orchestral treatment was developed by Mr. Grofé, Mr. Gershwin's manuscript being complete for the piano. It was a successful attempt to build a rhapsody out of the rhythms of popular American music. None of the thematic material had been used before. Its structure was simple and its popularity has been remarkable since we put it on the records. It is music conceived for the jazz orchestra and I do not believe any other kind of orchestra can do it full justice, though some have played it.

The audience listened attentively to everything and applauded wholeheartedly from the first moment. When they laughed and seemed pleased with "Livery Stable Blues," the crude jazz of the past, I had for a moment the panicky feeling that they hadn't realized the attempt at burlesque—that they were ignorantly applauding the thing on its merits. I experienced all sorts of qualms as the program went on, most of them unjustified, as it was.

A few of the men had accidents with their instruments, picking up one when they wanted another, but nobody noticed. This happens sometimes when one man plays five or six instruments. My twenty-three boys that day played thirty-six instruments.

Perhaps it would be interesting to list the instruments used in that first concert. The string section consisted of eight violins, two double basses, and a banjo. There were two trumpeters, two trombonists, two pianists, a drummer, three saxophonists, and two French horn players. All these men, except the violinists and one or two others, doubled on some instrument. These extra ones included accordion, bass tuba, flugelhorns, euphonium, celesta, flute, oboe, bass oboe, heckelphone, E-flat, B-flat, and bass clarinets, basset horn, Octavion, E-flat soprano, B-flat soprano, E-flat alto, and E-flat baritone saxophones.

It seemed as if people would never let us go. We played all the encores we knew and still they applauded. My heart was so full I could hardly speak, as I bowed again and again. The spark that a responsive audience can always kindle in the performers had been glowing all afternoon and, as a result, we played better than I had ever hoped.

When finally we bowed for the last time, the usher brought me a pile of notes from congratulating friends and the doorman said people were waiting to see me. There was a letter from Walter Damrosch that I particularly prize. He said he thought we had done wonders with our instruments and added that he had "enjoyed every minute of it."

This friendly praise was very sweet, but I knew I must wait for the papers to learn the best or the worst. Later that week, the *Musical Digest* published a sheaf of critical comments from the dailies, and the sentiment, not merely as we culled it for publicity press notices, was divided, but on the whole encouraging.

W. J. Henderson of the *Herald* described the concert as "one of the most interesting of a busy season. Mr. Herbert's music was delightful. Mr. Gershwin's composition proved to be a highly ingenious work, treating the piano in a manner calling for much technical skill and furnishing an orchestral background in which saxophones, trombones, and clarinets were merged in a really skillful piece of orchestration. If this way lies the path toward the development of American modern music into a high art form, then one can heartily congratulate Mr. Gershwin on his disclosure of some of the possibilities. Nor must the captivating cleverness of Zez Confrey be forgotten. And there was Ross Gorman, a supreme virtuoso in his field, who played ten reed instruments, and Roy Maxon and Paul Whiteman himself, a born conductor and a musical personality of force and courage who is to be congratulated on his adventure and the admirable results he obtained in proving the euphony of the jazz orchestra."

"To begin with," wrote Mr. Lawrence Gilman of the *Tribune*, "Mr. Whiteman's experiment was an uproarious success. This music conspicuously possesses superb vitality and ingenuity of rhythm, mastery of novel and beautiful effects of timbre. For jazz is basically a kind of rhythm plus a kind of instrumentation. But it seems to us that this music is only half alive. Its gorgeous vitality of rhythm and of instrumental color is impaired by melodic and harmonic anemia of the most pernicious kind. Listen to the compositions of the Messrs. Archer and Kern and Gershwin.

"Ignore for a moment the fascinating rhythm and the beauty and novelty of the instrumental coloring and fasten your attention on the melodic and harmonic structure of the music. How trite and feeble and conventional the tunes are, how sentimental and vapid the harmonic treatment. Old stuff it is. Recall the most ambitious piece, the *Rhapsody,* and weep over the lifelessness of its melody and harmony, so derivative, so stale, so inexpressive. And then recall for contrast, the rich inventiveness of the rhythms, the saliency and vividness of the orchestral color."

Deems Taylor of the *World* found "Victor

Herbert's four serenades not only charming in thematic material, but they demonstrated the fact that his skill in orchestration extends to handling the unusual instrumental combinations that a jazz band presents. George Gershwin's *Rhapsody,* in a way the most interesting offering, despite its shortcomings, chief of which were an occasional sacrifice of appropriate scoring to momentary effect and a lack of continuity in the musical structure—possessed at least two themes of genuine musical worth and displayed a latent ability on the part of this young composer to say something in his chosen idiom."

In the *Times,* Olin Downes mentioned "remarkably beautiful examples of scoring for a few instruments: scoring of singular economy, color, and effectiveness. . . . Mr. Gershwin's composition shows extraordinary talent, just as it also shows a young composer with the aims that go far beyond those of his ilk. In spite of technical immaturity, he has expressed himself in a significant and on the whole highly original manner. . . ."

Gilbert Gabriel of the *Sun* called the concert "one long, strong musical cocktail. Whatever it was, fun or fol-de-rol, glorious, gory, or just plain galumphing, it was wine that needs no bush.

"The title of the *Rhapsody* was a just one for Mr. Gershwin's composition, suitable to covering a degree of formlessness to which the middle section of the work, relying too steadily on tort and retort of the piano, seemed to lag. But the beginning and the ending of it were stunning. The beginning particularly, with a flutter-tongued, drunken whoop of an introduction that had the audience rocking. Mr. Gershwin has an irrepressible pack of talents. The *Serenades* were done in Mr. Herbert's ever-ready and bright style. Mr. Whiteman has some amazing musicians under him and he shines out as an extraordinarily well-rounded musician."

That was what they said. Not all compliments by any means—even in some places a suggestion of dissatisfaction with the newcomer. But after all, the critics had come to the concert instead of sending second-string men. They had devoted their lead paragraphs to it, too, and admitted its possibilities. Poor, imperfect, immature, it still was going somewhere, they said. And so the . . . magic worked on.

Gershwin's first trip abroad was in 1923. The celebrated composer of "Swanee" had been invited to write the score for The Rainbow Revue—*which was poorly received. His second trip was in 1924, to work in the summer on another purely British show,* Primrose. *Neither* The Rainbow Revue *nor* Primrose *was mounted in the United States.* Primrose *was a hit in London; Gershwin's score is amazingly British in style and tone, verging on Gilbert and Sullivan operetta. It includes a ballet, the jazzy "Boy Wanted" (imported from America from a previous show), and three numbers for which Gershwin himself provided the orchestrations.* Primrose *was the first of the Gershwin musicals to have its complete piano-vocal score published.*

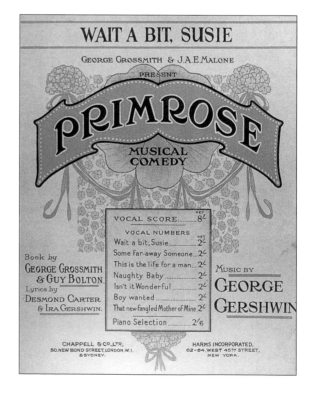

THE ASTAIRES, CATLETT, AND GERSHWIN ALL WIN

New York Telegram and Evening Mail, December 2, 1924

FRANK VREELAND

Fred and Adele Astaire returned to their New York public last night as fresh, unspoiled, and resilient as before their London dancing triumph, and life, especially at the Liberty Theatre, became particu-

Fred and Adele Astaire had been welcome performers in several shows in both New York and London, but with **Lady, Be Good!** *they gained tremendous popular and critical acclaim. They played a brother-and-sister dancing team, Dick and Susan Trevors, down on their luck and, in the opening scene, forced into the street.* **Lady, Be Good!,** *which opened on December 1, 1924, was also the first among many Gershwin shows (including* **Tip-Toes, Oh, Kay!, Funny Face,** *and* **Treasure Girl***) to be produced by the partnership of Alex A. Aarons and Vinton Freedley.*

larly worth living. The prankish Miss Astaire set a high mark for the season by scoring twelve unerring field goals by pillows kicked with her twinkling toe. This is all the more remarkable when you consider that none of the football stars who approached her standard in booting the ball did so while dancing. The rest of *Lady, Be Good!* was in keeping with that record. Alex A. Aarons and Vinton Freedley, in the second production of their youthful careers, have put over a wham of a musical comedy, with the sterling assistance of the Astaires, Walter Catlett, and George Gershwin's nervous music.

Several times during the evening the audience at the Liberty went mad over the Astaires and made them breathless up to the pulmotor stage with encores. Never have this brother and sister danced with such amazing, insouciant, and perfect unison, stamping them as the astral Astaires of musical comedy. They were all the more inspired because they seem to have found their true confederate in Cliff Edwards of the crooning ukulele and the amiable smile of the alligator in *Peter Pan*. Brooke Johns seemed to draw all the deviltry out of Ann Pennington with his mandolin. So "Ukulele Ike" last night with his yelping in "Fascinating Rhythm" seemed to rouse the Astaires to a sublime, crazy fervor.

The slyly demure Miss Astaire especially, with her antics as the society debutante who impersonated the widow of a Mexican magnate in order to turn a dishonest penny that would put herself and her impecunious brother in affluence again, was a constantly piquant sauce to the fare. When she warbled the enchanting "So Am I" with the crisp Alan Edwards as her lover, she caused numerous ladies in the audience to cluck over her cuteness. After she had been tossed with abandon in the arms of the gallant chorusmen and then kicked pillows at them, small wonder they slammed the pillows joyously back at her. She seemed like an absurd rag doll, just fit for such treatment.

With her goofy stare and her pertness, her grotesque drolleries, she suggested the tumbling Ray Dooley after she had been put through a refined finishing school. And her agile brother was equally adept, prancing and singing "The Half of It, Dearie, Blues" with the ingenuous air of a high school lad at his first dance.

The entertainment is so uniformly excellent that one can scarcely distinguish features, but Walter Catlett at his best is not to be gainsaid. His rapid-fire patter by Guy Bolton and Fred Thompson aroused such a comic din one forgave

him for reviving the sore and yellow gag about the lemon and the grapefruit.

Never did Kathlene Martyn seem so softly seductive, and in fact Gerald Oliver Smith, James Bradbury, and all the principals seemed raised above their ordinary terrestrial levels. Sammy Lee has staged the ensemble numbers with a fine frenzy. He has an uncommonly friendly, intelligent, and comely chorus at his command, and they never seemed to let their toes rest for a moment on the ground. Strong on dancing, the whole production was staged with a magnificent pace, a swirling momentum that scarcely faltered, even in the usually critical second act.

That was traceable to Gershwin's elfin music that tagged at the feet and plucked at the roots of the hair. The weirdly balanced trickeries of such syncopation as "Juanita" made it hard to remain staid and motionless. And the first musical settings of Norman Bel-Geddes, of *The Miracle* fame, beginning with the bizarre doll's-house street into which the Astaires were evicted, had a slightly nutty flavor appropriate to the rest of the delightful frolic.

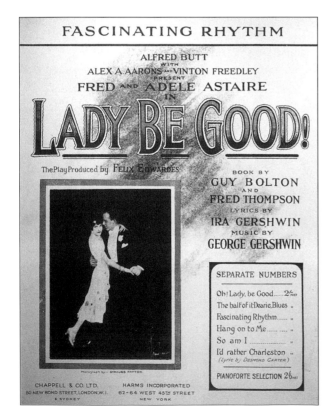

Lady, Be Good! *was the Gershwins'—George was now irrevocably linked with a nonpseudonymous Ira Gershwin as lyricist—first smash-hit musical. From this time forward, nearly every song in a Gershwin score would be stamped with the unmistakable Gershwin vitality, jazziness, and rhythmic and harmonic experimentation. The critics stood up and took notice.* **Lady, Be Good!**, *following its New York success, was imported to London (the first of several Gershwin musicals to travel overseas) with its principals, Fred and Adele Astaire. Gershwin went to London early in 1926 to help prepare the production, even adding a few more songs to the score, including the infectious "I'd Rather Charleston." Fred Astaire and Gershwin made recordings there of several songs from the show, one of which, "The Half of It, Dearie, Blues," incorporates the sounds of Astaire tap dancing as well as verbal banter between the two performers. These recordings provide some of the best extant examples of Gershwin's legendary piano style, full of vigor, surprises, and improvisatory embellishments.*

AN AMERICAN COMPOSER WHO IS WRITING NOTABLE MUSIC IN THE JAZZ IDIOM

Vanity Fair, **March 1925**

CARL VAN VECHTEN

I cannot recall the time when I did not feel an instinctive interest in American popular music. Before I could play a note on the piano I was humming or whistling such tunes as "Down Went McGinty" and "The Man Who Broke the Bank at Monte Carlo." A little later, the execrable, sentimental ballads of the early nineties, "Two Little Girls in Blue," "After the Ball," and "Daisy Bell," were tried on my piano along with two-hand arrangements of the symphonies of Mozart, Haydn, and Beethoven. When "At a Georgia Camp Meeting" and "Whistling Rufus" appeared in 1899, I appreciated this indication of a modest advance in the public taste. It is worthy of note that Debussy's sensibility to ragtime progressed no farther. His "Golliwog's Cakewalk" is an exact replica of the naive rhythmic forms employed in these pieces.

On the other hand, I gave a real welcome to Cole and Johnson's "Under the Bamboo Tree," which I admire to this day. I further enjoyed the primeval syncopations of "Bill Bailey" . . . "Ain't It a Shame?" . . . "When You Ain't Got No Money You Needn't Come Around" . . . and "Hiawatha," but when I heard "Alexander's Ragtime Band" (1911), I shouted.

Here, at last, was real American music, music of such vitality that it made the Grieg-Schumann-Wagner dilutions of MacDowell sound a little thin, and the saccharine bars of *Narcissus* and *Ophelia* so much pseudo-Chaminade concocted in an American back parlor, while it completely routed the so-called art music of the professors. At the time however, I was serving as assistant to Richard Aldrich, the music critic of the *New York Times.* In other words, I was a person of no importance whatever. Had I spoken, I should not have been heard.

Several years later, however, Irving Berlin's mas-terpiece having been succeeded by other popular airs worthy of attention such as "Everybody's Doing It" . . . and "Waiting for the Robert E. Lee," I wrote a paper entitled "The Great American Composer," published in *Vanity Fair* for April 1917, in which I outlined the reasons for my belief that it was out of American popular music that American art music would grow, just as the idiosyncratic national line of so much European art music has evolved from the national folksong. Nearly seven years passed before my prophecy was realized, but on February 12, 1924, a date which many of us will remember henceforth as commemorative of another event of importance besides the birth of our most famous president, George Gershwin's *Rhapsody in Blue* was performed for the first time by Paul Whiteman's orchestra with the composer at the piano.

There is, however, an historical prelude to the *Rhapsody.* In the spring of 1923, Eva Gauthier, indefatigable in her search for novelties, asked me to suggest additions to her autumn program. "Why not a group of American songs?" I urged. Her face betrayed her lack of interest. "Jazz," I particularized. Her expression brightened. Meeting this singer again in September, on her return from Paris, she informed me that Maurice Ravel had offered her the same sapient advice. She had, indeed, determined to adopt the idea and requested me to recommend a musician who might serve as her accompanist and guide in this venture. But one name fell from my lips, that of George Gershwin, whose compositions I admired and with whose skill as a pianist I was acquainted. The experiment was eventually made, Mme. Gauthier singing the jazz group on her program between a cluster of songs by Paul Hindemith and Béla Bartók on the one hand, and an air from Schoenberg's *Gurrelieder* on the other. This recital, given . . . [at Aeolian Hall] on November 1, 1923, marked George Gershwin's initial appearance as a performer on the serious concert stage.

The occasion did not pass uncelebrated. Newspapers and magazines commented at length on the phenomenon. Jazz, at last, it seemed, had come into its own. Presently, Paul Whiteman, weary of conducting for dancers more ready to appreciate a rigid tempo than variety in orchestration or the superlative tone quality of his band, had a pendent inspiration: he would give a concert to demonstrate the growth that jazz had made under ears too careless and indolent to distinguish the fine scoring and the intricate harmonic and rhythmic features of the new music from the haphazard, improvised performances of a few years earlier. His second idea was even more noteworthy: he commissioned George Gershwin to write a composition to be included in his first concert program.

As I had been out of the city when Mme. Gauthier gave her revolutionary recital, she very kindly invited me, late in January 1924, to hear a rehearsal of the same program in preparation for her Boston concert. It was at this rehearsal that Gershwin informed me of Whiteman's plan and added, in a rather offhand manner, that he had decided to compose a concerto in fantasia form for piano and jazz band, which he proposed to call *Rhapsody in Blue*. On that day, about four weeks before the date the composition was actually produced, he had only made a few preliminary sketches; he had not yet even found the now famous *andantino* theme! He played for me, however, the jazz theme announced by full orchestra, accompanied by figurations on the piano, and the ingenious passage, not thematic, which ushers in the finale (omitted from the phonograph record). At the first rehearsal of the program for the concert, the score was not yet ready. At the second rehearsal Gershwin played the *Rhapsody* twice with the band on a very bad piano. Nevertheless, after hearing that rehearsal, I never entertained a single doubt but that this young man of twenty-five (he was born in Brooklyn, September 26, 1898) had written the very finest piece of serious music that had ever come out of America; moreover, that he had composed the most effective concerto for piano that anybody had written since

Tchaikovsky's B-flat Minor.

Enthusiasm rewarded the first performance of the *Rhapsody*, but general and adequate appreciation of the glamour and vitality of the composition, exhibiting as it does a puissant melodic gift in combination with a talent for the invention of striking rhythms and a felicity in the arrangement of form, did not come so rapidly, perhaps, as a ready admiration for the composer's obviously rare skill as pianist. After Gershwin had performed the concerto several times in New York and other cities (Whiteman undertook a preliminary tour with his organization during the spring of 1924), recognition of its superior qualities became more widely diffused; the abridged phonograph disk (even both sides of a twelve-inch disk offer insufficient surface to record the piece in its entirety) added to its fame; and the publication of the score, arranged for two pianos, in December, sealed its triumph. It has since been performed, although seldom with the composer at the piano, at nearly every concert given by the Whiteman orchestra. Two causes have interfered with more general performances: first, the fact that the work is scored for a jazz band; second, the fact that the piano part is not only of transcendent difficulty but also demands a pianist who understands the spirit of jazz. I have no doubt whatever but that so soon as an arrangement is made for symphony orchestra the *Rhapsody* will become a part of the repertory of any pianist who can play it. Quite possibly, the work may have its flaws; so, on the other hand, has *Tristan und Isolde*.

The story of this young man's career is worthy of attention. Born in Brooklyn, George Gershwin was brought up on Grand Street in Manhattan. Until he arrived at the age of thirteen he never even thought about music. Shortly after his thirteenth birthday his mother bought a piano, for no other reason than because her sister-in-law had bought one and it seemed a proper thing to do. Once the piano was installed, somebody had to learn to play it, and young George was elected. After he had received four months' lessons, he already performed sufficiently well so that one of his father's friends advised that he be sent to Europe to study. This advice, fortunately, was not followed. Three neighborhood teachers, in turn, directed the course of his fingers. Then, by a fortuitous accident, he fell into the hands of a man who gave him his first real reverence for music. This was Charles Hambitzer, from whom he received his first lessons in harmony. He was working on the Chopin preludes when this teacher died. Gershwin was as yet unfamiliar with the work of Bach, Beethoven, Schumann, Schubert, or Brahms. A little later, he studied harmony with Edward Kilenyi, but the full course of his instruction with his several teachers occupied less than four years. In the meantime, George had become acquainted with Max Rosen, for whose playing he felt a deep admiration, but Rosen offered him no encouragement. "You will never become a musician. Give up the idea," was the violinist's candid advice.

Very early in his piano lessons he began to dabble in composition. A banal "Tango" appears to be the earliest preserved example. "Ragging the Traumerei," in 4/4 time, is written down in 2/4 and runs to twenty-one mediocre bars. At this same period he was almost fifteen—he started a song which began in F and wandered into G, from which region George found himself utterly unable to rescue it.

At the age of sixteen, George went to work as a song plugger for Remick, the music publisher, sometimes playing all day for vaudeville acts and until two or three in the morning at cafés. His remuneration was fifteen dollars a week. This irksome routine might have ruined his fingers for future concert playing but Charles Hambitzer had instructed him to play with a "loose wrist," a piece of advice which saved him his "touch." As a matter of fact, this engagement did him a real service, inasmuch as it taught him to transpose, no two performers ever being able to negotiate a song in the same key. Further vagaries of fortune led him to accept an opportunity to play the piano for the chorus rehearsals of Ned Wayburn's *Miss 1917*. It was here that he began to develop variety in his accompaniments, playing each repetition of a refrain in a different manner, a procedure which won encouragement from his employer, as it served to keep up the interest of the girls in their monotonous round of steps. It taught George the trick of lending individuality to the accompaniments of his songs. While he was playing for this

chorus, Vivienne Segal sang two of his songs at a Sunday night concert at the Century Theatre. Harry Askins, manager of *Miss 1917,* was so impressed with these tunes that he brought them to the attention of Max Dreyfus, of the firm of T. B. Harms, who immediately recognizing the ability of the young musician, put him under contract. Eight months later Gershwin wrote "I Was So Young . . . (You Were So Beautiful)" and found himself launched as the composer of a song hit.

Launched, but not satisfied. It usually happens that a manufacturer of jazz hits goes so far and no

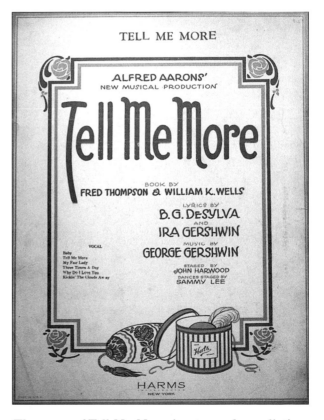

The score of **Tell Me More** *is, strangely, undistinguished; the musical was poorly reviewed but enjoyed a decent run. Gershwin produced a piano roll of a deservedly popular tune from the show, "Kickin' the Clouds Away." The composer again traveled overseas to help prepare the London production of* **Tell Me More,** *which opened there on May 26, 1925; it was a success. While in London, Gershwin also sketched themes for his new piano concerto, which had been commissioned by Walter Damrosch for the New York Symphony Orchestra.*

farther. Many popular composers are content to languidly pick tunes out with one finger on the piano, while an expert harmonizer sits by, ready to step in. It is not even an infrequent occurrence for a man's first success in this field to be his last. Gershwin apparently determined not only to hold on to his success but to improve upon it. His friends and business associates advised him not to study harmony. He answered them by working with Rubin Goldmark, from whom, he assures me, he received invaluable suggestions, especially in regard to form. He was warned that the *Rhapsody in Blue* would kill interest in his lighter music. It has had the opposite effect, as he instinctively felt that it would have.

I first became acquainted with Gershwin's music through his "Swanee," written in 1919 for the revue which opened the Capitol Theatre. With "I'll Build a Stairway to Paradise," written for the fourth of *George White's Scandals,* I completely capitulated to his amazing talent and nominated him to head my list of jazz composers. In this vein he has added to his fame with "The Yankee Doodle Blues," "Nashville Nightingale," "Do It Again," "I Won't Say I Will," "Somebody Loves Me," and the present ubiquitous "Fascinating Rhythm."

The time has not come, of course, to appraise the fellow's work. One can only predict his future in terms of his brief past. His career up to date, it will be observed, has been a steady crescendo of interest. What he will do in the future depends on no one but George Gershwin, but it is fairly evident that ample opportunity will be offered him to do many things that he ought not to do. He is unusually prolific in melodic ideas; his gift for rhythmic expression is almost unique; he has a classical sense of form. His gay music throbs with a pulse, a beat, a glamorous vitality rare in the work of any composer, and already he has the power to build up a thrilling climax, as two or three passages in the *Rhapsody* prove. Even his popular music is never banal. There is always something—if it is only two bars, as is the case in "Rose of Madrid"—to capture the attention of even a jaded listener. Tenderness and passion are as yet only potential attributes of his published music—it might be stated in passing that these are the two qualities that Stravinsky lacks—but some of Gershwin's finest inspirations have not as yet been either published or publicly performed. It is probable that the production of his twenty-four piano preludes and his tone poem for symphony orchestra, tentatively entitled *Black Belt,* will award him a still higher rank in the army of contemporary composers.

Ernest Newman has remarked, in reference to jazz, that there are no such things as movements, there are only composers. Obviously, quite true. Nevertheless, I am just as certain that the *Rhapsody* came out of the jazz movement in America as I am that Weber's *Der Freischütz* came out of the German folksong. Negro spirituals, Broadway, and jazz are Gershwin's musical godparents. Whatever he does, or however far he goes in the future, I hope that these influences will beneficently pursue him.

OUR NEW NATIONAL ANTHEM

Theatre Magazine, August 1925

GEORGE GERSHWIN

The true importance of jazz in American music is a subject over which controversy has raged back and forth. There are those who condemn the new idiom, root and branch, and there are those who profess to see in it the new musical evangel. The former brand jazz as expressive of all that is ugly in modern life, condemning it as destructive of beauty, taste, and all that goes towards artistic progress; the latter hail it as the germ of a new school of music, a school essentially American. I myself tend more to the latter than the former, but I am far from going to the extreme limit of believing that jazz is going to revolutionize music or even American music. Jazz will in time become absorbed into the great musical tradition as all other forms of music have been absorbed. It will affect that music, but it will be far from being a predominant element. It will in short find its place.

Indeed, there are many signs that it is already finding its place. The blatant jazz of ten years ago, crude, vulgar, and unadorned, is passing. In my *Rhapsody in Blue* I have tried to crystallize this fact by employing jazz almost incidentally, just as I employ syncopation. I realize that jazz expresses something very definite and vital in American

George Gershwin became the first composer to be featured on the cover of **Time** *magazine. The July 20, 1925, issue contained a short article on the Gershwin brothers, describing a typical series of events in the household and offering a brief profile of the brash young composer, stating: "Last year he composed the famed* **Rhapsody in Blue**, *a jazz concerto constructed after Liszt. It took him three weeks to write it. . . . It was . . . hailed by daring critics as 'the finest piece of music ever written in the U.S.' . . . Next season he will play his concerto with the New York Symphony." A paragraph was also devoted to Ira, who had only recently (with* **Lady, Be Good!**) *gained public recognition as a lyricist for his brother's music.*

life, but I also realize that it expresses only one element. To express the richness of that life fully, a composer must employ melody, harmony, and counterpoint as every great composer of the past has employed them. Not of course, in the same way, but with a full knowledge of their value. It was in this belief that I determined to make a serious study of composition. Many of my friends advised me not to do this, saying that it would destroy my originality. I replied that every composer of the past who had added anything vital to music had been a well-trained musician and that I was convinced that the native talent which can be killed by study must be too frail to amount to much. I felt the rhythms of American life, and in my music I had expressed them as best I could, but I knew I had gone as far as I could. To realize the richness of life, a knowledge of the past and of its technique was always needed. The future lies with the composer who, without forgetting the innate impressions of his youth, can employ in their expression the full resources of the masters of the past. It is only in this way that jazz can become of lasting value.

In speaking of jazz there is one superstition, and it is a

superstition which must be destroyed. This is the superstition that jazz is essentially Negro. The Negroes, of course, take to jazz, but in its essence it is no more Negro than is syncopation, which exists in the music of all nations. Jazz is not Negro but American. It is the spontaneous expression of the nervous energy of modern American life. . . .

The more one studies the history of jazz during the last fifteen years the more one realizes that it is following precisely the same course that all dances of the past have followed. Beginning with crudity and vulgarity, it has gradually been freeing itself and moving towards a higher plane. At first it was mere discord for the sake of discord, a simple reveling in animal vigor. But slowly the meaning of that discord, its color, its power in the depiction of American sentiment, has been brought to life. The discord of jazz is today no mere succession of meaningless and ugly grunts and wheezes. That these are still there is no doubt true, but then modern life is, alas! not expressed by smooth phrases. We are living in an age of staccato, not legato. This we must accept. But this does not mean that out of this very staccato utterance something beautiful may not be evolved. We all remember the ugliness of the early skyscraper architecture. We all remember the attacks hurled against this architecture, attacks justified in themselves yet oblivious to the beauty possible in the future. Today with such structures as the Woolworth Tower and the new Hotel Shelton we begin to realize that the skyscraper can be as beautiful as it is original. The same result will happen, I feel certain, in the case of jazz. Ugly at first, it is already feeling the touch of the beautiful. When at last it takes its proper and subordinate place in music, none of us will regret that it has come.

There is one great difficulty, however, in the employment of jazz that is extremely difficult for the composer to overcome. It is almost impossible to write down definitely, exactly, the effects wished, with the result that the musicians are only too apt to exaggerate their expression, and, if allowed to have their way, to twist the composition utterly away from the composer's intention. This is, of course up to the conductor, who must be continually on the lookout and who must rule his musicians' fancy with an iron hand. Indeed, when a conductor undertakes to direct a work in which jazz plays an important part, he must be even more jealous of the composer's intention than if he were conducting a classical symphony. Once give the musicians their head with jazz, and in a short while they will evolve something which the author himself will fail to recognize as his own offspring.

It is then as useless to deplore the triumph of jazz as it is to deplore the triumph of machinery. The thing to do is to domesticate both to our uses. The present craze for dancing will pass as everything human passes. The evil which that craze brought in its wake will also pass, but a residuum of good will remain. The employment of jazz will no longer dominate but only vitalize. It is for the trained musician who is also the creative artist to bring out this vitality and to heighten it with the eternal flame of beauty. When this time comes, and perhaps it is not so far away, jazz will be but one element in a great whole which will at last give a worthy musical expression to the spirit which is America. Meanwhile we can but do our best by writing what we feel and not what we think we ought to feel. And no one who knows America can doubt that jazz has its important place in the national consciousness.

Just as the acrobatic country dances are the expression of the vigorous life of the peasants of central Europe, just as the minuet expressed the stately grace of the civilization centered at Versailles, the popular dances of today express the nervous, somewhat unthinking vitality of present-day America. There can be little doubt that we are in a transitory stage. It is inconceivable that the present tension can continue forever. With its modification jazz will probably gradually take its proper and subordinate place. Jazz is, in short, not an end in itself but rather a means to an end. What that end will be the future musical development of the country will determine.

A JAZZ CONCERTO

The Outlook, **December 16, 1925**

Walter Damrosch has always been to the fore in the matter of presenting interesting musical programs. It is not surprising, therefore, that he should be the first symphonic conductor to experiment in earnest with an attempt to wed jazz to serious music. Under his direction, the New York Symphony Orchestra introduced to delighted audiences on December 3 and 4 a jazz concerto—George Gershwin's Concerto in F for piano and orchestra.

The youthful composer, who also officiated at the piano, has been known chiefly as a writer of popular songs and revues, and of the *Rhapsody in Blue,* performed by Paul Whiteman's orchestra more than a year and a half ago. So great was the interest created by the *Rhapsody,* Gershwin's first serious venture in jazz, that last spring Mr. Damrosch asked him to compose in the jazz idiom a piece of symphonic music. The Concerto in F is his result.

Its long-awaited performance at Carnegie Hall was received enthusiastically—and with very good cause, for, in spite of obvious shortcomings, the con-

certo displayed freshness, vitality, and audacious originality. It brimmed to overflowing with ideas, some good and some poor, and with a feverish delight in rhythm.

Yet in the rhythms employed, Gershwin's composition is new neither to jazz bands nor to symphony orchestras. Mr. Damrosch very cleverly

Ernest Hutcheson, who taught piano master classes at Chautauqua Institution (Chautauqua, N.Y.), invited Gershwin to work on his piano concerto in that peaceful enclave during July and August of 1925. Its orchestration completed in November, the Concerto in F premiered at Carnegie Hall, with Gershwin as pianist and Damrosch conducting, on December 3, 1925. Gershwin, with only two "classical" compositions to his credit, was included in a gallery of distinguished American composers assembled by the prestigious music periodical The Etude *for its booklet honoring the nation's 1926 sesquicentennial,* **Two Centuries of American Musical Composition.**

brought out this fact—and we cannot believe he did it unintentionally. He opened his program with Glazounov's Fifth Symphony, a composition of the nineteenth century; and, although none of the newspaper critics noticed the fact enough to comment on it, its finale burst forth with the identical "Charleston" rhythm which features so strongly in the Gershwin Concerto.

Gershwin's originality lies in something more than rhythm; it is an originality of language. In combining the vocabulary of serious music with that of the dance halls, he has at times gone outside the vocabulary of both. The result is stimulating. He has, so to speak, landed fish which nobody else had thought were in the stream.

On the other side of the balance must go several serious faults. The Concerto is less firmly bound together than might be hoped for. Gershwin might have used

the orchestra with greater resourcefulness and effectiveness. His critics were divided in opinion; some thought that he should forget what respectable composers in the past have said in the conventional forms, and express himself; others, that he should forget the vulgarities of his jazz, and write only respectable music. Both sides miss the mark. The only way in which Gershwin can climb to the heights for which he is striving is for him to remember every bit of jazz he ever knew, and at the same time learn all he can from the greatest composers of serious music, and particularly the masters of classical form.

Perhaps the outstanding feature of the performance of the Concerto in F was that a young American composer, unlike the vast majority, appeared to have something important to say. Or perhaps it was the even more outstanding fact that native American music was accepted by serious musicians to a further extent than has ever been done before.

Song of the Flame *is an oddity among George Gershwin's mature musicals—a pseudo-Russian, Viennese-style operetta cowritten with Herbert Stothart. Most of the tunes, including "Vodka," received joint credits; Gershwin alone wrote "Midnight Bells" and "The Signal." Although basically a critical failure,* **Song of the Flame** *proved surprisingly popular, even outdistancing the concurrent jazzy Gershwin brothers hit* **Tip-Toes** *in total performances.*

AND WHAT HE WROTE

from *So This Is Jazz* (1926)

HENRY O. OSGOOD

Reading the jeremiads that have been launched against jazz within the last few years by solemn bigwigs of the musical elite, one might imagine that the very existence of legitimate music was threatened. Nothing could be farther from the truth. What are the facts? That various composers who deserve serious consideration have written about a dozen or fifteen compositions purporting to be higher jazz and scored for a jazz orchestra . . . and that none of them promises to attain any degree of permanency on concert programs. This leaves, up to the present time, only the Gershwin works, the *Rhapsody in Blue* and the Piano Concerto in F, as representative of a successful attempt to graft upon the great trunk of legitimate music little offshoots of that vigorous sapling which is the only really original thing America has produced in music—jazz. Before looking at those two it will be worthwhile to consider another Gershwin experiment, the one-act operatic sketch *135th Street,* produced at the Whiteman concerts at Carnegie Hall [December 1925–January 1926].

There has been much talk for some time past of a "jazz opera." Reports insisted that Otto H. Kahn, chairman of the board of directors of the Metropolitan Opera Company, was looking for a jazz opera for production by that august organization; that he had commissioned one from Mr. Gershwin, from Mr. Smith, or from Mr. Brown. Mr. Kahn insisted that he wasn't looking for anything; that he had commissioned nothing. He said, however, that a jazz opera was bound to come some day and he is doubtless right in so thinking. . . .

One day there will be written an American libretto in which the spirit of jazz will predominate, forming the larger element of the story; then jazz, following the story, will predominate in the score. I do not believe there is sufficient basic musical value in jazz to allow any composer, however inge-nious, to construct an operatic score that shall be nothing else from beginning to end and still be interesting. It will be hybrid music, just as all other operatic music is hybrid.

And Gershwin was hybrid in his little jazz opera, which deserved a better fate than it met with, though the fault was not his. Under the title of *Blue Monday,* it started out as a sketch for one of *George White's Scandals* and had a continuous run of one night—the opening one—being promptly discarded as too highbrow. It lay neglected for several years until Whiteman decided to do it as a special feature of a concert program. Several things killed it as produced at Carnegie Hall. The cast was not ideal—for the most part, in fact, distinctly poor; it was found impossible to hang the scenery on the stage, so it was played on the front of the platform, with the orchestra itself for a background, utterly destructive of any theatrical effect there might have been in it. To see the wicked heroine wailing over the body of her dead lover out on the Carnegie Hall apron, while ample Mr. Whiteman waved his arms and his men blew and scraped behind them, was the height of the ridiculous. And above all, the book, of the Italian verismo, *Pagliacci / Cavalleria Rusticana* type, translated into blackface by its author, Bud DeSylva, was impossible.

The music, however, was distinctly interesting. It proved the possibilities of building up on some jazz tunes what would have done very acceptably for one act in a jazz opera. Mr. Gershwin's principal material was in two numbers, a slow tune, sort of a lament—"My Lovin' Henry" [*sic;* "Has Anyone Seen My Joe?"] was the title, I believe; and a real blues, called "Blue Monday Blues." Using snatches of these for the leading motives, he constructed a twenty-five-minute score that was varied, effective, and distinctly dramatic. It was cleverly done. There was, for instance, a comic dance for the entrance of the customers of the saloon

Henry O. Osgood was the editor of The Musical Courier *and an early champion of Gershwin and "jazz." His book* So This Is Jazz *contains two full chapters on George Gershwin.*

(the scene was laid in one of these obsolete places), which was afterward skillfully interwoven as counterpoint to the "Lovin' Henry" theme. Gershwin was greatly aided, too, by Grofé's instrumentation, full of variety and color. I remember, for instance, three-part chords in the lower register of three muted trombones, used for a special effect, recalling the ingenuity of Meyerbeer in inventing novel orchestral colors to support and heighten a dramatic situation.

The point is that, unsuccessful with the public as it was and must have been under the circumstances, Gershwin demonstrated the possibilities of jazz as legitimate operatic material when handled with imagination. After seeing *135th Street* (the title derives from the situation of that thoroughfare in the heart of New York City's largest colored section, Harlem) one was convinced of the possibility of a jazz opera, whether or not Gershwin shall be the one to produce it. . . .

[*Rhapsody in Blue.*] Gershwin purposely chose the title *Rhapsody* to leave himself unhampered by the rules of musical form, a rhapsody being, musically speaking, a free-for-all, catch-as-catch-can affair. It is interesting to note that, notwithstanding this, he fell into a regular form, for the composition, though played without pause, has the regulation three movements of the concerto for solo instrument and orchestra—the moderately paced opening allegro, a slow section, and a brisk finale. It is, in fact, a concerto for piano and orchestra with rather more allowance of piano than usual, as might be expected from the fact that Gershwin himself was the only one who knew and could play the piano part when the piece was new. In the

reduction for two pianos no less than eighteen pages out of forty-two are occupied by the music for the solo piano playing alone. Gershwin even adopts the classical proceeding of setting forth the principal themes in the introduction before the solo instrument is heard at all. . . .

The [musical] analyst . . . itches to analyze [the score] because somebody is speaking with a new voice, the voice of jazz, but jazz adapted to the proceedings of a day long before jazz existed.

The result is something absolutely original. Can anybody show pages from an orchestral score that preceded the *Rhapsody* and say, "Here is where Gershwin got his idea." I don't know any such pages. It isn't Debussy, it isn't Strauss, and it isn't any of the Russian Five, those three principal influences on the younger orchestral writers of today. It's jazz—jazz mulled over in a sensitive musical mind and coming out with a good deal of the dross removed. It isn't pure gold yet: it may never be. But with those first pages of the *Rhapsody*, George Gershwin produced something really new in music, to do which has fallen to the lot of exceedingly few composers in the long list. . . .

[*Concerto in F.*] How pleasant to leave to Walter Damrosch, who ordered it, the task of introducing, in one of his graceful and flowing periods, the second of Gershwin's serious jazz works—the Piano Concerto in F, first played at a concert of the New York Symphony Orchestra, Mr. Damrosch conducting, at Carnegie Hall, New York, December 3, 1925. The composer played the piano part—for one reason: because no one else could.

Thus Mr. Damrosch: "Various composers have been walking around jazz like a cat around a plate of hot soup, waiting for it to cool off, so that they could enjoy it without burning their tongues, hitherto accustomed only to the more tepid liquid distilled by cooks of the classical school. Lady Jazz, adorned with her intriguing rhythms, has danced her way around the world. . . . But for all her travels and her sweeping popularity, she has encountered no knight who could lift her to a level that would enable her to be received as a respectable member in musical circles. George Gershwin seems to have accomplished this miracle. He has done it boldly by dressing this extremely independent and up-to-date young lady in the classic garb of a concerto. Yet he has not detracted one whit from her fascinating personality. He is the prince who has taken Cinderella by the hand and openly proclaimed her a princess to the astonished world, no doubt to the fury of her envious sisters."

After this Mr. Gershwin came out amid tumultuous applause, sat down on the piano bench and "unto her did say" . . . what he said first. Very loud and noisy it was, and not especially effective, but it caught the attention, those four measures of percussion. Then came the first announcement of the Charleston rhythm which predominated in the first movement, followed by a tricky little figure on bassoon and clarinet, unison, with celli and basses holding a soft open fifth beneath. After this material, almost purely rhythmic in character, had been developed into quite a long introductory section for orchestra alone, the solo piano came in unobtrusively (as in the *Rhapsody*) with the principal theme of the movement, . . . strikingly original both in its melodic line and harmonic dress. Beneath it is a clever contrapuntal obbligato for English horn. This theme is certainly jazzy in its character, yet carries the burden of development put upon it later just as well as if its parent had been of a classic family from the noblest symphonic lineage. The contrasting lyric theme comes on the muted strings in the unrelated key of E major. . . . Then, while the strings play a simple variation of it in octaves, the piano has a rhythmically picturesque obbligato. . . . The movement, the longest of the three, is . . . very animated, with the vigorous rhythm of the Charleston predominating. There is a climax (*grandioso*) in which the whole orchestra . . . devotes itself to a *fortissimo* exposition of the first theme, the contrapuntal obbligato, on the first appearance of the theme. . . . On the whole, this first movement, though decidedly entertaining, is the least effective.

Phil Ohman and Victor Arden were duo-pianists whose sparkling sound Gershwin thought perfect for his shows. He insisted that they be prominent in the orchestra pit for many of his musicals, from Lady, Be Good! *onward, and including* Tip-Toes, *from which comes two of Gershwin's liveliest flapper-era tunes, "That Certain Feeling" (the composer's last piano roll) and "When Do We Dance?"*

The second movement begins with a passage which is one of the best and most original things Gershwin has done. After three measures of a solo horn, *pp*, which immediately establishes the mood, a solo trumpet, muted, above a three-part accompaniment of clarinets, sings one of the quaintest tunes imaginable, absolutely novel in line, a perfect expression of the tragicomic nature of the blues. The tune itself . . . is directly comic in some of its turns, as, for instance, in measure ten, where the wavering, indeterminate melodic phrase is suddenly succeeded by the drop of an octave and a sixth, with the muted trumpet buzzing like an angry bee on that entirely unlooked-for *sforzando* A-flat. This passage, in shape, form, orchestral color, melodic and harmonic lines is another one for which one seeks in vain a precedent in musical literature. It cracks the ear of the attentive (and musical) listener like a good joke. It is actually laughter provoking.

After the trumpet and its friends have got through with the theme, the composer hands it over to the solo piano to have a good time with, which it proceeds to do in merriest manner, . . . above thrummed pizzicato chords on the strings, sounding like a magnified guitar accompaniment. This goes on for some time, with various ingenious figures and variants for both piano and orchestra, until the simple beginning harmonies of the thrummed accompaniment suggest a new theme to the composer. . . . Using this for a base he works up a climax which ends abruptly on a crashing A minor tonic chord; then, after a single beat of silence, the short ten-measure coda begins with the first measure . . . in D-flat major. It reads like an abrupt and willful jump to a totally unrelated key—but the enthusiastic analyst will discover that the A minor–D-flat jump is perfectly legitimate and explainable; also it sounds well, which is the ultimate test.

The third movement, to speak technically, may be called a toccata in rondo form; to speak from experience, it is very exciting in its headlong dash to the finish, interrupted only once just before the final coda by a literal repetition of the *grandioso* passage from the first movement. The orchestra sets the pace in a twenty-measure introduction, then the piano takes up the rhythm, . . . which gives an idea of the vigorous briskness of the whole movement. For the most part, there is an ingenious reworking of themes from the preceding two movements. . . . Two themes from the slow movement appear in new guise, the second of them doubled in pace. . . . The piano part bristles with difficulties, many of the figures and devices suggesting the thought that George Gershwin had become more or less familiar with the works of Franz Liszt when he "took piano"—not so many years ago, at that.

Breathless is a good adjective to apply to this last movement. It has the rhythmic persistence of Stravinsky, though its thematic material does not suggest him. At the end the percussion instruments go to work again in that same figure that begins the Concerto, . . . and the work goes out in a blaze of noise, every instrument of the orchestra—except the trombones, which are unable to, for anatomic reasons—trilling on some note of the common chord of F major.

Messrs. Damrosch and Gershwin played the Concerto three times in New York and a few more on trips of the orchestra to outside cities. To judge by the enthusiasm displayed, the audiences heartily enjoyed it. In the nature of things it could hardly expect the popular success of that startlingly projected novelty, the *Rhapsody,* though from the musician's standpoint the Concerto is much better. Taking into consideration Gershwin's previous accomplishments and limited musical study, it is literally remarkable. It more than carried out the promise of the *Rhapsody* in proving the adaptabili-

ty of jazz elements to compositions in the larger form. I know of no other American work that has such a large percentage of originality. One can point to one or two things—though they are in no sense plagiarisms—that recall the Rachmaninoff of the Second Piano Concerto; there is a Debussy-like descending chord passage used two or three times in the second movement; but by far the greater part of it is Gershwin. He made the orchestration himself for straight symphony orchestra, without saxophones or banjos. Their omission seems rather a pity. As a whole the orchestration came off very well, though revision of certain passages, especially some for the strings (stranger, of course, to a jazz orchestrator, than the woodwind and brass) would brighten and lighten the score.

Certainly Gershwin has written a real piano concerto; certainly it is decidedly different from any other piano concerto. Some of my critical colleagues, because the work is labeled concerto, were befogged by memories of concerto writers from Tschaikovsky and Brahms back to Schumann, Beethoven, and even Mozart, and failed to discover what they were listening to; but until they advance stronger arguments than they so far have done, I shall continue to believe and preach that the Piano Concerto in F is one of the most important contributions to American musical literature ever made. It is better, even, than it sounded, as I discovered on a thorough study of the score after listening to four performances. All credit to Mr. Damrosch for having had the enterprise to order it. . . . There is more in the score than he got out of it—life, accent, vigor, spirit; also symphony players, willing and eager as they may be, are not ideal jazzists. Leopold Stokowski, the other night, made a Vienna Philharmonic out of his Philadelphia men to play Strauss's *Geschichten aus dem Wiener Wald;* perhaps his genius might even metamorphose them into a second Whiteman band, to the greater glory of himself, themselves, and Gershwin. It's worth thinking of.

MR. GERSHWIN'S LATEST

New York *World*, December 29, 1925

ALEXANDER WOOLLCOTT

Bright and gay and good-looking, the new musical comedy which came to the Liberty last night is made altogether captivating by the pretty, rebel, infectious music of George Gershwin—all told, the best score he has written in his days in the theater; all told, I think, the best score anyone has written for our town this season.

The piece is called *Tip-Toes,* and it is, for the most part, the work of the same people who gave us *Lady, Be Good!* last season. If, as I did, you liked *Lady, Be Good!,* you will, I am sure, be both pleased and surprised to hear that *Tip-Toes* is, by a hasty but expert calculation, here firmly reported as precisely three times as entertaining.

It was, of course, Gershwin's evening, so sweet and sassy are the melodies he has poured out for this *Tip-Toes,* so fresh and unstinted the gay, young flood of his invention. The new tunes range from the seductive, almost cloying waltz he wrote called "Looking for a Boy" to the hot, panting, exuberant Charleston tune, that "Sweet and Low-Down"—to say nothing of the pert ditty entitled "These Charming People," which is made memorable in the annals of Tin Pan Alley by its unblinking determination to rhyme "enjoy it" with "Detroit."

But all the good tunes ever trolled will not make a musical comedy. That calls for a hundred helping hands, and this scant review would need the literary style of the City Directory to distribute all the bouquets that are due to those who compounded this festivity. Why, care must even be taken to see that all the wreaths addressed to Gershwin do not go to the compos-

Queenie Smith was a notable theatrical star, a former dancer at the Metropolitan Opera, and a main attraction of Tip-Toes, *in which she played Tip-Toes Kaye and sang one of the hits of the show, "Looking for a Boy."*

er, for it is his elder brother, Ira Gershwin, who writes the lyrics which helped George Gershwin's tunes in their journey across the land. He has worked cleverly and engagingly this time. The result is good.

Then it struck some mad fellow in the management to insist that these lyrics might as well be heard, word for word. At all events it has worked out that way in the singing of them.

Finally, some other rash innovator seemed to think that just because the stock of melody ran high and the ensemble dances were certain of success was no good reason why the show should be no laughing matter. So they went out and tore Harry Watson Jr. from the bosom of the two-a-day, as funny a fellow as one could ask for.

Mr. Watson plays a rummy old vagabond of the type that was W. C. Fields's portion in *Poppy*. Like all the works of the masters this season (from Eugene O'Neill to George Kaufman), the scene of *Tip-Toes* is the love-lee land of Floree-dah. Master Watson arrives in shoes worn so thin that he can stand on a dime and tell whether it's heads or tails. Later you are rendered hilarious by his efforts to get his soup down, despite the necessity of rising to his feet every time a woman approaches him.

"And how," asks Mr. Tombes, "do you like your soup?"

"Well," says Mr. Watson pensively, "I kinda wish I hadn't stirred it up."

"And I," says a fair coryphée (hired at enormous expense, no doubt, just to make this impor-

tant observation) "am to sit on the right hand of the host at dinner."

"You are!" exclaims the bemused Watson in genuine surprise. "Then how's he going to stir his coffee?"

And perhaps you too would have rolled into the aisle when Tombes referred to the butler, Meadows, as "an old family container."

Perhaps these quips seemed more comical under the spell of the show's own communicable glow. The glow enveloped Queenie Smith till she seemed at least four times as engaging as ever in her life before. It embraced that capital juvenile, Allen Kearns.

It even reached down into the orchestra pit, on which a great amount of character and piquancy was bestowed by the presence of Victor Arden and Phil Ohman, adding the staccato of a trained tandem piano to the orchestration, and once going it alone, with a very tumult of applause ensuing. And it reached a high point when, to the lisping of a hundred tapping feet in "Sweet and Low-Down," a forest of trombones suddenly added their moans. Then the Liberty Theatre quietly but firmly went mad.

December 1925 was the culmination of an incredibly busy—and artistically productive—period for George Gershwin. His second major serious composition, the Concerto in F, was premiered by the New York Symphony; **Tip-Toes** *opened, containing one of the Gershwin brothers' jazziest and strongest scores; the musical* **Song of the Flame** *began its successful run; and Paul Whiteman presented a new staging of Gershwin's 1922* **Scandals** *one-act opera, now entitled* **135th Street** *and reorchestrated for the occasion by Ferde Grofé.*

DOES JAZZ BELONG TO ART?

Singing, July 1926

GEORGE GERSHWIN

No student of singing can afford any longer to ignore jazz music or to sniff at it as being of low estate and of negative cultural value. The study and practice of jazz has a very important contribution to make toward the complete training of any modern disciple of the musical art. It can be of positive benefit to the vocalist in every department of his profession. The new understanding of rhythm which it imparts will simplify and amplify all his repertoire.

In the above sentences I have been bluntly dogmatic. Purposely so, because I believe the time has come when these statements can be made flatly and without apology, as matters of proved truth.

I have no intention of "defending" jazz. I am no propagandist, and I have no time to waste in "converting" those who hide their heads in the sand like the ostrich, and decline to see things as they are. Let jazz speak for itself. It is here, and all the tirades of our musical jeremiahs cannot take it from us or abate its profound influence on the music of the present and future.

There has been too much argument about jazz—most of it from people who are not even clear in their terminology. To condemn jazz, for example, because there is much bad jazz in the world, is as absurd as to condemn all music because much bad music exists. I hold no brief for those compositions of the Dada school, which employ the instrumentation of electric fans or couple fifty synchronized electric pianos in a riot of noisy cacophony. That is not jazz; it is merely delirium. But if you take the best of our modern serious jazz music and study it, you can come to only one conclusion—that it is, in the words of Madame D'Alvarez, "America's greatest contribution to the musical art."

The most vicious opponents of jazz bring the impartiality of complete ignorance to their judgment seat. "Of course I know very little about music," naively remarked Dr. John Roach Straton at the Town Hall Club, "but I am sure that jazz singing comes from the Devil and will have no place in the heavenly choir."

A few days later, a distinguished scientist, president of one of our greatest universities, ventured to deliver a commencement address before his University School of Music. For the greater part of his address he stuck to his own bailiwick and talked paternally, but sensibly, about science. But finally he slipped into the abyss of trying to speak with equal authority on a subject outside his ken. "My dear children," he said over his spectacles, "beware the dreadful jazz. Cultivate good music. While there may be art in these modern rhythms, it certainly is a different art than that portrayed in the established and recognized classics. Hold fast to that which has been proved by time." He continued with a great deal more of the same kind of twaddle. Words, empty words, revealing nothing save a complete ignorance of his subject.

What would the learned prexy say if a musician of note should rise before the commencement class in his Scientific School and proclaim: "Boys and girls, beware the modern in science. Shun evolution and the studies and investigations of recent years. Give your time to Lucretius and the established classics of the golden age of King Tut. There is no such thing as progress. All that is good is old. All that is new is bad."

Every musician who has studied modern music knows that jazz already has made a real contribution to our art. How much this contribution will mean in the next decade nobody can predict, but assuredly its part will be large and important. Every composer of the present day has given a great deal of time and study to this musical development, although many of them cannot themselves write jazz successfully.

The successful jazz artist, whether he be composer, instrumentalist, or singer, should get the rhythm into his blood early in life. Acquisition of the jazz art in one's riper years is always difficult and sometimes impossible. One of our most distinguished American singers, who has made a profound study of jazz and who sings a great deal of it, has never been quite able to get the genuine rhythm of it. He comprehends it intellectually, and it delights him, even though the complete thrill and abandon of the composition is somehow lacking. But he has deliberately specialized in the intellectual interpretation of jazz, and his contribution has been unique and important, because he has been able to show that there is a real musical soul in jazz, entirely apart from the powerful reaction of its native rhythms.

The late Amy Lowell, great New England poet and seer, was one of those who loved jazz, although she could neither sing it nor play it nor dance it. "I can only move my toe to it," she told me once, "but if I couldn't do that, I think I should burst with the rapture of it."

Jazz had a hard row to hoe in England for many years. The English are conservative to a fault, and they dislike to make even the slightest effort to comprehend anything which is new to their experience. But jazz has at last won its way to their hearts, and today I think the English understand its essential musical virtues better even than we do in America. Paul Whiteman last year packed Albert Hall fuller than it had ever been before in its musical history, and his audience was symptomatic of a change that pervades every stratum of English musical appreciation.

"Jazz is the music of the street," said a learned divine the other day, apparently feeling that this was the final word in condemnation. It is true that many

Singing, a serious music magazine, heralded Gershwin's article on its July 1926 cover. A counter-article questioning the artistic validity of "jazz" by A. Walter Kramer appeared in the September issue. The debate continued when Gershwin replied with a lengthy refutation, published in the October issue.

of the street songs of today are jazz in character, but our best jazz is far too good musically to be popular in the street. Practically none of my own songs can boast of that wide popularity which entitles them to be called "songs of the street."

In the very dignified and sedate program which I shall give with Mme. D'Alvarez in the Hotel Roosevelt recital series this fall, my own part will consist of selections from the *Rhapsody in Blue,* supplemented by two or three jazz preludes on which I am now working and which will come before the public for the first time on that occasion. Later in the program, I shall accompany Mme. D'Alvarez in several songs selected from my later musical comedies, such as *Lady, Be Good!* and *Tip-Toes.*

Not one of the numbers on that program will be cheap or trashy in character, I am sure. They are all of sound musical value, and worthy of a place on any sober and dignified program. This partnership of Mme. D'Alvarez and myself in support of modern music comes as the result of her recent defense of jazz in a debate with the Reverend John Roach Straton. She sings jazz better, I believe, than any other great singer on our concert or opera stage today, because she interprets with fidelity and enthusiasm, not merely the notes, but the spirit and the rhythm of the music.

It's marvelous what a really great voice can do, musically speaking, with a good jazz air. The greater the voice, the greater its effectiveness in jazz interpretation, provided only that the singer has a superlative sense of rhythm. Rhythm is the very life of music. "Without perfect rhythmical feeling," we are told, "you can never move an audience to tears nor stir an army to action."

Jazz is no child's play. Good jazz music needs as much effort and ability for its mastery as any other music. I suspect that many first-class musicians are forced to adopt an air of supercilious contempt toward it because they cannot master it. Perhaps they started too late; perhaps they never started at all; perhaps they lacked the "divine spark" which, after all, is an essential of good jazz performance. If you think that jazz is easy, try Kern's "They Didn't Believe Me" as a studio exercise: there are some passages in that song that will prove difficult hurdles for any voice.

I have been asked to recommend a list of jazz songs which a concert singer might study, either as an introduction to jazz rhythms or with a view to public performance. . . . "Siren Song" (Kern); "Japanese Sandman" (Whiting-Egan); "St. Louis Blues" (Handy); "The Jazz City" (Souvainc); "International Rag" (Berlin); "I Want to Be Happy" (Youmans); "Carolina in the Morning" (Donaldson); "They Didn't Believe Me" (Kern); "Stairway to Paradise" (Gershwin); "Swanee" (Gershwin); "Nashville Nightingale" (Gershwin).

For any singer, an excellent training in jazz rhythms is the study of the phonograph records made by singers like Marion Harris, Al Jolson, and the Revelers. The quartet singing of the Revelers is marvelous, not merely in their perfection of rhythm, but also in their unique ability to get unusual and skillful orchestral effects with the voice.

There are some singers who will not find, in the present jazz vocal repertoire, anything which they will desire to add to their platform programs. But there are none of them who will not benefit greatly, in the broad sense of musical culture, from the serious study and practice of the rhythmic gymnastics which jazz supplies.

I close with the moral of this little tale: If you are a singer, don't ignore jazz music. Study it, love and cherish it, give it free rein in your heart. It will repay you a hundredfold. It will help you over many tough spots in your classics. It will add a new rhythmic meaning to your whole repertoire, old and new. It will be your good friend and companion through sunshine and shadow.

Don't condemn jazz on the say-so of any old fogy. Avoid musical snobbery. Think for yourself. Live in the musical present and the past will be even more significant and precious.

A Note from the Editors of *Singing*

Born in Brooklyn in 1898, George Gershwin was educated in the New York schools, studied harmony with Rubin Goldmark and piano with Charles Hambitzer. He wrote his first musical comedy, *La La Lucille,* at the age of nineteen. During the nine years which have followed, he has written the scores of twenty-two musical comedies, operettas, or revues. More serious works, in which he has "sublimated" jazz, have claimed a share of his attention during the past three or four years. A one-act opera, *135th Street,* was produced for one performance at the Globe Theatre, New York, in 1922, and was revived in 1925 at Carnegie Hall. The *Rhapsody in Blue* was written in 1924, and the Concerto in F in 1925. The Concerto is to be published in full this winter.

We are presenting Mr. Gershwin's article not because we agree with his viewpoint but simply because we wish to give a respectful hearing to the arguments of the foremost creative artists of the jazz school. Our own views on the subject of jazz were clearly set forth in our editorial columns a few months ago. We agree that jazz is a vital expression of certain phases of our modern life: a rhythmic reflection of the ugliness and clatter. Moreover, most jazz composers are overrated and overpraised, thanks to the high-powered publicity and propaganda fathered by zealous members of our literary intelligentsia, writers who detect sanctified art in the pleasantries of Messrs. Mutt and Jeff, the Katzenjammer Kids, and the delightful antics of Mr. Charlie Chaplin. The hackneyed character of the programs offered by solemn-eyed exponents of "serious" music may also be responsible for the vogue of jazz—but this is another story.

Mr. Gershwin is an earnest young musician with sophisticated ways. His earnestness and inventive gifts set him in a special niche far removed from the serried rows of Broadway commercialists. We look for a truly representative American operetta from the Gershwin pen one of these days; perhaps after the jazz flood has subsided.

Anyhow, we intend to be present when Mr. Gershwin and the mercuric Mme. D'Alvarez begin their invasion of our tranquil recital halls.

MR. GERSHWIN REPLIES TO MR. KRAMER

Singing, October 1926

GEORGE GERSHWIN

I have just read Mr. A. Walter Kramer's article in the September issue of *Singing*. Mr. Kramer's sympathies are in no way antijazz; he merely feels, he says, that jazz ought to "stay in its place."

The most painful thing about any discussion of jazz is the seemingly inevitable confusion of terminology. The word *jazz* ought to be limited to a certain type of dance music. The word has been used for so many different things that it has ceased to have any definite meaning.

For instance, here are some of the widely different things that just now go under the heading of jazz: popular songs like "Papa Loves Mama"; adaptations of the classics to dance rhythms; Negro spirituals; even a waltz number like Irving Berlin's "What'll I Do?"; the *Rhapsody in Blue*.

Some people go so far as to affix the jazz label to my Concerto in F, in which I have attempted to utilize certain jazz rhythms worked out along more or less conventional symphonic lines.

We need a new set of words for each of these widely divergent types, because much of the present discussion degenerates into a mere quibbling over words and definitions. The same word trouble surrounds the colloquial use of the phrase *classic*[*al*] *music*. It means as many things as there are people who say it. A man writes a piece of music which he considers serious, but which really is pretty awful; he labels his work classic[al] and an unsuspecting public accepts the label. From any sound critical standpoint, labels mean nothing at all. Good music is good music, even if you call it oysters.

Mr. Ernest Newman, who denounced jazz recently in no uncertain terms, was apparently speaking mainly about adaptations of the classics to dance rhythms. He heard the *Rhapsody in Blue* last year and wrote: "Mr. Gershwin's *Rhapsody* is by far the most interesting thing of its kind I have yet met. It really has ideas, and they work themselves out in a way that interests the musical hearer."

In other words, ideas are the things that count, not mere labeling of form.

Mr. Newman continued: "But is this really jazz? The *Rhapsody* certainly begins as jazz, and every now and then in its later course it behaves as such. But it seems to me to forget to live up to its name for a great part of the time. Jazz, in fact, is now obeying a universal law of musical evolution. Why did so many passages in the *Rhapsody* sound so Brahms-like? I should not be surprised in five or ten years to find Mr. Gershwin writing classical music. What is at present certain is that he has written something for a jazz orchestra that is really music."

As long as there is such a thing as music known as jazz, which is understood and appreciated by millions of people—some highbrow, but mostly lowbrow—the musician should at least know what it is and what it is all about. His musical education is incomplete if he refuses even to recognize that it exists. When I recommended jazz studies to singers, all that I maintained was that certain numbers written in the jazz idiom would do them a lot of good from the standpoint of rhythm and accent. Here is a type of material which they can get in no other songs or vocal exercises.

There are one or two specific points in Mr. Kramer's article which I would like to correct. He is entirely right in saying that the song "They Didn't Believe Me" is not jazz. I do not consider it jazz either, and the mention of it in my article was an error in the transposition of my dictation, which I did not have the opportunity to correct owing to my departure for England. The song which I had in mind was Irving Berlin's "Everybody Step," which because of its very interesting rhythmical qualities would help any singer who is at all interested in rhythmical variation for the voice.

Mr. Kramer does me an injustice in stating that my piano concerto was orchestrated by anyone but myself. The *Rhapsody in Blue* was orchestrated by

Ferde Grofé, but this was done because the Whiteman orchestra is such a unique combination. And yet Mr. Grofé worked from a very complete piano and orchestral sketch, in which many of the orchestral colors were indicated. Even so fine an orchestrator as Deems Taylor gave his *Circus Days* to Grofé to orchestrate for Whiteman.

But the Concerto was orchestrated entirely by myself. I should be delighted to arrange a meeting with Mr. Kramer at his earliest convenience and go over with him the full score of this concerto. . . .

And by the way, Mr. Kramer's point about the importance of orchestration seems to me a little overstressed. He says: "It is the *arranger's* instrumental version that one hears. And instead of applauding *him,* one applauds the composer, who may have done little more than write the tune." Bach's *Passacaglia* was a great piece of music before Stokowski orchestrated it. Rimsky-Korsakov reorchestrated in great measure Moussorgsky's *Boris Goudonov.* Chopin, although one of the world's greatest musicians, was a notably poor orchestrator.

The ability to orchestrate is a talent apart from the ability to create. The world is full of most competent orchestrators who cannot for the life of them write four bars of original music.

To sum up, a final quotation from Mr. Newman, slightly abbreviated to conserve space: "There is no virtue in any particular form of music. If the art of fugue writing had been discovered only a few years ago, there would probably have happened to it just what has happened to jazz: everybody would be writing fugues, and 999 out of every thousand would be very bad fugues. There is no salvation for music in forms or fashions or coteries; there is salvation only in composers."

A Note from the Editors of *Singing*

In the September issue of *Singing,* A. Walter Kramer, the American composer, threw his hat vigorously into the ring by declaring that "jazz does not belong" to musical art. His article was in reply to an earlier one from Mr. Gershwin, who pleaded for a serious appraisal of syncopated composition.

Writing irks Mr. Gershwin, and he has no desire to participate in any long-drawn controversy which would draw him out of his musical medium into the toils of the unfamiliar typewriter. The letter from him which we print above is, he suggests, merely an explanation of certain points brought up by Mr. Kramer. His real reply to critics of his position regarding jazz will be made, he avers, in musical notation, through a group of six new piano preludes, which he will present to the public for the first time in his appearance with Mme. D'Alvarez at the [Hotel] Roosevelt recitals on December 4.

In 1926 Gershwin accompanied Marguerite D'Alvarez in an evening of classical and popular songs, along the lines of his 1923 concert with Eva Gauthier. The recital at the Hotel Roosevelt on December 4 also premiered a two-piano version of the **Rhapsody in Blue** *plus five Gershwin piano preludes. One of these, the Novelette in Fourths, is an early composition that Gershwin recorded in 1919 on a Welte-Mignon piano roll. This prelude was combined with a second novelette (1923) by noted violinist Samuel Dushkin in* **Short Story,** *a piece for violin and piano that was introduced at the University Club of New York on February 8, 1925. To these two preludes were added three others for the group of five on the D'Alvarez program (a sixth briefly surfaced at the January 16, 1927, D'Alvarez concert in Boston). The three newer pieces, which seemed more of a unit, were published in 1927 as Preludes for Piano—a work that has since become a favorite in concert halls the world over.*

DALE FINDS MUCH GOOD IN 'OH, KAY!'

New York American, **November 9, 1926**

ALAN DALE

I suppose that at least one-half of the rampant and rollicking mob at the Imperial Theatre last night went thither to see Gertrude Lawrence, late of the *Charlot's Revue* and translated into musical come-

Gershwin's friendship with Gertrude Lawrence began in 1924 and was cemented during his stay in London in 1926. An English performer who had gained an American following with her appearances in two **Charlot's Revues** *on Broadway, Lawrence sang what would become one of George and Ira Gershwin's most enduring ballads, "Someone to Watch over Me," to a rag doll in the brothers' new hit show,* **Oh, Kay!** *Lawrence presented George with an autographed photo at Christmas 1926, during the musical's run.*

dy by one of the metamorphoses not uncommon in the theater. That was my reason for selecting this entertainment entitled *Oh, Kay!* and leaving even such a star as Fay Bainter for future consideration.

But if the truth must be told—and I suppose it must—Miss Lawrence didn't seem particularly happy in her new translation.

Always the artist, always delightful, humorous, piquant, and other adjectives of equal import, Miss Lawrence scarcely lent herself to the constant interruptions of chorus, funnymen, plot, and the other accessories of the unchanging entertainment "with music."

To be sure, everything she did last night she did well, and superwell. But there was hardly enough of her, and she is positively no musical comedy scintillation. She had various songs; she splashed through a stupid plot, she looked admirable, and she was incessantly charming.

Oh, Kay!, however, boasted some really nice and clever and unusual music by George Gershwin—music far removed from molasses and stickiness and the usual saccharine doses of the musical show—music that had charm, orchestration, pep, agility, alertness, freshness, and intricacy—music that it was a pleasure to hear after the sugary drippings of the average musical show. Gershwin was the outstanding feature of last night.

The "book" by Bolton and Wodehouse was sad to the verge of tears. It oozed a gentle melancholy, and sometimes listening to the brilliant music of Mr. Gershwin, silly tears seemed to be imminent when the "plot" intruded itself. It appeared to have something occult to do with bootleggery, and it enclosed a silly Dook, a more silly revenue officer, and a funnyman who did the booze ad nauseam. But this book didn't matter. It was only occasional.

For the most part they sang and danced and did both excellently. The dancing, even in these days of hyperterpsichoreanism, was awfully good and distinctly held its own. One felt happy when the story was silenced and the vocal and muscular activities of the cast were called into play.

Miss Lawrence was marvelously modest. She had a first "entrance" that many a featured "performer" would have kicked at. In fact, she came on in the dark, when none but the ushers recognized her—and they did! They broke into applause and warned us that Miss Lawrence was there. But the unaffected sincerity of the artist soon won.

After Miss Lawrence, I should say that Harland Dixon was the most interesting feature. He danced till every inch of his flesh quivered, and he assuredly made good. Then there were the Fairbankses, looking twinny and cute, but not freighted with very important missions to an expectant world. Gerald Oliver Smith was the Dook, and the role was somewhat doleful, not to say lugubrious.

Oh, Kay! was gorgeously staged. In fact, nothing prettier than the settings, designed by John Wengel, have been seen this season. The costumes were dreams of artistic charm.

Gershwin by 1926 had stopped making piano rolls after ten years. However, he continued to concentrate on phonograph recording as a means of reproducing his music. He had already recorded the **Rhapsody in Blue** *and accompanied Fred Astaire in London recordings of* **Lady, Be Good!** *music. He recorded a number of his own songs as piano solos both before and after* **Oh, Kay!** *First called* **Mayfair,** *then* **Miss Mayfair,** *and then* **Cheerio!, Oh, Kay!** *spawned Gershwin's sprightly and idiosyncratic piano rendition, for Columbia records, of "Maybe," backed by "Someone to Watch over Me."*

GERSHWIN AND MUSICAL SNOBBERY

The Outlook, February 2, 1927

CHARLES L. BUCHANAN

A vote of thanks should be tendered Mr. Walter Damrosch and the Symphony Society for their courage in having recently given us another chance to hear George Gershwin's piano concerto. This composition, written for the Symphony Society, and performed for the first time by Mr. Damrosch last season, shows an increasingly clear title to be ranked the one composition of indubitable vitality, and authentic progressiveness, that this country has produced.

Hearing this work the other day made me wish to abase myself and retract the nonsense I wrote about it last season. At that time it had seemed to me self-conscious, tongue-tied, partially sterile; although even at a first hearing, the unprecedented, queer beauty of the second movement made itself felt unmistakably. I am now inclined to assert that this work can hold its own with the finest examples of this form of composition that we have. Given a fair trial (which is precisely what one fears it will not be given), its second and third movements will go miles ahead of such outstanding and popular works as the Tchaikovsky B-flat Minor Concerto or the Rachmaninoff C Minor Concerto. The persistent hammer and thud of the last movement, with its fascinating thematic material, and the grotesque, devious beauty of the second movement make for a point of view and a kind of sound for which there is no exact parallel.

There is grave reason for assuming, however, that this work will fail to obtain the high measure of praise and encouragement it deserves. Mr. Gershwin, as most people know, is a highly successful writer of "popular" music. He is implicated in that monstrous thing, jazz. He has supplied tunes for those adroit and entertaining shows *Lady, Be Good!, Tip-Toes, Oh, Kay!* As a result, he is already "placed," "labeled," "tagged," so to speak. In other words, the chances are that if Mr. Gershwin gave this country a superlatively fine piece of music (and, for my part, I think he has

already done so in this concerto), he would nevertheless remain unfavorably associated in the average consciousness with the dubious activities of the White Light district.

It is for the purpose of directing attention to the absurd fallaciousness of this very general attitude of mind that this article is written. There is a comfortable and convenient notion, old as the hills, that, in the last analysis, intrinsic merit will obtain recognition. "Water finds its level" and "You can't keep a good man down" are popular crystallizations of this easygoing philosophy. This erroneous assumption is a part of that superficial and slovenly sort of optimism which is more often than not a smokescreen thrown out to cloak inertia and indifference. Preeminence is possibly eight times out of ten a question of circumstance, precedent, propinquity. The work of art, for instance, is usually accepted insofar as it approximates a standard upon which consensus of respectable opinion has set its seal of approval. If it deviates from this standard, it is usually viewed with suspicion. Professional critical opinion, even, does not venture far from the rules of artistic deportment sanctioned by the "best people." Your average critic knows that it is safer to go with the tide of conventional opinion than it is to take up the cudgels for anything outside the beaten path of standpattism.

We see this tendency already at work in the case of Gershwin. Looking over the next morning's reviews of his performance, we note an evasiveness on the part of our critics. Mr. Lawrence Gilman took the curiously negative attitude of dismissing the affair with a more or less perfunctory gesture, delicately and tactfully witty, and then proceeded to a lengthy discussion of a Sibelius tone poem which followed, and which appealed to him as disappointingly boring and negligible. Mr. Olin Downes went a little farther, and conceded that we may have "underestimated" the work; but he, too, perpetrated the absurd inconsistency of giving

Gershwin one paragraph to the three paragraphs given the Sibelius tone poem. Mr. Henderson refused to commit himself, and Mr. Peyser shrugged his shoulders contemptuously. Many of the members of the orchestra were frankly antagonistic to the composition, even to the point of reviling it.

Why, one asks, must this perverse attitude of resistance to the new persist in human nature? For years we have been striving to encourage, develop, produce an American music. When someone gives us a music which may or may not be American (whatever that is or ought to be), but which is beyond the shadow of a doubt a new, vital, propulsive kind of sound, musical snobbery is up in arms against it, and the old deadly steamroller of classical routine goes over the achievement and extinguishes it. In one breath our intelligentsia are deploring the fact that our art is a mere sterile replica of European standards, and then when we produce something that is individually spicy and racy and partially indigenous, the same intelligentsia throw up their hands in holy horror because the affair does not approximate European standards. "This is all right insofar as it goes," they say, "but keep it in its proper environment. Segregate jazz; it belongs to the cabaret; how dare it knock at the doors of the sacred temples of sound!"

It is time someone had the courage to call emphatic attention to the counterfeit quality of this attitude. It is not genuine. It is bogus. It is the attitude of artistic social climbers, not sure of themselves. The blueblood, to-the-manner-born musical aristocrat should be able to enjoy jazz in its proper proportion as he enjoys the third act of *Tristan* in its proper proportion. Unfortunately, most persons are incapable of independent reactions. They cannot estimate a thing for whatever degree of particular intrinsic merit the thing may possess. They are dependent on signposts and preconceived ideas. Their opinions are formed

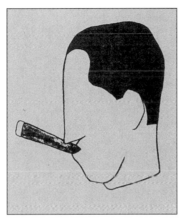

A caricature of Gershwin by William Auerbach-Levy appeared with the composer's article in the July 1926 **Singing** *magazine.*

through a sort of social register, so to speak, of the artistic proprieties. When Chabrier's *España* is played at Carnegie Hall, it is "good" music. If the tunes upon which it is based were heard at the Biltmore, they would be "popular" music. When Stravinsky adroitly exploits a number of ordinary Russian tunes in his *Petrushka,* the affair is hailed as an outstanding event in the history of music. When Gershwin is alleged to have done the same thing in his piano concerto, something is said about Tin Pan Alley, and the matter is dismissed as of negligible importance.

As a matter of fact, the Gershwin Concerto [in F] has no more to do with jazz than the Grieg Concerto has to do with Norwegian folk music. It is not to be viewed condescendingly, as an interesting experiment or a freak exhibition; it is an assured accomplishment; and, as Mr. Walter Damrosch pointed out in conversation with the present writer, it can hold its own with universal competition. Emphasis should be laid upon this point. Let us forget jazz and Tin Pan Alley (wherever precisely that is), and the fact that Mr. Gershwin wrote *Oh, Kay!,* and judge this composition as we would judge a composition of Honegger's or Stravinsky's or someone else's. It may then become clear that Gershwin has given us one of the few gestures of vivid, enticing sound that music has had to offer since Stravinsky's *Sacre du Printemps.*

Plain speaking of this sort may be looked upon as evidence of a critical instability on the part of the writer. But someone has got to come out in the open, wholeheartedly and fearlessly, if music in this country is to be saved from the deadening influences of class distinction, of conventionality, of academic snobbery and hair-splittings. It is a fallacy to believe that a genuine musical beauty will survive on its merits alone. Grieg, one of the most penetratingly beautiful harmonists of all time, is seldom, if ever, played by the professional musician. Grainger, one of the most fervent, potential, natural musical talents we have today, is still tethered to his reputation as the composer of "Country Gardens" or "Irish Tune." Shall we allow this inequitable kind of fate to impede Gershwin?

Unfortunately, there is every reason to predict that Gershwin will not receive sufficient encouragement to "carry on," as we say. We shall probably continue our fulsome habit of overlooking a genius in the hand while we are searching for problematic geniuses in the bush. It is a way we have. Only a short time ago I read in one of our prominent magazines an article consisting of elaborate surmises as to the inception and growth of some problematic future American music; and a little later on Mr. Henderson quoted the article with eulogistic comment. What the writer of the article was driving at is more than I know; for I could find nothing but a series of highly theoretical and philosophic speculations, without a single concrete and specific reference or recommendation. I move that we let the future take care of itself and give our attention to the present. Then we may come to appreciate the vivid aptness of a cinema score such as that supplied *The Big Parade*, for example, or the kind of raw, harsh beauty that we hear in Gershwin at his top-notch.

In conclusion, it is hardly necessary to point out that no one in his sober senses suggests that the Gershwin Concerto should be placed on a par with Bach or Brahms or Beethoven. The claim is made, however, that if you were to hear Gershwin's *Rhapsody in Blue* or this Concerto with an absolutely unprejudiced pair of ears, you would concede that this music is rattling good fun, to begin with, and fascinating, at times exquisite music, to end with. It is not going too far to say that, even including the Rachmaninoffian melody in the strings, there is nothing in all music quite like the second movement of this Concerto. Not beautiful in the classic or romantic sense, it yet possesses a peculiarly hoarse, tart, stunted charm that touches at least the exclusive fingertips of an alien loveliness. One may not soon forget its far-off stuttering trumpet, and the spruce, jaunty piano passage that follows.

Here is a piece of music generated, if you will, by jazz, but valuable intrinsically as a thing in itself. Its virtues are threefold: it has charm, it is techni-

cally expert, and it has used jazz merely as a springboard from which to project itself into the mystical areas of a distinct individuality. It is not essentially American in the sense that Thanksgiving Day or [the] Fourth of July are essentially American. It is not American in the sense that a song of Stephen Foster's is American. It is music of the pavement rather than of the soil. . . . But it is, in company with the collective popular music of our time, the one unmistakably live impulse in contemporary music. And there is grave reason to believe that such an impulse, from whatever source it comes, is indispensable to the present well-being of music.

Scan the entire musical horizon today, and no single vital, dominating figure is in sight. Ravel, in France, appears to have touched the summit of his talent in his exquisite and entrancing, if somewhat sophisticated *La Valse*. Stravinsky has done nothing of significance since his memorable *Sacre du Printemps*, which work, incidentally, appears more and more to have been the outcome of a fortuitous experimentation rather than the inevitable expression of a consistently unfolding genius. I cannot agree with those persons who look hopefully towards Bloch; his *Israel* Symphony seemed to me to be merely in line with music's tiresome modern tendency in the direction of extreme and illegitimate inarticulateness.

Music, I believe, is going to seed. Preoccupation with tonal and harmonic complexity has rendered it an alien and artificial thing. It must be taken out of the sacrosanct confines and superrefinements of philosophic theory, of technical hair-splittings, and given an airing. It is in need of revitalization. Never a believer in the national music idea to the fallacious extent to which some persons carry it, I yet suggest the advisability of a blood transfusion, so to speak, and recommend for this purpose a recognition of the merits and importance of so-called popular music. In the case of Gershwin, I do not know whether he has the cultural inheritance, the artistic morale, to grow largely and finely. But by all means let us give him his chance. It is to be hoped that progressive musicians like Mr. Stokowski, Mr. Sakoloff, Mr. Reiner, and so on will interest themselves in this work.

JAZZ IS THE VOICE OF THE AMERICAN SOUL

Theatre Magazine, **March 1927**

GEORGE GERSHWIN

The peak of my career was not, as my friends and the public think, when I played in my own Concerto in F in Carnegie Hall with the New York Symphony Orchestra, Walter Damrosch conducting. That was an event which amiable contemporary biographers are recording as notable. And I may say, with gratitude and humility, it was.

But there are invisible peaks that anticipate the visible. There are spiritual fulfillments that precede the physical. The peak of my highest joy in completed work was when I listened to that concerto played by the fifty thorough musicians I had engaged for it. Two weeks before the evening when the Concerto was heard in Carnegie Hall, there was a reading of it on an afternoon in the Globe Theatre. Charles Dillingham had permitted the reading in his playhouse. I enjoyed it, not as one of my fair and mischievous friends said, as the mad king Ludwig enjoyed Wagner, being the sole audience in his theater; for Mr. Damrosch was there, and about a dozen others who I wished to hear it. Four of these were music critics. The rest were personal friends. That was the [first] time I heard my most serious work with my own ears. On this occasion I played the piano myself, and was listening, as it were, with the multiple ears of the audience. Another peak will be the evening of this day in which I am preparing these impressions for the *Theatre Magazine,* when I play my biggest composition with the New York Symphony Orchestra, for the radio and a million listeners.

When, last year at Carnegie Hall, I played my first concerto, I was twenty-seven years old. For eight years I had been writing compositions, so I was not totally surprised when great musicians came to the piano and paid me compliments upon my efforts as a composer. What caused a surprised smile, however, was that all of them—Rachmaninoff, Heifetz, Hofmann—complimented me upon my piano execution. For I had had but four years of piano study, and those not with teachers of celebrity. My facility had come not from tuition but from a habit I had consciously cultivated since I was in my early teens. I mean my habit of intensive listening. I had gone to concerts and listened not only with my ears but with my nerves, my mind, my heart. I had listened so earnestly that I became saturated with the music.

Then I went home and listened in memory. I sat at the piano and repeated the motifs. I was becoming acquainted with that which later I was to interpret—the soul of the American people.

Having been born in New York and grown up among New Yorkers, I have heard the voice of that soul. It spoke to me on the streets, in school, at the theater. In the chorus of city sounds I heard it. Though of Russian parentage, I owed no sensitiveness to melodious sounds from that source. My father was a businessman. No one in my family save my brother Ira and myself had an interest in music.

Wherever I went I heard a concourse of sounds. Many of them were not audible to my companions, for I was hearing them in memory. Strains from the latest concert, the cracked tones of a hurdy-

Theatre Magazine, *a high-quality chronicler of the New York stage, devoted an impressive layout to Gershwin's article in its March 1927 issue.*

gurdy, the wail of a street singer, the obbligato of a broken violin, past or present music—I was hearing within me.

Old music and new music, forgotten melodies and the craze of the moment, bits of opera, Russian folk songs, Spanish ballads, chansons, ragtime ditties combined in a mighty chorus in my inner ear. And through and over it all I heard, faint at first, loud at last, the soul of this great America of ours.

And what is the voice of the American soul? It is jazz developed out of ragtime, jazz that is the plan-tation song improved and transformed into finer, bigger harmonies. . . .

I do not assert that the American soul is Negroid. But it is a combination that includes the wail, the whine, and the exultant note of the old "mammy" songs of the South. It is black and white. It is all colors and all souls unified in the great melting pot of the world. Its dominant note is vibrant syncopation.

If I were an Asia[n] or a European, suddenly set down by an aeroplane on this soil and listening with fresh ear to the American chorus of sounds, I

Gershwin's article for **Theatre Magazine**—*accompanied by two striking photographs of the composer—reiterated his belief about the importance of jazz in forging a uniquely American music. The essay was also notable for its author's expression of unmitigated delight at hearing the Concerto in F played for the first time at an orchestra rehearsal. Also in 1927 Gershwin produced one Broadway hit,* **Funny Face,** *and the first version of* **Strike Up the Band,** *which did not last beyond tryouts in Long Branch, N.J., and Philadelphia.*

should say that American life is nervous, hurried, syncopated, ever *accelerando,* and slightly vulgar. I should use the word *vulgar* without intent of offense. There is a vulgarity that is newness. It is essential. The Charleston is vulgar. But it has a strength, an earthiness, that is an essential part of symphonic sound.

When I realized beyond any possibility of error, or need of recantation, that the voice of America, the expression of its soul, is jazz, a determination to do the best possible in that idiom filled me.

Jazz is young. It is not more than ten years old. Ragtime is dead. It was dying when my ear began to be attuned to the voice of the spirit of America. I began to write songs. My first published one had the singular and unabbreviated [*sic*] title "When You Want 'Em You Can't Get 'Em." I was seventeen when I offered it to an indifferent world. The publishing house for which I was working showed its estimation of the merits of the song by deciding to publish it. But the house of Von Tilzer was willing also to print my second song, with the title "You[-oo], Just You." The first that pleased the sweetheart we all woo, that coy damsel, Miss Public, was "I Was So Young (You Were So Beautiful)." The melodious brother and sister, Mollie and Charles King, sang it in a musical version of *The Magistrate,* called *Good Morning, Judge.* When I was twenty my first "show," *La La Lucille,* was produced. It was at Henry Miller's Theatre.

The best song I have written, measured by its reception, was "Swanee," sung by Al Jolson. Mr. Jolson interpolated it in *Sinbad.* I have written the music for twenty-two musical comedies, the next to the last, now in its third year, being *Lady, Be Good!,* and the last and most popular, *Oh, Kay!* Of

my record for industry I am not ashamed. My average is about three musical comedies a year.

I shall go on writing them. They make it possible to flit away, as I shall do after writing this, to Lake Placid in the Adirondacks for a rest. My work is agreeable and remunerative. But to my compositions that most gratify the inward seeking, they are as numbers sung by Al Jolson and by a Caruso. That statement does not decry Mr. Jolson. In his realm he is king. But the creator longs to write what is worthy the voice of a master vocal musician.

My best works therefore are my *Rhapsody in Blue* and my Concerto in F. The *Rhapsody in Blue* represents what I had been striving for since my earliest composition. I wanted to show that jazz is an idiom not to be limited to a mere song and chorus that consumed three minutes in presentation. The *Rhapsody* was a longer work. It required fifteen minutes for the playing. It included more than a dance medium. I succeeded in showing that jazz is not merely a dance; it comprises bigger themes and purposes. It may have the quality of an epic. I wrote it in ten days; it has lived for three years, and is healthy and growing.

I do not know what the next decade will disclose in music. No composer knows. But to be true music it must repeat the thoughts and aspirations of the people and the time. My people are Americans. My time is today. Of tomorrow, and of my tomorrow, as an interpreter of American life in music, I am sure of but one thing: that the essence of future music will hold enough of the melody and harmony of today to reveal its origin. It will be sure to have a tincture of the derided yesterday, which has been accepted today and which perhaps tomorrow will be exalted—jazz.

GERSHWIN AND FRED ASTAIRE

New York *World,* November 23, 1927

ALEXANDER WOOLLCOTT

The managerial partnership between Alex A. Aarons and Vinton Freedley, which has busied itself of late years with the crass business details behind the Gershwin harlequinades, solemnized the union last evening by inaugurating a brand-new playhouse, recently flung to the stars in a desperate effort to relieve the theater famine in this unfortunate city. It is called the Alvin (a name cunningly compounded of their own given names), and you will find it, wide and handsome, right across the street from the chastely, offended Guild Theatre.

And what may possibly take you to the Alvin these autumn nights is the work of still another partnership—that of George Gershwin and Fred Astaire. These two marked children of their time make up a partnership as inevitable as that of Gilbert and Sullivan. I do not know whether Gershwin was born into this world to write rhythms for Fred Astaire's feet or whether Astaire was born into this world to show how the Gershwin music should really be danced. But surely they were written in the same key, these two, and the dancing last night to the tune of "What Am I Going to Do?" rewarded one for much patient sitting through a rather tedious musical comedy.

It is called *Funny Face,* and in it Fred and Adele Astaire come loping back to town, assisted by a well-regimented set of coryphées and by others—notably, to my mind, the engaging Victor Moore, who is superb in one scene when, as a too-tender-hearted and confiding gunman, he tries ever so gently to kill a man his gang has doomed.

For *Funny Face* Gershwin has written a clever, sparkling, teasing score. I can imagine that there are many who would find such a *sauce piquante* of odd dissonances and stumbling measures a little trying as steady fare, like a whole meal made out of Worcestershire sauce. But it is tickling music, all of it, and for once in a way the brothers Gershwin (it is Ira, you know, who writes the lyrics) have the satisfaction of hearing their songs sung.

It is all very well to adorn one's troupe with the incomparable Astaires for purposes of charm and tap dancing, but Gershwin, in seasons past, must have been gnawed by a certain discontent at hearing his beloved tunes inhaled by two such reticent vocalists. The audience at *Funny Face* is not allowed to go home until the entire score has been sung through once by a police glee club of twenty voices, with a quartet roaring in the middle and with the priceless Ohman and Arden at the two pianos. Then you hear such lusty volume and such harmony and such loving swipes as seldom reward our songwriters until their songs have reached the campus.

The book of *Funny Face* is credited to Fred Thompson and Paul Gerard Smith. It struck me as singularly perishable, although I shall personally cherish in my memory book that moment where the hero cries out to the shrinking coward, "Why, man, where's your chivalry?" and he replies, in a quivering voice, "Oh, I sold the old thing and got me a Cadillac."

It was, I believe, in the concoction of some earlier version of the same libretto that the previously carefree Robert Benchley was summoned into conference. After some weeks he withdrew from the collaboration and attended last night's premiere with all his old insouciance. But when he lifts his hat one notices that his hair has turned snow white since last summer. I have heard that no vestigial traces of his humor remain in the present script, no memorial of his passing whatsoever. Unless, possibly, those were a few of his aunts I couldn't help noticing in the chorus.

In the summer of 1927 Gershwin worked on his first watercolor, wrote the score for **Strike Up the Band,** *and made his initial appearance as soloist with the New York Philharmonic in the* **Rhapsody in Blue** *and Concerto in F, playing to a capacity crowd at City College's Lewisohn Stadium in uptown Manhattan.* **Funny Face,** *which opened in New York on November 22, 1927, boasts one of the Gershwins' most characteristic and interesting Jazz Age scores, featuring the songs "The Babbitt and the Bromide," "My One and Only," and "'S Wonderful."* **Funny Face** *reunited* **Lady, Be Good!**'s *Fred and Adele Astaire with the Gershwins, librettist Guy Bolton, and producers Alex Aarons and Vinton Freedley, who were counting on it as a major production to inaugurate their newly built theater, the Alvin. First called* **Smarty,** *and one of the 1920s' most reworked shows during its out-of-town tryouts (half of the original songs were dropped), it eventually became a critical and popular hit, running for 244 performances.*

The British staging of **Funny Face** *added comic Leslie Henson (who had been in the overseas productions of* **Primrose** *and* **Tell Me More**) *and premiered in London on November 8, 1928. Gershwin recorded three of the* **Funny Face** *songs as piano solos during the show's London run.*

GEORGE GERSHWIN; OR, A DRUNKEN SCHUBERT

from *Are They the Same at Home?* (1927)

BEVERLEY NICHOLS

I am going to begin right in the middle, because until I have made George Gershwin play you his first piano concerto you will probably regard him (as do most of our half-baked critics) as a mere peddler of common tunes, like his "Swanee" and "[Oh,] Lady, Be Good!" So you must imagine a swarthy young man of twenty-seven, seated at a piano by the open window of a room in Pall Mall not long ago, lifting his fingers and beginning to play. The twilight was fast fading when he sat down, and by the time he had finished it was almost dark, and the street lamps were lit. Yet in that brief period I had passed through one of the most singular musical experiences I have known. I ought to be slightly drunk to be able to describe it properly, for it was the music of intoxication. Only by ragged words, by a mass of stage effects, by strident and jagged adjectives could one hope to recapture on the printed page the entangled and enticing rhythms which floated across the darkening room.

How can I describe those rhythms? Everybody is acquainted, of course, with the ordinary jazz tricks. Most of them consist in making a tune hiccup, by a judicious administration of quavers at the beginning of a bar. Or else, a simple phrase of six quavers, demanding a 3/4 tempo, is put into a strait-waistcoat of common time, and made to wriggle about with most entertaining antics. Everybody knows these little devices. They are as old as Bach, and probably older.

I realized in the first five minutes that Gershwin was going far beyond that in his concerto. It would need a very complicated series of mathematical charts to explain exactly what he *was* doing; and even when one had explained it, the number of people who could play the result would, I imagine, be not greater than those who, according to Mr. Einstein, comprehended the theory of relativity. To

put it in a nontechnical way, he was taking a quantity of strictly opposed rhythms and, by some magic counterpoint of his own, weaving them into a glittering mass which was at once as well ordered as a route march and as drunken as an orgy.

Yet beautiful. *Really* beautiful. The visions that this concerto called up before me! I loathe people who make pictures out of music, who grin vacuously and refer to waterfalls when they hear a Liszt cadenza, who poignantly recall their first seduction when listening to a sentimental waltz by Chaminade, and to whom the preludes of Chopin mean nothing more than rain dripping on a roof or George Sand having the vapors. The world is full of such people, and I have always flattered myself that I was not of their number. Apparently I was mistaken.

For as I listened it seemed that the whole of new America was blossoming into beauty before me. The phrases swept up the piano with the stern, unfaltering grace of a skyscraper. Ever and anon the bass would take it into its head to go mad. . . . There were passages vivid and humorous—a sort of chattering of Broadway chorus girls drinking mint julep[s] at Child's. There were slow, secretive melodies that had in them something of the mystery of vast forests. The tunes clashed and fought, degenerated, were made clean again, joined together, and scampered madly over the keyboard in a final rush which was as breathless as the thundering herd over the prairies of the West.

When it was all over, and the aftermath of silence had gradually been penetrated by the noises of everyday life from the streets outside, I felt that the occasion was one for repeating what Schumann said after hearing Chopin for the first time: "Hats off, gentlemen—a genius." Only there were no hats to take off, and we should both have been embarrassed by so un-English a display of emotion. I therefore turned to one of the most complicated pages and asked him, quite bluntly, how it was done.

"I don't know."

"Please play this bit very slowly."

He played it. There were three distinct rhythms fighting each other—two in the treble and one in the bass. I began to laugh.

"What are you laughing at?"

"All those rhythms—scrapping. How do you make them fight like that?"

He shook his head, and went on playing.

"I feel things inside, and then I work them out—that's all."

"You must have felt pretty volcanic when you wrote this. Do you always feel volcanic?"

"No. An ordinary jazz tune's different."

While he had been talking, he had been occasionally dabbing at the keyboard with his right hand. Little bits of tunes were born, floated away, died. Now and then he would play a phrase twice, three times, and then smother it with a discord, as though he did not wish to claim its paternity. Then, suddenly, a rather fascinating phrase came out.

"I say," I said, "I rather like that."

"So do I." He played it again, improvising a "following" theme. "It's got possibilities. But it's really a Charleston tune, and it hasn't got a Charleston rhythm."

At which he proceeded to maltreat that poor tune as few tunes have been maltreated. Over and over again he played it, until I felt that I never wanted to hear it again. Then, when it seemed perfect, he said: "Well, at any rate, that's a beginning."

When I went to the first night of *Lady, Be Good!* I heard the tune that had been begun that evening. You have probably heard it, too.

There—I am writing on silent paper, which has no power of harmony or discord, and I will cease from these descriptions of an art which cannot be described. But before I end, I want to tell what I should have told in the first few lines—how Gershwin, who has now an income much greater than the president of the United States, began. He said: "I began a few years ago in a little music-publishing house on Broadway. Every day at nine o'clock I was there at the piano, playing popular tunes for anybody who came along. Colored people used to come in and get me to play them 'God Send You Back to Me' in seven keys. Chorus ladies used to breathe down my neck. Some of the customers treated one like dirt. Others were charming. Among the latter was Fred Astaire.

"It was at a time when Fred and Adele were doing a little vaudeville show of their own. Fred used to come in sometimes to hear the new songs. I remember saying to him once, 'Wouldn't it be wonderful if one day I could write a show of my own, and you and Adele could star in it?' We just laughed then. But it came true."

It certainly did.

George Gershwin's ultramodern penthouse apartment was located at 33 Riverside Drive in Manhattan. From 1928 to 1933 he lived, worked, played, and entertained there, enjoying his ever-growing collection of modern art and his gymnasium (complete with punching bag). Beside his bed was a screen painted with **An American in Paris** *themes by his artist cousin, Henry Botkin. Gershwin's next apartment—on 72nd Street—was decorated in a somewhat more "traditional" style.*

GEORGE GERSHWIN AND JAZZ

The Outlook, **February 29, 1928**

GEORGE NEWELL

For many empty years serious creative music in America was a sort of catch-as-catch-can affair. The muse of the lyre was looked upon as the anemic sister of the American arts, that robust art which had produced Walt Whitman and Sargent. Somehow Europe had us musically buffaloed. There was talent, to be sure, but they could not get their composing machinery to function originally.

They would pilgrimage to Paris or Berlin. There they would study, drink beer, and affect "Flying Dutchman" hats—soon to return to their native land neatly done up in a French or German bandbox. They would write just that sort of music too, the only difference being that it was then called "American."

But was it? Listen to the ten bars of the *Rhapsody in Blue* before you answer. George Gershwin seems to be at last the American who can express his native land and its life in terms of notes, trombones, or what have you.

But you will say, "Is this African stuff any more American than the imitation European music?"

The way it is done by Mr. Gershwin, I believe it is.

For that matter, what European school is free from foreign influence? The music of Spain is a volatile blend of Moorish, Basque, and gypsy. The profound influence of Hungarian-gypsy music on the work of the German composer Brahms is well known. The similarity of the wild glamour so red-headedly existent in Celtic folksongs is startling in its Slavic resemblance.

"Very well, then; but tell me, what is this jazz, anyway?"

Some say jazz is this, some say jazz is that. The name itself was found by Lafcadio Hearn in the Creole *patois* of New Orleans. It meant "to speed up," particularly in reference to syncopated music. In Africa the word *jas,* or *jazz,* has a corresponding meaning among the natives. But I say fiddle-de-dee for all these learned definitions. Jazz is

American, and that's that. Now let's hear you define America.

Difficult, isn't it?

Some of the components of America may be more or less defined, though: nervous energy, joy, humor, youth, lack of repression, freedom of expression. It is because the spirit of jazz so admirably paints this musical picture of America that the coming of George Gershwin at this time is so propitious.

A bumptious English wit of the nineteenth century said: "American musicians are at present too gentlemanly to faithfully portray their motherland. When a good husky rail-splitter comes along and turns to music, you will then have a man sufficiently equipped by experience and character to write American music."

One needs the copious probing of the figurative thumbnail to scratch through the veneer of this false statement. For in recalling the personalities of Lincoln, Bret Harte, and Blakelock we are tempted to ratify the Englishman's definition. That is, we would be so tempted if we hadn't met George Gershwin.

Every inch of this tall young man is that of a gentleman. He is poised, quiet, and well-mannered. He is genuinely polite, kind, and considerate. He is always willing to listen to the work of any other composer and advise him. The names of the men and women whom he has helped along the barbed road to success would give our typesetter a dizzy morning. Yet he is not a rail-splitter, nor has he the arrogant, temperamental qualities of a Wagner or a Debussy.

As a man, I should say he is more like that kindly, naive composer Mozart. Mozart, you will recall, was that fastidious gentleman so patently at home in either the glittering court of Vienna or the smoky cottage of a roadside peasant.

If any harassed process server ever has occasion to search out the presence of Mr. Gershwin, I advise him to look either at Mrs. Astor's or "Pop" Connolly's lunch wagon. If he is at the wagon, Mr. Gershwin will be the only diner whose elbows do not garnish the counter!

George Gershwin was born twenty-nine years ago in Brooklyn. He was no child musical prodigy. He assures us that he played nothing during his first thirteen years—nothing except hookey or precarious one-eyed-cat around the fireplugs and the neighborhood pushcarts.

That he might possess musical talent never occurred to his hard-working mother and father. There had never been any musician in the family. What would they do with a musician, anyhow?

At the age of thirteen, however, the affairs of the father took a turn toward the near-prosperous. A piano was acquired—an upright of uncertain vintage. Still, the varnish was nice and shiny and the keys pushed up and down beautifully.

Ira, George's older brother, was to take piano lessons—the same Ira who is now one of Broadway's cleverest lyric writers. He will enter our story farther on.

Ira was to take lessons at fifty cents an hour from a "lady teacher." The younger brother was never considered; but one day he climbed upon the stool and proceeded, in his usual experimental fashion, to see what made the thing go. He found out.

It was immediately apparent to his mother that the fifty-cent investment would not be wasted on George. Ira would become a doctor, maybe.

For four months the marvelous musical absorptive qualities of George's quick mind kept the "lady teacher" in a state of breathless pedagogy. And at the end of ten dollars' worth of lessons she was "all taught out."

Rosalie *was produced by master showman Flo Ziegfeld, who enlisted the help of the Gershwins to furnish half of the score when the musical's composer, Sigmund Romberg, was unable to complete it in time. The book and songs were all tailored to the show's star, Marilyn Miller, who helped make the artistically weak* Rosalie *a popular success, with 335 performances.*

But George was anything but "all taught in," so he went to study with "a funny old Dutchman who used to be a bandmaster." He taught the young Gershwin such musical pastries as the *William Tell* Overture, with wedding-cake variations and other brassy favorites of bandmasters reduced to teaching pianoforte.

Thanks to a few discerning friends and his own intuitive instincts to gravitate in the right direction, he soon left this harbinger of the brass band.

He then went to study with the late Charles Hambitzer. George was fifteen then. To this day he speaks of this teacher with genuine awe and affection. "He was a fine musician—and I really began to learn something."

These piano lessons of the first few years were about the only lessons (in the common meaning of the word) that George Gershwin ever had. For the most part his facility for brilliant piano playing has been self-taught.

Self-taught is surely the correct term for his technique as a composer. Like Wagner and Schubert, he seems to have studied with no one in particular, preferring to abide by the counsel of his own ear. He is decidedly an aural musician. He listens to everything, attending concerts religiously, that his ear may be a true teacher. No formulae-bound academician ever superimposed his agglutin[at]ed conventions upon the soul of George Gershwin.

To be sure, he did treat himself to the luxury of a few harmony lessons (weekly inoculations from a textbook of correct church harmonies).

When he was seventeen, he began to earn his living. He started in as a song plugger for the popular-music firm of Remick.

Do you know what a song plugger is? He is

the anvil-chorus, high-pressure, robotlike salesman of the ragtime music publisher. All day long, often for ten hours, he must sit and "swat out" syncopated ditties on a piano—a sort of musical demonstration to "the trade" of the latest "hits." Fine for the nerves and the piano tuners' union.

I forgot to mention that the song plugger was paid fifteen dollars a week for his musico-gymnastic efforts.

In the evenings, if he had any energy left from his work in the music iron foundry, George composed—but nothing of much consequence. As a composer he was still going through the incubator stage: soaking it up—blues, spirituals, . . . ballads, and mixing them with the Chopin and Beethoven of his piano lessons.

Two years of this song plugging, and then one day he quit.

"I just walked out," he said. "It wasn't what I wanted.

"No, I didn't have any other job in view. That fifteen dollars was all I was making."

The same intuitive instinct that sent him from the poor teaching of the bandmaster to the door of Hambitzer was again evident. This time it took him to Will Vodery, that dynamic Negro musician and orchestrator.

The kindly Will got him to try out for pianist at the rehearsals of *Miss 1917*, a Jerome Kern–Wodehouse show.

It was a fortunate tryout—for George, that is; the other pianist was fired. George could put lots more pep into *his* work. He could play the music up in the treble, down in the bass, and in countless original ways of his own invention, to the great delectation of the chorus and the dancing director.

"You can't make up new dance steps to a lot of melodious opium," was the dancing man's comment.

"That tip of Vodery's got me a thirty-five-dollar-a-week job."

And now came another friend in need—Vivienne Segal. At the Sunday night concerts of the Century Theatre she sang two of Gershwin's songs. The success of these two songs was the beginning of an easier trail for George. The firm of Harms & Company, who control 90 percent of all the American show music, signed him on the dot-

For Rosalie, *the Gershwins quickly dusted off songs previously discarded from other musicals—notably the wonderful "How Long Has This Been Going On?"—and added three new tunes, "Say So!," "New York Serenade," and "Oh Gee! Oh Joy!"*

ted line—the first man to be so contracted since Jerome Kern. And soon, in 1919, came his first big success, *La La Lucille*.

Since then he has written all or some of the music for twenty-five shows. At present he has music in two shows on Broadway, *Funny Face* and *Rosalie*; one, *Oh, Kay!*, on the road; another company in London, and one in Australia.

In almost all these shows his lyrical collaborator has been his older brother, Ira, the one George sidetracked from the fifty-cent lessons.

The family really had tried to make a doctor out of Ira. He even got to the premedic course at City College. But he had too much of his brother's spirit to stay where he was not happy. So he too "walked out on them" to be treasurer and secretary of Colonel Lagg's Great Empire Shows—a

Midwest tent carnival to which a hamlet of a thousand inhabitants was a big stand.

"I was lucky to get that job," Ira told me. "The other treasurer had absconded. And I got thirty-five dollars a week, too, only five dollars less than the highest-paid man in the show—the fire-walker. But I had to put up my own tent, and that title, secretary-treasurer, is just a lot of hokum for ticket seller."

George had already won his spurs as a musical-comedy composer before Ira entered the field. And rather than be known as the brother of a famous brother who got his job via the convenient alleyway of fraternal politics, Ira wrote his first lyrics under the name of Arthur Francis. For a long time he insisted that his brother refer to his lyrics as the work of "a college boy I know, who isn't so bad."

Arthur Francis had quite achieved success in his own right before he collaborated officially with George, though the plan that Ira become a lyric writer was first sponsored by his brother. But Ira had fully cut his teeth on the show *Two Little Girls in Blue* before he dropped the pen name. He and George then wrote *Lady, Be Good!*

It was in the year of *Lady, Be Good!* (1924) that George Gershwin wrote the epochal *Rhapsody in Blue*. Here was something truly new in music. Jazz had indeed come into its syncopated own. . . .

So confident . . . was [Walter Damrosch,] the conductor of the New York Symphony, [of the composer's ability to raise jazz] . . . to the level of musical respectability . . . that the next year, 1925, he commissioned Mr. Gershwin to write a jazz piano concerto. Gershwin accepted this commission the day before sailing to England to produce a show. "I didn't have any idea if I could write one, of course," he told me, "but I'd heard a few concertos at concerts."

He returned from England, and in one month he wrote the concerto—fully scored by himself for 110 symphony players.

Practically no other jazz composer orchestrates any of his work. Many of them, the "one-finger composers," must have a professional arranger to write the notes down on paper for them. Very few of even the literate popular-song writers ever bother to write their own harmonies.

The success of the Concerto [in F], while not as sensational as that of the *Rhapsody in Blue,* was very solid indeed. Since the Concerto, a one-act operatic sketch, *135th Street,* has been produced. It was written long before, however.

I saw Mr. Gershwin a few weeks ago, following the New York opening of *Rosalie,* and I can best characterize his present condition as imminently volcanic. Something is going to happen soon. He is so calm outside that his insides must be seething. Something big is coming. Is it another *Rhapsody in Blue?*

No one can say but George Gershwin himself, as he writes high up in the soundproof studio at the top of his New York home.

GERSHWIN PRESENTS A NEW WORK

Musical America, **August 18, 1928**

HYMAN SANDOW

George Gershwin has been to Paris, written a new symphonic piece, visited with the ultramodernists, acquired a Mustel reed organ, considered writing a jazz opera, has a complete set of everything Debussy ever wrote, and finds that his favorite composers are Bach, Wagner, and Stravinsky.

And he is now reported to have accepted an offer of a hundred thousand dollars from the Fox Movietone Company to write a new musical comedy, to be used exclusively for the talking moving pictures.

I chatted with Gershwin the other day about his new symphonic work.

"This new piece, really a rhapsodic ballet, is written very freely and is the most modern music I've yet attempted," Mr. Gershwin said as we glanced through the pages of the penciled manuscript.

"The opening part will be developed in typical French style, in the manner of Debussy and the Six, though the themes are all original. My purpose here is to portray the impressions of an American visitor in Paris as he strolls about the city, listens to the various street noises, and absorbs the French atmosphere.

"As in my other orchestral compositions, I've not endeavored to present any definite scenes in this music," he continued. "The rhapsody is programmatic only in a general impressionistic way, so that the individual listener can read into the music such episodes as his imagination pictures for him."

Flipping over a few pages, Mr. Gershwin indicated the next section with his pipe.

"The opening gay section," he explained, "is followed by a rich 'blues' with a strong rhythmic undercurrent. Our American friend, perhaps after strolling into a café and having a few drinks, has suddenly succumbed to a spasm of homesickness. The harmony here is both more intense and simple than in the preceding pages. This 'blues' rises to a climax followed by a coda in which the spirit of the music returns to the vivacity and bubbling exuberance of the opening part with its impressions of Paris. Apparently the homesick American, having left the café and reached the open air, has downed his spell of the blues and once again is an alert spectator of Parisian life. At the conclusion, the street noises and French atmosphere are triumphant."

An American in Paris will require about twenty minutes to perform. Mr. Gershwin began its composition in New York in January of this year, continued working on it while abroad last spring, and is now completing the score in this city.

The premiere performance is already scheduled for some time in November, when Walter Damrosch and the newly consolidated New York Philharmonic Symphony Orchestra will play the work in Carnegie Hall. It is scored for a straight symphony orchestra, piano, three saxophones, and several French taxi horns. Gershwin's newest jazz piece differs from his previous orchestral compositions, the *Rhapsody in Blue* and the Concerto in F, in relegating a comparatively unimportant role, rather than the dignity of a solo part, to the piano. The composer will not play this instrument at the premiere.

As I entered the little electric elevator that sedately lifted me up to Mr. Gershwin's studio on the top floor of the family residence on West 103rd Street, just off Riverside Drive, I heard the sonorous notes of an organ, which he was playing. Later he called my attention to the instrument, a Mustel reed organ, and enthusiastically told of having discovered and purchased it in France and of its arrival on the steamer *Paris* just the day before.

"Here's something else I prize very much that I also bought in France," Mr. Gershwin said as he turned to a nearby bookshelf. From it he took down one of eight handsomely bound volumes that contain everything which Claude Debussy, whose music Mr. Gershwin greatly admires, ever wrote.

Among his other deeply cherished mementos are a photograph of Prince George of England, whom he met in London in 1925, bearing the inscription "From George to George," and a gold cigarette case, signed by twenty-eight friends, which was presented to him by Otto Kahn at a party after the first performance of his Concerto. Mr. Gershwin likewise is the happy owner of five of the late George Bellows's famous lithographs, *Splinter Beach, River Front, Dempsey Through the Ropes, Prayer Meeting,* and *Between Rounds.* These recently acquired lithographs now decorate the walls of his studio, which contains one of his three grand pianos.

Mr. Gershwin said he had been highly pleased by the excellent manner in which Vladimir Golschmann and a picked orchestra interpreted his Concerto in F, with Dimitri Tiomkin playing the piano solo, at the Paris Opera House on May 29. This performance was not only the first rendition of his

Concerto abroad but also the first occasion on which Mr. Gershwin listened to a performance of his work with a musician other than himself at the piano.

Writing of this concert in the *Christian Science Monitor* for July 7, Emile Vuillermoz, the French critic, declared: "By the character of his (Gershwin's) style and also by the dignity and distinction of Tiomkin's playing, this very characteristic work made even the most distrustful musicians realize that jazz, after having renewed the technique of dancing, might perfectly well exert a deep and beneficent influence in the most exalted spheres."

Mr. Gershwin composed the Concerto in 1925. Before he wrote a note of the score, he had been booked for six performances of the work by the New York Symphony Orchestra under Walter Damrosch, with himself as soloist, in New York, Brooklyn, Washington, Philadelphia, and Baltimore. His only previous experience in orchestration was in writing three numbers for his musical show *Primrose,* which was presented in London in 1924. Prior to orchestrating the Concerto, he had had no academic instruction in counterpoint, form, or instrumentation.

Simultaneously, he composed two Broadway musical successes, *Song of the Flame* and *Tip-Toes.*

Last summer Mr. Gershwin appeared as soloist in the concerts and his *Rhapsody in Blue* was played at a Philharmonic concert in the Lewisohn Stadium with Willem Hoogstraten conducting. The crowd of eighteen thousand was the largest, and probably the most enthusiastic, ever attracted to a Stadium concert.

The Gershwins followed one of their biggest successes—Rosalie—with a dismal flop. Treasure Girl premiered just as the composer was putting the finishing touches on a major orchestral work, An American in Paris. This cynical-themed musical (greed and double-crossing are the essential elements) was panned by the critics and closed after sixty-eight performances, despite the attraction of its star, Gertrude Lawrence. Its best song, "I've Got a Crush on You," eventually turned up in the 1930 version of Strike Up the Band.

I asked Mr. Gershwin if jazz is favorably regarded abroad.

"Decidedly so," was his quick and ardent reply. "Both from what prominent composers and musicians told me and from the music I heard there, I am convinced that American jazz is in a class by itself. It is absolutely unique. And mainly because of its originality, it is strongly admired in Europe.

"It was quite a paradox to me to find that, although I went abroad largely to benefit my technique as much as possible from a study of European orchestral methods, much more attention is paid there to the originality of musical material than to the excellence of its technical development."

"Did any aspect of music abroad particularly impress you?"

"One of the high spots of my visit," he said, as he walked across the room to a music cabinet from which he returned with a small pocket score, "was my meeting with Alban Berg, an Austrian ultra-modernist composer almost unknown in this country, who wrote this string quartet."

He showed me the score, which bears an inscription from Mr. Berg, who is forty years old and a pupil of Schoenberg.

"Although this quartet is dissonant to the extent of proving disagreeable to the average music lover's consonant-trained ear," Mr. Gershwin remarked, "it seems to me the work has genuine merit. Its conception and treatment are thoroughly modern in the best sense of the word."

"When I talked with you in February," I said, "I asked you if you were planning to write a jazz opera, and you replied that you didn't contemplate doing so, at least in the near future. Are you any closer to definitely undertaking such a composition now?"

"No, I'm not," Mr. Gershwin answered. "I hope someday to write a jazz opera, but before undertaking it, I want to write more orchestral music so that I can get into the mental swing of serious composition and improve my technique. I realize that I have so far written very little music for symphonic performance, but I plan to spend more and more time on such work from now on."

Though a tireless worker, Mr. Gershwin composes without following any set time schedule. In fact, he instinctively shrinks from the slightest resemblance of routine. Yet I would not call him a temperamental person, for his manner is the epitome of urbanity, true gentlemanliness, sincerity, and good humor.

He talks enthusiastically about his work, music, and other interests in a pleasantly modulated voice. He punctuates his words with occasional staccato beats of his left hand, tightened at such times about the bowl of his ever-present briar pipe, momentarily removed from his mouth. When in the mood, he plays piano for hours at a time, while one friend or a dozen listen delightedly. . . .

Mr. Gershwin's swarthy complexion and well-knit body reflect his interest in tennis, riding, and golf. His tastes vary from the writings of Shaw to ping-pong or a good prizefight, and his dislikes include nightclubs and oversentimentalized music. . . .

In answer to a question, Mr. Gershwin said that he has often thought of reorchestrating the *Rhapsody* and that he plans to do so when time permits. The present instrumentation is scored in the published version for only twelve band instruments. When Mr. Gershwin reorchestrates the *Rhapsody,* he will score it for a full symphonic orchestra.

Almost exclusively on the broad shoulders of this young American composer now rests the burden of establishing beyond reasonable question the intrinsic merit of jazz as a modern expression. That is why George Gershwin's forthcoming orchestral work, *An American in Paris,* will be listened to with keen expectancy.

'AN AMERICAN IN PARIS': NARRATIVE GUIDE

Concert Program, Carnegie Hall, New York City, December 13, 1928

DEEMS TAYLOR

You are to imagine . . . an American, visiting Paris, swinging down the Champs-Élysées on a mild sunny morning in May or June. Being what he is, he starts with preliminaries, and is off at full speed at once, to the tune of the First Walking Theme, a straightforward, diatonic air, designed to convey an impression of Gallic freedom and gaiety.

Our American's ears being open, as well as his eyes, he notes with pleasure the sounds of the city. French taxicabs seem to amuse him particularly, a fact that the orchestra points out in a brief episode introducing four real Paris taxi horns (imported at great expense for the occasion). These have a special theme allotted to them (the driver, possibly?),

which is announced by the strings whenever they appear in the score.

Having safely eluded the taxis, our American apparently passes the open door of a café, where, if one is to believe the trombones, *La Maxixe* [*sic*] is still popular. Exhilarated by the reminder of the gay 1900s, he resumes his stroll through the medium of the Second Walking Theme, which is announced by the clarinetist in French with a strong American accent.

Both themes are now discussed at some length by the instruments, until our tourist happens to pass—something. The composer thought it might be a church, while the commentator held out for

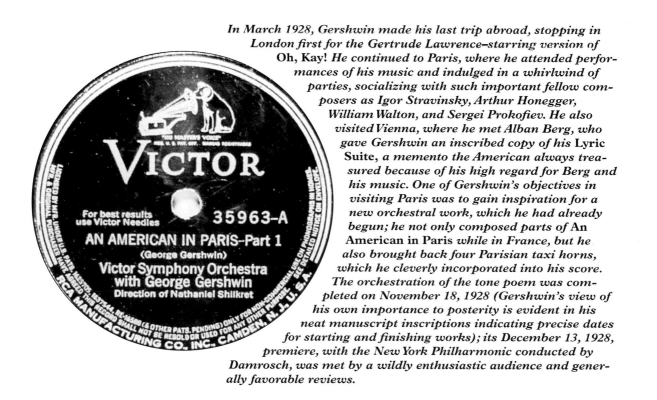

In March 1928, Gershwin made his last trip abroad, stopping in London first for the Gertrude Lawrence–starring version of Oh, Kay! *He continued to Paris, where he attended performances of his music and indulged in a whirlwind of parties, socializing with such important fellow composers as Igor Stravinsky, Arthur Honegger, William Walton, and Sergei Prokofiev. He also visited Vienna, where he met Alban Berg, who gave Gershwin an inscribed copy of his* Lyric Suite, *a memento the American always treasured because of his high regard for Berg and his music. One of Gershwin's objectives in visiting Paris was to gain inspiration for a new orchestral work, which he had already begun; he not only composed parts of* An American in Paris *while in France, but he also brought back four Parisian taxi horns, which he cleverly incorporated into his score. The orchestration of the tone poem was completed on November 18, 1928 (Gershwin's view of his own importance to posterity is evident in his neat manuscript inscriptions indicating precise dates for starting and finishing works); its December 13, 1928, premiere, with the New York Philharmonic conducted by Damrosch, was met by a wildly enthusiastic audience and generally favorable reviews.*

the Grand Palais, where the Salon holds forth. At all events, our hero does not go in. Instead, as revealed by the English horn, he respectfully slackens his pace until he is safely past.

At this point, the American's itinerary becomes somewhat obscured. It may be that he continues on down the Champs-Élysées; it may be that he has turned off—the composer retains an open mind on the subject. However, since what immediately ensues is technically known as a bridge passage, one is reasonably justified in assuming that the Gershwin pen, guided by an unseen hand, has perpetrated a musical pun, and that when the Third Walking Theme makes its eventual appearance our American has crossed the Seine and is somewhere on the Left Bank. Certainly it is distinctly less Gallic than its predecessors, speaking American with a French intonation, as befits the region of the city where so many Americans forgather. *Walking Theme* may be a misnomer, for despite its vitality the theme is slightly sedentary in character, and becomes progressively more so. Indeed, the end of this section of the work is couched in terms so unmistakably, albeit pleasantly, blurred, as to suggest that the American is on the *terrasse* of a café, exploring the mysteries of an Anise de Lozo.

And now the orchestra introduces an unhallowed episode. Suffice it to say that a solo violin approaches our hero (in soprano register) and addresses him in the most charming broken English and, his response being inaudible—or at least unintelligible—repeats the remark. The one-sided conversation continues for some little time.

Of course, one hastens to add, it is possible that a grave injustice is being done to both author and protagonist, and that the whole episode is simply a musical transition. The latter interpretation may

well be true, for otherwise it is difficult to believe what ensues: our hero becomes homesick. He has the blues; and if the behavior of the orchestra be any criterion, he has them very thoroughly. He realizes suddenly, overwhelmingly, that he does not belong to this place, that he is the most wretched creature in the world, a foreigner. The cool, blue Paris sky, the distant upward sweep of the Eiffel Tower, the bookstalls of the quay, the pattern of the horse-chestnut leaves on the white, sun-flecked street—what avails all this alien beauty? He is no Baudelaire, longing to be "anywhere out of the world." The world is just what he longs for, the world that he knows best: a world less lovely—sentimental and a little vulgar perhaps—but for all that, home.

However, nostalgia is not a fatal disease—nor, in this instance, of overlong duration. Just in the nick of time the compassionate orchestra rushes another theme to the rescue, two trumpets performing the ceremony of introduction. It is apparent that our hero must have met a compatriot; for this last theme is a noisy, cheerful, self-confident Charleston without a drop of Gallic blood in its veins.

For the moment, Paris is no more; and a voluble, gusty, wisecracking orchestra proceeds to demonstrate at some length that it's always fair weather when two Americans get together, no matter where. Walking Theme Number Two enters soon thereafter, enthusiastically abetted by Number Three. Paris isn't such a bad place after all: as a matter of fact, it's a grand place! Nice weather, nothing to do till tomorrow. The blues return, but mitigated by the Second Walking Theme—a happy reminiscence rather than homesick yearning—and the orchestra, in a riotous finale, decides to make a night of it. It will be great to get home; but meanwhile, this is Paris!

GEORGE GERSHWIN AND AMERICAN YOUTH: AN APPRECIATION

The Musical Courier, **January 22, 1929**

OTTO KAHN

George Gershwin is a leader of young America in music, in the same sense in which Lindbergh is the leader of young America in aviation. And in more than one respect, he has qualities similar to those of the gallant and attractive colonel, qualities which we like to consider characteristic of the best type of young America. He has the same unspoilableness—if I may coin a word—the same engaging and unassuming ways, the same simple dignity and dislike of show, the same absence of affectation, the same direct, uncomplicated, naive, "Parsifalesque" outlook upon life and upon his task.

They are a fine lot, take them by and large, these American "kids" of our day, male and female. They are full of talent and of courage. They have a peculiar inner cleanliness and freshness and spontaneousness. . . .

Crude and turbulent sometimes, and a little bit too cocksure, they are serious in purpose, and many of them—more indeed than surface appearance would indicate—are determinedly seeking to aim high. There is no better raw material to be found anywhere. Below their apparent "hardboiledness" and sophistication, there is a groping, unadmitted, sometimes uncouth, often unconscious prompting of idealism—a note welcome and needed in the midst of the colossal sweep of the nation's material occupations. . . .

And George Gershwin, without self-seeking or self-consciousness, and just because of that, is one of their typical examples, and in his art, thoroughly and uncompromisingly American as it is, one of their foremost spokesmen. In the rhythm, the melody, the humor, the grace, the rush and sweep and dynamics of his compositions, he expresses the genius of young America.

Now, in that genius of young America, there is one note rather conspicuous by its absence. It is the note that sounds a legacy of sorrow, a note that springs from the deepest stirrings of the soul of the race. . . . The path of America—since she became a nation—has been all too smooth perhaps, too uniformly successful. Mercifully, she has been spared . . . the ordeal of deep anguish, besetting care, and heart-searching tribulations, which mark the history of the older nations—except only the epic tragedy of the Civil War. . . .

Now, far be it from me to wish any tragedy to come into the life of this nation for the sake of chastening its soul, or into the life of George Gershwin, for the sake of deepening his art. But I do want to quote to him a few verses (by Thomas Hardy, I believe) which I came across the other day and which are supposed to relate to America: "I shrink to see a modern coast / Whose riper times have yet to be; / Where the new regions claim them free / From that long drip of human tears / Which peoples old in tragedy / Have left upon the centuried years."

The "long drip of human tears," my dear George! They have great and strange and beautiful power, those human tears. They fertilize the deepest roots of art, and from them flowers spring of a loveliness and perfume that no other moisture can produce.

I believe in you with full faith and admiration, in your personality, in your gifts, in your art, in your future, in your significance in the field of American music, and I wish you well with all my heart. And just because of that I could wish for you an experience—not too prolonged—of that driving storm and stress of the emotions, of that solitary wrestling with your own soul, of that aloofness, for a while, from the actions and distractions of the everyday world, which are the most effective ingredients for the deepening and mellowing and the complete development, energizing, and revealment of an artist's inner being and spiritual powers.

TROUBADOUR

The New Yorker, May 25, 1929

S. N. BEHRMAN

When I first knew George Gershwin he was living with his family in an apartment in 110th Street. To me, who am forced when I want to write so much as a postcard to shut all doors, cut off the telephone, and cere myself carefully in an immutable silence, it was a perpetual wonder that Gershwin could do his work in the living room of this particular flat, the simultaneous stamping ground of the other members of the family and the numberless relatives and visitors who would lounge through, lean on the piano, chat, tell stories, and do their setting-up exercises. I have seen Gershwin working on the score of the Concerto in F in a room in which there must have been six other people talking among themselves, having tea, and playing checkers.

In those days Gershwin used to mumble ineffectually that what he needed was privacy. This mild protest went on for several years and resulted finally in the purchase of a five-story house in West 103rd Street. The top floor was the composer's study; here his treasures were transplanted: the Steinway grand, the Great Composers Series drawn for him by Will Cotton, the photograph of Prince George of England informally inscribed "From George to George," the framed poster announcing the performance of the Concerto at the Paris Opera, the specially bound scores of Debussy and Wagner.

At one time, during those 110th Street days, Gershwin was working simultaneously on the Concerto and the scores of *Song of the Flame* and *Tip-Toes.* During this triple creation he would occasionally emigrate to a suite of rooms in a hotel at Broadway and 100th Street. But even here the "privacy" he achieved was only comparative; here, too, the rooms were generally full of admirers, voluntary secretaries who asked nothing further than to be allowed to copy out a score—and relatives.

The electrical success of the *Rhapsody in Blue* (first played by Paul Whiteman in Aeolian Hall,

February 12, 1924) made Gershwin an international figure, and the house in 103rd Street, with its presumably sacrosanct top floor, was a symbol of the composer's new dignity.

My last visit to the house in 103rd Street demonstrated vividly the futility of symbols in the face of an overpowering reality. I hadn't seen the Gershwins in a long time and I telephoned to ask if it would be convenient for me to call. It was a sweltering night in September and I arrived at the house about nine o'clock. For a long time I rang the doorbell but got no answer. Through the screened, curtained door window I could see figures moving inside, and I kept ringing impatiently. No answer. Finally I pushed the door open and walked in. Three or four young men I had never seen before were sitting around the hall smoking. Off the hall was a small reception room which had been converted into a billiard room. I peered in— there was a game in progress but I knew none of the players. I asked for George, or his brother Ira. No one bothered to reply, but one of the young men made a terse gesture in the direction of the upper stories. I went up one flight and there I found a new group. One of them I vaguely recognized from 110th Street, and I asked him where George and Ira were. He said he thought they were upstairs. On the third floor I found Arthur, the youngest brother, who had just come in and didn't know who was in the house, but on the fourth I got an answer to my—by this time agonized—cry. I heard Ira's voice inviting me up to the fifth. I found him and his wife, Leonore, trying to keep cool in George's study. I told them of my adventures coming up the stairs. "Who under the sun," I asked, "are those fellows playing billiards on the first floor?"

Ira looked almost guilty. "To tell you the truth," he said, "I don't know!"

"But you must," I insisted. "They looked perfectly at home."

"I really don't," he said. "There's a bunch of fellows from down the street who've taken to dropping in here every night for a game. I think they're friends of Arthur's. But I don't know who they are."

"Where," I demanded sternly, "is George?"

"He's taken his old rooms in the hotel around the corner. He says he's got to a have a little privacy."

And, lest I deduce from this that George had become unbearably temperamental, Ira—who is the *fidus Achates* of his younger brother as well as his lyricist—added apologetically, "You see, George had to do some work on *Funny Face*."

As a matter of fact I had long since come to the conclusion that George doesn't in the least need "privacy"—at any rate not for composition. His talent is so amazingly prodigal that he hasn't, like the less favored of us, to dig and prod for it. Possibly his training in Tin Pan Alley when he plugged songs for Remick accustomed him to working under conditions that the average creative artist would find impossible. The *Rhapsody in Blue* was written in a few weeks because he had promised Paul Whiteman a piece for his first concert. The Concerto in F was written and scored while he was at work on two musical shows; *An American in Paris,* during a few hectic weeks on the Continent. Mr. Gershwin is thirty; his first show, *La La Lucille,* was produced when he was twenty. Since then he has written thirty [*sic*] full musical scores; three important orchestral works ("*An American in Paris* is the most important American composition since the Concerto in F"—I quote from the review written on the morning after the first performance by the music critic of the *World*); a series of piano preludes which, I am told by the same authority, are first-rate; and besides that, literally scores of songs which have never appeared in shows.

Among these last are some of his loveliest. "The Man I Love" was one until it was stuck into the ill-fated *Strike Up the Band*. There was talk once of making up a score of Gershwin's songs which, for

The lavishness of 1929's **Show Girl**—*another Ziegfeld production—overwhelmed its plot. Ruby Keeler (soon to become famous in the great Busby Berkeley film musicals) starred, one of her attractions being that she was married at the time to Al Jolson (who actually joined his wife in song during many performances of the show). Also featured were comedian Jimmy Durante, the Duke Ellington Orchestra, and a ballet that used music from* **An American in Paris.**

one reason or another, had been thrown out of shows, and the list made one feel like going out at once to raise the money. At the mercy of banal librettists and the exigencies of "show business," Mr. Gershwin has to take out songs because the prima donnas can't sing them, or because it's time for the slapstick men, or because they're too intricate for the chorus to dance. Almost anyone who knows him well will tell you that much of his stuff which sounds magnificent when he plays it on the piano is dimmed and muffled by the time it reaches the theater.

But Gershwin's active repertory at the piano is practically endless; besides the well-known ones, from "Swanee" to "My One and Only" and "Feeling I'm Falling," there is a succession not generally known—among which two prime favorites are the incomparable "Mischa, Jascha, Toscha, Sascha," written for a party at Jascha Heifetz's, and "My Little Ducky." It is a seemingly inexhaustible fecundity.

The house in 103rd Street has only recently been abandoned, and Gershwin is installed now in a penthouse apartment in Riverside Drive. To complete the gesture of emancipation, the place is done in ultramodern style—a rather swooning, Mélisandish bedroom, terraced bookshelves and elongated wall-lights in the living room, and over the dining room table a weirdly crenelated electric lamp that reminds me somehow of the last act of *Dynamo.* One room, though, is fitted as a gymnasium, with old-fashioned punching bags and fencing foils.

Personally I regard the breakup of the Gershwin ménage with considerable regret, because it will probably minimize my contacts with Gershwin père. He is short, rotund, inclined to literalness, and he has that singular and unerring faculty which certain originals have for saying, in any situation, that final thing beyond which there is nothing left to be said. There has accumulated gradually a saga of anecdotes emanating from him; when I meet George or Ira I simply say, "What's the latest?" and I am generally told.

The latest happens to be this. The family was discussing the new Einstein paper and George commented on the astonishing compactness of scientific vocabulary:

"Imagine working for twenty years and putting your results into three pages!"

"Well," said Mr. Gershwin calmly, "it was probably very small print!"

The rest of the family consists of Mrs. Gershwin and a younger brother and sister, Arthur and Frances. Mrs. Gershwin is level-headed and practical; I imagine it was she who steered the family through the early years and who helped Gershwin père to the eminence of a restaurant proprietor. I gather that it was not her fault that prosperity dwindled in the era immediately before George became famous. When George was growing up

Although **Show Girl** *had a reasonable 111 performances, for Ziegfeld it was a box-office flop; blaming the Gershwins, he actually refused to pay them their royalties, causing the brothers to sue.*

the family was so poor it couldn't afford a piano, and it was at some sacrifice that one was secured for him when he was thirteen years old. The sister is sporadically on the stage and at Palm Beach, and Arthur does something in the commercial side of films and practices the piano. It is the family joke that one day Arthur will outdistance George, but so far this speculation remains in the region of humor.

This is the background of Gershwin's electrifying genius—a background which has this in common with the environment of most genius—that it remains inscrutable and explains nothing. I use the expression deliberately, for this good-humored, ingenuous young man is one of the most thrilling artists now alive. Because I have no authority to write about music, I have spoken with circumspection of Gershwin's achievements as a composer. I come now to a side of his talent of which I can speak because I have been under its spell—his immediate talent as a pianist, as an interpreter of his own songs. Josef Hofmann says of Gershwin that he has "a fine pianistic talent . . . firm, clear . . . good command over the keyboard." To the layman it seems a positive domination. You get the sense of a complete mastery, a complete authority—the most satisfactory feeling any artist can give you. When he sits at the piano and plays his own songs in a roomful of people, the effect that he evokes is extraordinary. I have seen Kreisler, Zimbalist, Auer, and Heifetz caught up in the heady surf that inundates a room the moment he strikes a chord. It is a feat not only of technique but of sheer virtuosity of personality. At the piano Gershwin takes on a new life and so do his auditors. He sings. He makes elaborate gestures. When he comes to a line in "My Little Ducky"—"Gloria Swanson is hot for me, / Look at the pin she got for me"—hand flies to his tie to convey the better Miss Swanson's magnanimity. Described, this sounds grotesque, but actually it is as beautifully interpreted as a clever harmony. Gershwin becomes a sort of sublimated and transplanted troubadour, singing an elemental emotion, an unabashed humor. . . . (What a stunt it would be for someone to take a slow movie of a group of people crowded around a piano while Gershwin is playing and run it off without music!) Illuminated and vitalized by his own music, his own voice, his own eager sense of the rhythm of life, Gershwin instantly conveys that illumination and that vitality to others, and that is why he can at once pick up the confused and disparate elements of the average New York party and precipitate them—willy-nilly—into a medium warm and homogeneous and ecstatic.

Of course, Gershwin enjoys his own playing and his own music and his own talent. It is part of the integrity of his effect. There are people who will tell you that Gershwin can't write a tune and there are people who will tell you that he plays too long at parties. There are, in fact, all sorts of people. As a matter of fact, Gershwin has been exploited mercilessly by hostesses—and hosts—whose parties he has saved from irredeemable dullness. I have referred to Gershwin as ingenuous. This is a condescension with which articulate people often indulge themselves when speaking of the less articulate. There are moments when I gather that Gershwin is not unable to evaluate nicely his own place in society. He told me once that his mother had cautioned him against playing too much at parties. With engaging candor Gershwin admitted that there might be some truth in this; but was it ingenuousness or sophistication which prompted him to add, "You see, the trouble is, when I don't play, I don't have a good time"?

WAR WITH THE SWISS

New York *World,* January 15, 1930

ROBERT LITTEL

Strike Up the Band is the swellest phoenix that ever rose from the ashes. Not so very long ago this same show, with much the same music and lyrics, by George and Ira Gershwin, was abandoned not far from Atlantic City. It has come to life again, to gay and silly life, and may immediately be set down as one of the few musicals that you must see.

Last night was particularly memorable because the leader of the orchestra which played some of the best tunes was George Gershwin himself, who seemed to be enjoying things hugely, as well he might. In spite of a particularly graceful and well-drilled chorus and innumerable other good things which shall be mentioned in due course, it was almost impossible to keep one's eyes off Mr. Gershwin, in the world's largest white tie and boutonniere, having as good a time as anyone in the audience. You could see him—and sometimes hear him—singing along with the chorus, and every once in a while a certain pursing of the lips indicated that he was no longer singing but whistling, as many others will do from now on; for such tunes as "Strike Up the Band" and "[I Want to Be a] War Bride," not to speak of half a dozen others, are about as good as tunes can be.

But George Gershwin has a brother, Ira, whose contribution to last night's party was hardly less remarkable. It has always been his ill luck that people hum tunes long before they memorize words. It has also been his ill luck that few choruses and fewer singers let us hear the extraordinarily gay, neat words and endlessly resourceful

The first version of **Strike Up the Band** *closed during tryouts in Philadelphia in September 1927; the era was still too optimistic for George S. Kaufman's stinging antiwar scenario. For the 1930 version Morrie Ryskind joined Kaufman in lightening up the book, which still dealt with a fictional American war with the Swiss, instigated by greedy capitalists, this time over chocolate rather than cheese.*

rhymes of his lyrics. And, last night, to our sorrow, was no exception.

The Gershwins were most of it, and the best of it, but by no means all of it. The book, based by Morrie Ryskind on a libretto by George S. Kaufman, is an amusing piece of satirical foolishness on the subject of a mock war between the Swiss and the United States over a high tariff on chocolate. It isn't always as good as that idea, a veritable Einstein among ideas for musical comedy books, sounds. Too frequently it is much like all the rest of them. And while we are dealing with the minus column, let it be said, though not too loud, that the production is not all it might be, that some of the singing is very feeble, and that there are moments when the only thing worth watching—and if you are near enough, hearing—is George Gershwin putting the orchestra through its paces.

There are some grand performers in *Strike Up the Band,* and of course the first prize goes to that most peerless team, Clark and McCullough. Mr. Clark is funny enough to keep you laughing even when what he has to say isn't much, which happens more than once throughout the evening. And here is Blanche Ring in person, very capable indeed. And Dudley Clements as Fletcher, the chocolate manufacturer whose machinations start the war rolling, extremely good too. And the speedy and nimble dancing of Doris Carson.

It is all so good that one wishes it could rise from the ashes a second time and be perfect.

GEORGE GERSHWIN AND JAZZ: A CRITICAL ANALYSIS OF A MODERN COMPOSER

Theatre Guild Magazine, **March 1930**

ISAAC GOLDBERG

The theater is darkened, all but the stage. In the auditorium, only a few spectators: Edgar Selwyn, Morrie Ryskind, Ira Gershwin and his wife, a few friends—scattered, perhaps strategically, about the lower house. Ruth Selwyn is there, too, half her mind upon this dress rehearsal of *Strike Up the Band* and the other half upon her own debut as a producer with the *9:15 Revue*. The composer of *An American in Paris* and the insufficiently heard Concerto in F has just ducked his way through the low door leading from under the stage to the orchestra pit. His gray felt hat and his fur-lined overcoat are thrown across the top of the piano; his cigar . . . is already going full blast. Later in the evening it will serve as a baton; or George will blow songs through it. Director Leftwich stands fidgety in the wings, glaring like a martinet from under his eyeshade. . . .

Tomorrow night—which is Christmas—the show opens in Boston. Tonight it must proceed without a hitch. No stops for anything. Georgie Hale, arms crossed tightly, alert to see the boys and girls of the ensemble go through their paces, will not be seated there quietly for long. An ad hoc overture, opening chorus, and up bobs Hale, never to rest until the final curtain. . . . A word to Leftwich, an imploring look at George, back over the double-bass's head . . . repeat, ad libitum.

And George, conducting, is imperturbable. It is a paradox, but he is at once enthusiastic and unexcited. Between numbers he sits back and laughs youthfully at the antics of Clark and McCullough. He comes back to talk to a friend and misses a cue. His cigar is forever going out. And when the band strikes up, he hums his music, whistles it, sings it out lustily.

"My voice," he will tell you, "is what is known as small but disagreeable." As a matter of fact, it is neither. He conducts with his baton, his cigar, his shoulders, and his hips. . . . His conducting is a dance.

And now, with the pride of one who has been virtually self-taught in orchestration, he listens for the various effects that he is always planning. So far as concerns the kind of listening that a composer gets from nine-tenths of a musical-comedy audience—are my figures too optimistic?—this sort of thing is self-indulgence. A bouncing figuration in the strings, for example, against a slow flow of melody from the woodwinds . . . a figure in the bassoon that shoots through the harmony like a short thread of coarse silk and disappears into the air . . . a sudden fanfare that portends an antic war—on the stage, in the voices, there is a new subtlety that betokens a new, an expanding, composer. The melodic line is more plastic, it is longer, it does not fear angles, it has a delightful habit—always the sign of a fresh, original spirit—of reaching out to unexpected notes. Gershwin's later tunes, even when they keep true to certain jazz formulas, are more dynamic than the songs that first made him known. They are . . . unpredictable.

Let us take, as pertinent examples, some of the songs from *Show Girl*. The score of that piece cannot compare, for extended writing, with the score of *Strike Up the Band*. The individual songs, however, were insufficiently appreciated, and not by Mr. Ziegfeld alone. In the refrain of "So Are You" there is a delightful and unobtrusive moment when the tonic of the key suddenly becomes the leading note of the new, temporary key. That the tune itself is an excellent representation of mock coyness we may pass over; notice, however, the feeling of unrest created by the chord that immediately precedes the refrain; notice how the psychological resolution—as distinguished from the harmonic—is not complete until the word *red* in the line "Roses are red."

The *trouvaille* of *Show Girl,* however—and I should call it one of the happiest touches in our contemporary popular music—is to be found in the first four bars of the refrain to "Liza." I can't conceive of this melody as having been written down separately and afterwards harmonized. Music like this grows all of a piece. Melodically, the tune represents nothing but an incomplete rising pentatonic scale, in terms of the singer: "sol, la, do, re." As it is played over the radio, this effect is usually smeared by a tempo that has the dancer and not the singer in mind. Even in the sheet-music arrangement, however, the harmonies may be fully appreciated. The music mirrors perfectly the rising anxiety of the words. . . . Such a setting—four bars such as these—are in the finest tradition of song, popular or classical. And so, for that matter, are such Gershwin "numbers" as "'S Wonderful" from *Funny Face* and, of course, that masterpiece of modern song, "The Man I Love," which it took our public some four years to discover.

It is a peculiarity of "Liza"—Gershwin did not realize it until it had been pointed out to him—that the refrain begins with half-notes, continues with quarter-notes, and then dissolves into eighths. As I look through George's very first songs I find it to be almost a habit with him to start on a long note and then let it spatter into shorter ones. For recent examples, I might indicate the "blues" in *An American in Paris,* the chorus of "Soon" in *Strike Up the Band.* For early ones, how about the refrain to "Swanee"? And how about the first conscious "blues" that Gershwin wrote, only ten years ago, for the second *George White's Scandals*? The name of it is "On My Mind the Whole Night Long."

Speaking of "Liza," Gershwin ought to make a record, whether phonographic or on the piano rolls, of his variations upon this theme. If you find him in a good mood he will keep them up for a quarter of an hour. At moments something demonic possesses him and the variations of "Sweet and Low-Down," from *Tip-Toes,* leap into a flame of rhythms. These, like the happy touches in the orchestrations, are among the things that never get into the sheet music.

The Gershwin songs are not happy accidents. They are not solely the productions of a born melodist. . . . They are the work of a born composer—of a young man who thinks, not in terms of tunes, or even in terms of jazz, but in terms of tone.

Gershwin's jazz is not a stencil. In a stricter sense, it is not even an aim. He is not committed to glorifying jazz. What he cares about is music. His writing, whether in the more popular forms or in the quasi-symphonic media, is peculiarly honest because it is peculiarly himself. It is himself in tone. To see him, after an arduous rehearsal, challenge Georgie Hale to a hoofing duet, or match strength with one of his principals, or to hear his passing comments upon musical affairs in general is to realize how unforced is his humor in his melodies and harmonies, how simply true they are to the fellow behind the music.

In George's jazz there is not a little mathematical calculation. For his processes he can give specific formulas. In a word, his head is in constant cooperation with his heart. At the same time—an examination of his early songs bears witness—as he has become more conscious of the mathematical element, he has become—need it be paradoxically?—more spontaneous, more flexible. He sees his music—I do not say feels it—preeminently as design, as structure. Jazz is, and has been, all things to all ears. It has been regarded as merely a form of treatment, as color in harmonies, as free counterpoint in tones and in rhythms, as a form of release from oppressive routine, as a symbol of our latter-day sexual freedom, as a phase of the new primitivity. . . .

George is distinctly of his day, of his city. His roots, if not his branches, are in the present, and of Gotham. His jazz is more complex than that of his early brothers in Tin Pan Alley because his own nature is restless and experimental. If jazz, among other things, symbolizes an escape from routine, even Gershwin's most popular music exemplifies that escape in the form of more meaningful melodies, more intricate accompaniments, and since he began to orchestrate for himself, more significant instrumentations.

In *Strike Up the Band* he has added new colors to his palette. It is not every musical comedy that, for its music, and especially for the orchestral treatment of the music, easily bears three hearings within a week. Gershwin, in this madcap production, has written not only some of his best tunes but he has demonstrated in the finale to the first act a capacity for remaining long on the wing. Given a true libretto, an integrated scenario, he could create for us—with the economic consent of the producers—the American equivalent of the Gilbert-Sullivan operetta. The proof of this lies in the selfsame finale. It is easy to suggest, of course,

Given the recent stock market crash and the beginnings of the Depression, by early 1930 the popular mood was more receptive to the type of satire in the revised **Strike Up the Band.** *Gershwin was very involved in the rehearsals, and he conducted the Red Nichols band on the opening nights in Boston (December 24, 1929) and New York (January 14, 1930). The show was a critical and popular success, with 191 performances. The Gershwins, who created whole scenes of music and long "songs" that were essential to the dramatic structure of the book, were hailed in many quarters as originators of a new and unique form of musical theater and as the American Gilbert and Sullivan. "Soon" was the hit number, and* **Strike Up the Band** *became the second Gershwin musical to have its entire score published.*

that George and brother Ira have been listening with both ears to the words and music of England's heavenly twins. In *Strike Up the Band* the Savoyard will find intimations of *Pinafore, The Pirates of Penzance,* of *Iolanthe.* And I am surprised that no one has heretofore noticed, in the book itself, as well as in some of the words and situations, a general indebtedness to that neglected score, *Princess Ida.*

It is important to point out, however, that the Gershwins have not been merely imitating Gilbert and Sullivan. They are on the way to translating them into American. Better still, they are on the way to fashioning an indigenous satirical strain for our musical stage. Here is a symptomatic example, which I have from George himself.

You will recall the stammering tune, ". . . The Unofficial Spokesman . . ." This may have been one of the few instances in which Ira's words preceded George's music. In any case, as George considered the piece, something balked him. The words were right; there was something wrong, something "unrealized," about the simple tune. As it stood, it was too closely in the Gilbert-Sullivan tradition—a topical, political song, visiting good-natured ridicule upon the singer and the song. It needed something to Americanize it, as it were. And then, as so often, George suddenly hit upon what was trying to force itself into his consciousness. He would make that music undergo a sea-change: it would be transformed from a British subject into an American citizen. How? By jazzing up its line; by repeating the word *unofficial* (and all other words that stood in a similar position) in a stammering rhythm that was unmistakably of this soil. This peculiar effect was the composer's contribution to the words. . . .

The commentary of the orchestra upon the progress of the action is particularly rich in *Strike Up the Band.* It is, in tones, the very image of Gershwin sitting on the sidelines and offering a fire of wisecracks. Recall the trio of elderly gentlemen trying to win the affections—and the imaginary fortune—of the not-too-old lady represented by Blanche Ring with "How About a . . . [Boy] Like Me . . . ?" Now, if you listen carefully to the orchestra when this line is first sung, you will hear a series of descending chords that is delightfully uncertain in key. Two measures of sour observation—and yet they are sufficient to "debunk," musically, the amorous pretensions of the faded Lotharios on the stage.

There is another moment in which Gershwin's orchestra is at the same trick. This was, I believe, an eleventh-hour thought of the composer. A few days before the premiere of the comedy I discovered him in bed at the Ritz-Carlton, Boston, orchestrating a short line that was needed for the entrance of [Bobby] Clark at the head of his Fletcherized army. The ordinary composer, if he is up to his routine, has his head stored with marches, waltzes, tangos, and the familiar rest, and can supply these upon demand. George, however, remembered that this was no ordinary army. So that his greeting to the soldiers begins rightly enough with a trumpeted *ra-ta-ta*; and suddenly this brave flourish collapses. The music ends, again, upon a series of descending chords that have all the effect of a tire that has been punctured. And, surely, their purpose is to deflate this puffed-up army of Fletcher's milk-chocolate soldiers.

It is little touches such as these that make a second visit to the piece so delightful. Near the close, when the girls step to the footlights and sing their resume of the plot, the music to the words is also a thematic resume of the tunes. This, of course, is more obvious stuff, but it is cleverly joined. As obvious, but as cleverly articulated, is the call of the trumpet intoning, in double time, the phrase from ". . . A Typical Self-Made American," when Fletcher falls into his long, deep dream of war. . . .

These touches, delicate or harsh as the case may be, do not get into the sheet-music versions, more's the pity. Some of them are too intricate or too rhythmically subtle. Even the refrain to the song "I Mean to Say" is frequently sung and whistled, away from the theater, as if it began on the downbeat—the accented first beat of the bar. As a matter of fact it begins on the second beat—the one beat of silence that precedes the tune adds to the vitality of the whole. ". . . Hangin' Around with You" presents the chiefly rhythmic difficulty of mastering the repetitions of the melody on the words *hanging around with you,* when Gershwin, as is his fond habit, telescopes the tune. . . .

Nor is all that is Gershwin jazz. It is in his orchestral accompaniments that we may notice in *Strike Up the Band* evidence of a new richness in his musical personality. He is no slave to a label, and he is not fond of repeating himself if he can help it. The more regrettable, then, if we may not have the musical comedy printed as a score in its entirety. The usual practice is to issue a few of the "hits." But it is precisely in the less hummable songs, in those that less lend themselves to whistling, that Gershwin has done his best work here. He has composed no act in his career that can match the first act of *Strike Up the Band* for general tunefulness, for variety of thematic material, for harmonic and orchestral versatility, for sheer spirit. Especially at the opening and the close. The march "Strike Up the Band" is quite as effective and dramatically in place as the glorious tune that Sullivan devised for the end of the first act in *Iolanthe,* in which the victory of Strephon is presaged. Observe how it pushes its way up chromatically through an octave drive; how it then makes a partial descent, only to reach its climax on a whole note above the octave.

Oh, yes, jazz may be good, and when it is Gershwin, it is usually good, if not better. Here, too, more may be meant than meets the ear, or than finds its way into print for popular sale.

SOME THINGS
ABOUT A YOUNG COMPOSER

New York *World*, May 4, 1930

ARTHUR KOBER

George Gershwin believes that the best music he has ever written is contained in the score of *Strike Up the Band.*

He is fully aware of his own ability and is his own severest critic. He values the critical opinion of his brother Ira above all others.

He will play for you without having to be asked twice. Once he plays, it will be hours before he stops. His favorite composition when entertaining is "Liza" . . . [from *Show Girl*]. He has as many as twenty interpretations of this melody.

He received only one amusing wire the night *Strike Up the Band* opened. It was from Florenz Ziegfeld, who wrote, "Why didn't you conduct for me at *my* opening night?"

He is proud of his father and his father's stories. When the latter was introduced to Jerry Goff, leading man in *Strike Up the Band,* after the opening, George said, "Pop, you know Mr. Goff. He's the leading man in the show." "Sure," said Mr. Gershwin to his son. "He was on the Americans' side."

He suffered from stomach trouble for a long time. That trouble went flying with the acquisition of a new house man, Dindle, who placed him on a diet of agar. George becomes positively eloquent on the subject of agar.

His favorite avocation is painting. He has just learned to use watercolors. He turns every attractive female visitor into a model.

He believes that if his public-school teacher hadn't laughed when he showed her a drawing he had made, he would have been a very successful artist today.

He is wildly enthusiastic about conducting. When *Strike Up the Band* opened in Boston he telephoned to Max Dreyfus of Harms. The only one in that office at the time was the telephone operator. "I conducted last night," he told her, "and I was very good."

He has a habit of twitching his neck. He explains this by saying that his bones there are dry and that he cracks them much in the manner of a person cracking his fingers.

He thinks that he made his biggest financial gesture in asking fifty thousand dollars for the talking-picture rights to the *Rhapsody in Blue*—and getting it.

He spent several hours one morning in flattering a person just because he wanted him to "purr." That person actually purred.

He is tender about people who ask him for his autograph because "they must get little fun out of life to be able to get such a big kick out of that."

His day is continually punctuated by naps. Yet on the eve of an important opening or event he will stay up until dawn, a method of avoiding stage fright.

He loves, above all else, big black cigars.

He is so prolific when composing a score for a show that he actually chafes at the slowness of his associates.

He has never outgrown certain juvenile qualities. He still loves to impress people—not as a mere display of ostentation, but because he himself is slightly bewildered by it all. . . .

He has been caricatured by many. His favorite caricature of himself is by Auerbach-Levy. His favorite caricaturist is Will Cotton.

His choice of a book writer is S. N. Behrman, with whom he hopes to collaborate on a musical romance.

He is proud of the line he gave Bobby Clark in *Strike Up the Band.* "I just left Gideon at 146 West Forty-eighth Street," shouts Clark. "What's there?" asks someone. "I don't know" is the answer. "You just ask for Schulz."

King of Jazz *(Universal, 1930) was designed as a movie-musical extravaganza, featuring Paul Whiteman's orchestra, an animated cartoon with Whiteman as the hero, comedy routines and songs, and increasingly popular crooner Bing Crosby. In the early days of the talkies, musicals were the rage and were often given lavish treatment; Whiteman's movie was accorded the luxury of primitive Technicolor, making for an almost surrealistic experience when viewed today. Although Gershwin is not in the film, his* **Rhapsody in Blue** *(for years Whiteman's signature piece) is— and for its use the composer was paid the astronomical sum of fifty thousand dollars. The movie opened in New York at the Roxy Theatre in May 1930 and was paired for a limited engagement with a stage show featuring Whiteman conducting the enormous Roxy Orchestra, with Gershwin himself, for a week, at the piano for several shows a day.*

MAKING MUSIC

New York *Sunday World Magazine,* May 4, 1930

GEORGE GERSHWIN

"There are so many songwriters today that if placed end to end, it wouldn't be a bad idea!"

This futile but perhaps sage suggestion, presented the other day by a well-known Broadway wag, is being echoed up and down the Great Blight Way. And with no little reason. Never, in all our history of popular music, has there been such a plethora of composers—professional, amateur, and alleged—as we have today. Responsible, of course, are those two fresh hotbeds, the soniferous cinema and the radio. The merciless ether, by unceasing plugging, has cut down the life of a popular song to but a few weeks, with the result that anyone who thinks he can carry a tune—even if it's nowhere in particular nowadays takes a "shot" at music-making. "I care not who makes the nation's laws, if I may make its theme songs" appears to be the general attitude. One music publisher facetiously declares that songwriting may someday displace the anagram!

With this enormous increase of interest in songwriting I find that I am being asked more often than ever by laymen as well as by aspiring composers for my formula, if any: just how, where, why, and when I write my music. In placing it all on the record here, I only wish to correct a few of the many popular misconceptions about songwriting.

Often I am given to understand that composing a song is an easy affair. All a number needs for success, it seems, is thirty-two bars; a good phrase of eight bars used to start the refrain is repeated twice more with a new eight-bar added which is much less important. It sounds simple, of course, but personally I can think of no more nerve-wracking, no more mentally arduous task than making music. There are times when a phrase of music will cost me many hours of internal sweating. Rhythms romp through my brain, but they're not easy to capture and keep; the chief difficulty is to avoid reminiscence.

Inspiration, commonly considered the main-spring of composition, is as elusive as it is illusive. I might call it an unconscious something that happens within you which makes you do a thing much better than if it were done self-consciously. When it does come it may be truly called a gift from the gods. Out of my entire annual output of songs, perhaps two—or at the most, three—come as a result of inspiration. When I want it most, it does not come, so I never rely on it; that is, I don't sit around and wait for an inspiration to walk up to me and introduce itself. What I substitute for it is nothing more than talent plus my knowledge. If a composer's endowment is great enough, the song is made to sound as if it were truly inspired.

After all, making music is actually little else than a matter of invention. What causes me to write is only my inventiveness, aided and abetted by emotion. I combine what I know of music with what I feel. I see a piece of music in the form of a design. With a melody I can take the whole design in one look; with a larger composition, like a concerto, I have to take it piece by piece and then construct it so much longer. No matter what they say about "nothing new under the sun," it is always possible to invent something original. The songwriter takes an idea and adds his own individuality to it; he merely uses his capacity for invention in arranging bars his own way. Though it can hardly be said that I come from a musical family, my grandfather really was an inventor in Russia, while my father at one time was a devotee of opera and showed an authentic love for music, I think, by being able to imitate a trumpet almost perfectly and to whistle very beautifully.

Just as a creator of fiction or of poetry, a composer of music smells symphonic ideas in every fact. To me they are represented by both abstract and concrete ideas. Though I am a great lover of nature, none of my music comes from viewing detached scenes, no matter how beautiful or "inspiring" they may be; most of my ideas arise

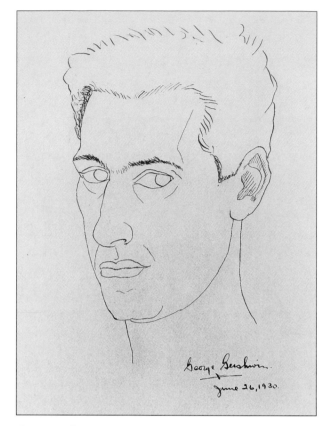

By 1930 George Gershwin was becoming increasingly self-assured in his forays into the visual arts. He often created pen-and-ink portraits of himself, his family, and his friends.

from contact with people, from personalities and emotions of men and women I meet.

The idea for the *Rhapsody in Blue,* for example, came to me quite suddenly. The vivid panorama of American life swept through my mind—its feverishness, its vulgarity, its welter of love, marriage, and divorce, and its basic solidity in the character of the people. All of the emotional reactions excited by contemplating the American scene, with all its mixtures of races, . . . were stuffed into the first outline of the *Rhapsody,* with a dominant theme derived from the fashionable "blue" or melancholy rhythm.

I really prefer writing serious music. A serious composition is either a success or a failure because of what the composer does to it. I may write a good score for a musical comedy, but if the book or cast is poor my work registers a flop. A symphony, on the other hand, lives or dies according to its real

worth. While popular music may be tricked very easily, serious music offers so many more interesting problems in construction, in orchestration, in other details. For a long time—as far back as my eighteenth year—I have wanted to work at big compositions. I am glad I can do it now. Nor will the contention of Madame Galli-Curci that opera is old-fashioned deter me from writing my opus.

Of extreme importance to the concocter of tunes is his mood. Without the proper mood it is almost impossible to compose satisfactorily. Frequently I have to force myself into a mood. Although, to write a happy song, for example, I do not actually have to be happy, I must try to feel like one who is happy. To get into the proper frame of mind I sit at the piano and play. Thus I find myself most frequently at the piano while composing.

Composing at the piano is not a good practice. But I started that way and it has become a habit. However, I give my mind free rein and use the piano only to try what I can hear mentally. The best method is one which will not permit anything to hold you down in any way, for it is always easier to think in a straight line, without the distraction of sounds. The mind should be allowed to run loose, unhampered by the piano, which may be used now and then only to stimulate thought and set an idea aflame. The actual composition must be done in the brain. Too much, however, should not be left to the memory. Sometimes, when I think the phrase is safe in my mind, I will find that I have lost it the next day. So that when I get a phrase which I am not sure I will remember the following day I set it down on paper at once. Occasionally I dream a composition, but rarely can I remember it when I wake. On one occasion I did get out of bed and write a song. That number, incidentally, is one of my recent compositions, "Strike Up the Band."

What comes first, the words or the music? Odd, how this question is the first which enters the mind of most people when the art of writing songs is under discussion. In my own case most frequently the music is written first. Often, however, my brother Ira will write the lyric first, but always in a definite rhythm. These songs are mainly of the comedy variety.

Like the denizens of the prize ring, the songwriter must always keep in training. He must try to write something every day. I know that if I don't do any writing for several weeks I lose a great deal of time in catching my stride again. Hence I am always composing.

My creative work is done almost exclusively at night, and my best is achieved in the fall and winter months. A beautiful spring or summer day is least conducive to making music, for I always prefer being out than at work. I don't write at all in the morning, for the obvious reason that I'm not awake at the time. The afternoon I devote to physical labor—orchestrations, piano copies, etc. At night, when other people are asleep or out for a good time, I can get absolute quiet for my composing. Not that perfect peace is always necessary; often I have written my tunes with people in the same room or playing cards in the next. If I find myself in the desired mood I can hold it until I finish the song.

"To be a songwriter you must live a songwriter," a famous popular composer once remarked. I can think of no more apt dictum for those who are seriously contemplating composing music as a profession. You can't be something else—a butcher, a baker, or a broker—and then suddenly write a successful song. One must write, rewrite, and then write again. Knowing Tin Pan Alley, living in the atmosphere of words and music, tells the beginner what not to do. The outsider looking in will find it extremely difficult to break through to recognition.

I learned to write music by studying the most successful songs published. At nineteen I could write a song that sounded so much like Jerome Kern that he wouldn't know whether he or I had written it. But imitation can go only so far. The young songwriter may start by imitating a successful composer he admires, but he must break away as soon as he has learned the maestro's strong points and technique. Then he must try to develop his own musical personality, to bring something of his own invention into his work.

For some songwriters it is not even absolutely essential that they know anything about music. Many of the composers with the greatest number of successes to their credit—among them Walter Donaldson and Irving Berlin—can't read a line of music. What they have is an innate sense of melody

and rhythm; all they seek is to write a simple tune that the public can easily remember. In order to write longer compositions, the study of musical technique is indispensable. Many people say that too much study kills spontaneity in music, but I claim that, although study may kill a small talent, it must develop a big talent. In other words, if study kills a musical endowment, it deserves to be killed. I studied piano for four years, and then harmony. And I shall continue to study for a long time.

Above all, the aspiring composer should write something every day, regardless of its length or quality. Continued writing offers greater chances for achieving something original and important. Perhaps the tenth—or the hundredth—song will do the trick.

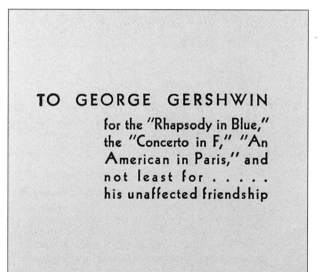

TO GEORGE GERSHWIN

for the "Rhapsody in Blue," the "Concerto in F," "An American in Paris," and not least for . . . . . his unaffected friendship

*Isaac Goldberg, George Gershwin's friend and biographer, dedicated his important book on American popular music, **Tin Pan Alley** (1930), to Gershwin. The composer provided the volume's introduction, which Goldberg seems to have edited somewhat and to which he obviously added opening and closing comments. A version of the same essay appeared in the New York **World** in May 1930, sans the Goldberg additions, and in language a bit closer to the rough-around-the-edges writing style exhibited by Gershwin in his other articles.*

'GIRL CRAZY' MAKES HIT AS DIVERTING NEW SHOW

New York Telegram, October 15, 1930

WILLIAM BOEHNEL

Simply and straight to the point, without indulging in any preliminary explosion of superlatives, I should like to go on record as stating that *Girl Crazy,* at the Alvin Theatre, is one of the few diverting entertainments of the new season.

It is a big and breathless musical show, full of excellent tunes by George Gershwin, and contain-ing among others in its cast that amazing young lady, Ethel Merman, who, it is said, formerly amused the more jaded habitués of the gilded nightclubs—and who can fondle a blues song in such as way that it becomes a combination of both Helen Morgan and Libby Holman without sug-gesting either.

In addition to the aforementioned Miss Merman, Messrs. Aarons and Freedley have gathered together for your amusement such enjoyable per-formers as Allen Kearns, Ginger Rogers, Willie Howard, and William Kent. And what with its young, comely, and lively chorus, its varied and pretty costumes and handsome settings, *Girl Crazy* is a play worthy to be patronized by the most fastidious drama lover.

There is a plot, too, the offspring of Guy Bolton and John McGowan. It is the customary plot, but since it is sub-merged in favor of such more important items as specialty dances, songs, and girls, it will do. It concerns itself with young Danny Churchill, a Manhattan playboy, who comes to his father's ranch

Girl Crazy, *which opened on Octo-ber 14, 1930, was the last—and the apogee—of the Gershwins' lighthearted Jazz Age musicals. A favorite with crit-ics and audiences, it ran for 272 perfor-mances. Ethel Merman, making her stage debut, became a Broadway legend overnight. She played Frisco Kate, singing the torrid blues ballad "Sam and Delilah" and belting out "Boy! What Love Has Done to Me!" and "I Got Rhythm." Ginger Rogers also appeared, as postmistress Molly Gray; it was her second show.*

in Arizona, falls in love with a cowgirl, turns the ranch into one of those known as the dude, and after the usual complications wins the girl.

The first half is full of vitality, and it moves at such a terrific pace that it never for a moment lets you catch your breath. In contrast, the second half not only seems but is frequently dull. But not enough to make one particle of difference.

Last night Mr. George Gershwin, who conducted the orchestra, must have been pleased with the manner in which his songs were sung and played. It is an excellent score, one of his best, and if I know my radio as well as I think I do, you will hear "Embraceable You," "I Got Rhythm," and "But Not for Me" being played and sung about the same time this report appears, if not sooner.

The very attractive and charming Ginger Rogers does nicely, very nicely indeed, as the girl in the case, and Allen Kearns makes a likable and believable hero. Willie Howard is there to throw

you into hysterics with his imitation of George Jessell, and William Kent helps to make matters a good deal livelier.

Last night's audience applauded long and vigorously. And rightly so, too, for *Girl Crazy* is a grand show.

*The **Girl Crazy** pit orchestra was an all-star jazz band led by Red Nichols and featuring Benny Goodman, Gene Krupa, Glenn Miller, Jimmy Dorsey, and Jack Teagarden. Gershwin again conducted on opening night. The arrangements are by Robert Russell Bennett, one of the great Broadway and Hollywood orchestrators, who during his career worked on the finest scores of Porter, Kern, and Gershwin. The original watercolor set designs for **Girl Crazy** were painted by Donald Oenslager.*

WORDS AND MUSIC

New York Times, **November 9, 1930**

IRA GERSHWIN

Twenty, thirty years ago men like Blossom, McClellan, and Harry B. Smith would write both the libretto and lyrics for their musical comedy and operetta offerings, but today the librettist is rare who, in concocting plots, embellishing dialogue, and pacifying comedians, can spare the time necessary for fitting a collection of highly involved and intricate rhythms with suitable words. Lyric writing, like tea testing and hitting the chimes for half-hour station announcements, has become a profession. A precarious profession, no doubt—one that the East Side marriage broker has as yet put no valuation on, one that is looked down on as a racket in some literary fields, but one which, nevertheless, requires a certain dexterity with words and a feeling for music on the one hand and, on the other, the infinite patience of the gemsetter, compatibility with the composer, and an understanding of the various personalities in a cast.

The librettists above mentioned and some others were lyric writers of the first water, but their work was more or less taken for granted. It was only when P. G. Wodehouse began writing for Kern and the Princess Theatre that the critics realized that here were lyrics worthy of attention; here, a writer who, if not a Gilbert in incisiveness, warranted recognition because of his quaint conceits and lighthearted tomfoolery. And when men like Brian Hooker and Berton Braley were infected with the virus *lyricus* or *lyrica,* as the case may be (I studied French and German), it was felt that possibly words were added to the music not only because the singers would look silly singing "tra-la-la" but because the words themselves might have entertainment value. I will not say that everyone in an audience is, for want of a better phrase, lyric conscious, but there are enough listening with a critical ear to make the lyric writer strive to get away from the banal and hackneyed.

One would imagine that after doing fifteen shows, the lyrics for my latest one, *Girl Crazy,* would flow easily from the Faber, the Waterman, and the Corona (I use all three). But instead of becoming easier, there is so much one cannot repeat, so much snow of yesterday that is slush today, so many trick rhymes that have become secondhand, so many titles that creak, and so few new angles on Jack and Jill, the Pied Piper, and little Goody Two-Shoes that working on a score and trying to set reasonable ideas to unreasonable rhythms becomes four months of intensive crisscross word puzzling. However, what with a pot of black coffee at hand, a box of cigars in reach, and a wolf at the door, one manages.

Since musical-comedy lyrics are written, for the greater part, to the melodies, let us consider the composer. In this case he is a musician whom we shall call George Gershwin, although that is his real name.

He composes, so far as routine is concerned, at no regular hours. Sometimes he is at the piano early in the afternoon, sometimes at three in the morning. When he gets eight bars he likes, he can finish a chorus in a couple of minutes. I have known him to write four tunes in an afternoon, tunes I thought he would put down for future use, only to find next day that he had discarded them. Once, we returned from *Funny Face,* which was playing the road prior to the New York opening, when George discovered that he had left two notebooks containing at least forty tunes in the hotel at Wilmington. After calling the hotel and learning that the notebooks could not be located, he did not seem greatly perturbed. His attitude is that he can always write new ones.

Between shows my brother and I write very little, preparing not more than three or four songs of a general nature that can be introduced into any show. In *Girl Crazy,* there were three such: "Could You Use Me?," "Embraceable You," and "I Got Rhythm." These we had before the contract was signed, and, with a line changed here and there, they later were easily cued in the story.

Once we receive the outline of the plot we really get down to work. We decide that such and such a tune is best for this or that situation. The tune decided on, I go to work alone. I do not use a "lead sheet," as I can't read music, but this is no handicap, as after the melody is heard a few times I can play it with one finger. After getting the title, about which more later, I skip, nine times out of ten, to the last line and try to work the title in again, with a twist, if possible. Every time I get a line I sing it to myself to see how it sings.

We had a maid last year who, continually discovering me at a desk singing to myself, asked my wife, "Don't Mr. Gershwin never go to work?" When I first began writing lyrics a tune would haunt me for days, even after I had finished working on it. The song was over but the melody lingered on. After a couple of years, however, this phase disappeared and I can now completely dismiss a tune and lyric when the song is finished.

We are both pretty critical and outspoken, George about my lyrics and I about his music. Praise is very faint. But at that we are far from being as bad as one songwriting team who used to spend most of their time in vituperation. Occasionally I suggest that a note or a "middle" (the seventeenth to twenty-fourth bar of the chorus) be changed, while now and then a line is thrown me.

The important thing about a lyric to me is the title and idea. You get an idea, you put it as a theorem in your title, you prove it, Q.E.D., to the listener's satisfaction in the lines that follow. There is probably little literary value to the present lyric. With the limited vocabulary permitted us, we know not the bosky dells of the poet, and if we did the audience wouldn't. When people read poetry they can study the printed page, but each song lyric is hurled at them only once or twice in the course of an evening, and the audience has no chance to rehear or reread it. Thus, good lyrics should be simple, colloquial, rhymed, conversational lines. It is up to the lyric writer to take the few hundred words allotted him and use whatever ingenuity he has in turning them neatly and trying to get a phrase here and there which will get over to the customers in the theater and be quotable on the dance floor. But the song itself is the important thing, not the words or the music as separate entities, and often too great a straining for cleverness in lyric will make too cerebral an offering that should be light and jingly.

As for titles, one gets them from thin air, figuratively and literally. Unlike good children, titles should be heard, not seen. I mean that listening to the argot in everyday conversation results in paydirt for lyric writers. It is inconceivable that a few years ago a girl, after her third highball, might have confided in you in this fashion: "I've got a crush on Tom, but he's not k-ra-zy for me. Here I am, feeling I'm falling, and he high-hats me. What causes that?"

It probably is inconceivable, but you get the idea. "[I've Got a] Crush on You," "What Causes That?," "Feeling I'm Falling," "K-ra-zy for You," and "High Hat" were introduced in *Treasure Girl* and *Funny Face* to general dancing in the streets and almost resulted in a hurried summons to members of the Nobel committee on literature.

Comedians are invaluable. Hearing Bill Kent say, "Heigh ho, that's life!" gave me the idea for "The Babbitt and the Bromide." Hearing Walter Catlett use words like *pash* for *passion*, *delish* for *delicious* gave me the notions for half a dozen songs like "Sunny Disposish" and "'S Wonderful."

THE COMPOSER IN THE MACHINE AGE

from *Revolt in the Arts* (1930) by Oliver M. Sayler

GEORGE GERSHWIN

Unquestionably modern musical America has been influenced by modern musical Europe. But it seems to me that modern European composers, in turn, have very largely received their stimulus, their rhythms and impulses, from Machine Age America. They have a much older tradition of musical technique, which has helped them put into musical terms a little more clearly the thoughts that originated here. They can express themselves more glibly.

The Machine Age has influenced practically everything. I do not mean only music but everything from the arts to finance. The machine has not affected our age in form as much as in tempo, speed, and sound. It has affected us in sound whenever composers utilize new instruments to imitate its aspects. In my *American in Paris* I used four taxi horns for musical effect. George Antheil has used everything, including aeroplane propellers, doorbells, typewriter keys, and so forth. By the use of the old instruments, too, we are able to obtain modern effects. Take a composition like Honegger's *Pacific No. 231*, written and dedicated to a steam engine. It reproduces the whole effect of a train stopping and starting, and it is all done with familiar instruments.

There is only one important thing in music, and that is ideas and feeling. The various tonalities and sounds mean nothing unless they grow out of ideas. Not many composers have ideas. Far more of them

Oliver M. Sayler's 1930 book **Revolt in the Arts** *brought together a disparate group of important twentieth-century figures in the arts and industry to discuss cultural "modernism." George Gershwin, Lillian Gish, Martha Graham, John Sloan, Frank Lloyd Wright, Hart Crane, David Sarnoff, John Erskine, and Jesse Lasky, among many others, contributed essays.*

know how to use strange instruments which do not require ideas. Whoever has inspired ideas will write the great music of our period. We are plowing the ground for that genius who may be alive or may be born today or tomorrow. If he is alive, he is recognized to a certain degree, although it is impossible for the public at large to assimilate real greatness quickly. Take a composer like Bach. In his lifetime, he was recognized as one of the greatest organists in the world, but he was not acclaimed as one of the greatest composers of his time or of all time until generations after his death.

I do not think there is any such thing as mechanized musical composition without feeling, without emotion. Music is one of the arts which appeals directly through the emotions. Mechanism and feeling will have to go hand in hand, in the same way that a skyscraper is at the same time a triumph of the machine and a tremendous emotional experience, almost breathtaking. Not merely its height but its mass and proportions are the result of an emotion, as well as of calculation.

Any discussion of the distinction between presentation and representation in music resolves itself into an attempt to determine the relative values of abstract music and program music. It is very difficult for anyone to tell where abstract music starts and program music finishes. There must have been a picture of something in the composer's mind. What it was nobody knows, often not even the composer. But music has a marvelous faculty of recording a picture in someone else's mind. In my own case, everybody who has ever listened to *Rhapsody in Blue*—and that embraces thousands of people—has a story for it but myself. *An American in Paris* is obviously a program piece, although I would say half of it or more is abstract music tied together by a few representative themes. Imitation never gets anyone anywhere. Originality is the only thing that counts. But the originator uses material and ideas that occur around him and pass through him. And out of his experience comes this original creation or work of art, unquestionably influenced by his surroundings, which include very largely what we call the Machine Age.

It is difficult to determine what enduring values, esthetically, jazz has contributed, because *jazz* is a word which has been used for at least five or six different types of music. It is really a conglomeration of many things. It has a little bit of ragtime, the blues, classicism, and spirituals. Basically, it is a matter of rhythm. After rhythm in importance come intervals, music intervals which are peculiar to the rhythm. After all, there is nothing new in music.

I maintained years ago that there is very little difference in the music of different nations. There is just that little individual touch. One country may prefer a peculiar rhythm or a note like the seventh. This it stresses, and it becomes identified with that nation. In America this preferred rhythm is called jazz. Jazz is music; it uses the same notes that Bach used. When jazz is played in another nation, it is called American. When it is played in another country, it sounds false. Jazz is the result of the energy stored up in America. It is a very energetic kind of music, noisy, boisterous, and even vulgar. One thing is certain. Jazz has contributed an enduring value to America in the sense that it has expressed ourselves. It is an original American achievement which will endure, not as jazz perhaps, but which will leave its mark on future music in one form or another. The only kinds of music which endure are those which possess form in the universal sense and folk music. All else dies. But unquestionably folksongs are being written and have been written which contain enduring elements of jazz. To be sure, that is only an element;

it is not the whole. An entire composition written in jazz could not live.

As for further esthetic developments in musical composition, American composers may in time use quarter notes, but then so will Europe use quarter notes. Eventually our ears will become sensitive to a much finer degree then they were a hundred, fifty, or twenty-five years ago. Music deemed ugly then is accepted without question today. It stands to reason, therefore, that composers will continue to alter their language. That might lead to anything. They have been writing already in two keys. There is no reason why they will not go further and ask us to recognize quarter or sixteenth notes. Such notes, whether written or not, are used all the time, only we are not conscious of them. In India they use quarter tones and, I believe, consciously.

Music is a phenomenon that to me has a very marked effect on the emotions. It can have various effects. It has the power of moving people to all of

"The Man I Love" is a song whose greatness was recognized only after years of rejection. It was originally written for Adele Astaire's character in Lady, Be Good! *in 1924 but was dropped from the show; it was also dropped from both versions of* Strike Up the Band *and rejected by Marilyn Miller for* Rosalie. *Its great popularity developed as a song unrelated to the theater, when Gershwin gave a copy of the music to Lady Mountbatten in London, who encouraged dance bands play it, so that first England and then France became enamored of the tune. It finally made its way back to America, achieving such popularity that Harms's Max Dreyfus heavily promoted the piece in 1928, selling 100,000 copies of the sheet music in six months. Helen Morgan, the famous torch singer, adopted the song as her own.*

the various moods. Through the emotions, it can have a cleansing effect on the mind, a disturbing effect, a drowsy effect, an exciting effect. I do not know to what extent it can finally become a part of the people. I do not think music as we know it now is indispensable, although we have music all around us in some form or other. There is music in the wind. People can live more or less satisfactorily without orchestral music, for instance. And who can tell that we would not be better off if we weren't as civilized as we are, if we lacked many of our emotions? But we have them and we are more or less egotistic about them. We think that they are important and that they make us what we are. We think that we are an improvement over people of other ages who didn't have them.

Music has become a very important part of civilization, and one of the main reasons is that one does not need a formal education to appreciate it. Music can be appreciated by a person who can neither read nor write, and it can also be appreciated by people who have the highest form of intelligence. For example, Einstein plays the violin and listens to music. People in the underworld, dope fiends and gunmen, invariably are music lovers and, if not, they are affected by it. Music is entering into medicine. Music sets up a certain vibration which unquestionably results in a physical reaction. Eventually the proper vibration for every person will be found and utilized. I like to think of music as an emotional science.

Almost every great composer profoundly influences the age in which he lives. Bach, Beethoven, Wagner, Brahms, Debussy, Stravinsky. They have all recreated something of their time so that millions of people could feel it more forcefully and better understand their time.

The composer, in my estimation, has been helped a great deal by the mechanical reproduction of music. Music is written to be heard, and any instrument that tends to help it to be heard more frequently and by greater numbers is advantageous to the person who writes it. Aside from royalties or anything like that, I should think that the theory that music is written to be heard is a good one. To enable millions of people to listen to music by radio or phonograph is helpful to the composer. The composer who writes music for himself and doesn't want it to be heard is generally a bad composer. The first incursion of mechanized reproduction was a stimulus to the composer, and the second wave has merely intensified that stimulus.

In the past, composers have starved because of lack of performance, lack of being heard. That is impossible today. Schubert could not make any money because he did not have an opportunity through the means of distribution of his day to reach the public. He died at the age of thirty-one and had a certain reputation. If he had lived to be fifty or sixty, unquestionably he would have obtained recognition in his own day. If he were living today, he would be well off and comfortable.

The radio and the phonograph are harmful to the extent that they bastardize music and give currency to a lot of cheap things. They are not harmful to the composer. The more people listen to music, the more they will be able to criticize it and know when it is good. When we speak of machine-made music, however, we are not speaking of music in the highest sense, because, no matter how much the world becomes a Machine Age, music will have to be created in the same old way. The Machine Age can affect music only in its distribution. Composers must compose in the same way the old composers did. No one has found a new method in which to write music. We still use the old signatures, the old symbols. The composer has to do every bit of his work himself. Handwork can never be replaced in the composition of music. If music ever became machine-made in that sense, it would cease to be an art.

To write the score for their first sound movie, **Delicious** (Fox, 1931), *George and Ira Gershwin traveled to California in November 1930; they set up headquarters in a Beverly Hills house and embraced a leisurely lifestyle, George enthusiastically engaging in tennis and golf. The composer gathered songs from his files of previously written material, and worked on the most ambitious part of the score, an orchestral rhapsody to accompany a nightmarish sequence in which the star, Janet Gaynor, wanders through the streets of Manhattan. Gershwin's* **New York Rhapsody** *(a.k.a.* **Manhattan Rhapsody** *and* **Rhapsody in Rivets***), effectively used in the movie, was soon to become a concert hall sequel to his* **Rhapsody in Blue.** *Another sequence in the film, "Welcome to the Melting Pot," is especially notable for its operettalike structure, echoing* **Strike Up the Band** *and prefiguring the musical organization of the Gershwins' Broadway masterpiece,* **Of Thee I Sing.**

AMERICAN OPERETTA COMES OF AGE: 'OF THEE I SING' AND ITS MERRY MAKERS

Disques, March 1932

ISAAC GOLDBERG

It looks like a great year on Broadway for the Irish and the Jews. And, by that same token, like a great year for the American drama, light or serious. In a way it is a most astounding occurrence, and certainly a heartening one. Consider the simple facts. We have been accustomed to hearing the ever-recurrent statement that the American people do not care for art. Almost as frequently we have had it dinned into our ears that, since such things as

plays and books are after all a luxury, they and the art for which they stand are the first to suffer in a period of depression. Yet the year that has just come to a close, disastrous as it was from the standpoint of economic maladjustment and world embroilments, has produced two of the most important dramatic entertainments in the history of the American stage. And despite the financial chaos, these works have been patronized so lavish-

In Broadway's 1931 political operetta **Of Thee I Sing,** *Lois Moran played the first lady, Mary Turner, and William Gaxton, the president of the United States, John P. Wintergreen. A platform of "love" propelled Wintergreen into the White House, despite his jilting the winner of an Atlantic City beauty contest whom he had promised to marry. A more obviously comic presence was Victor Moore, a familiar face in many Gershwin shows, who played the hapless and ignored vice president, Alexander Throttlebottom.*

ly as to bring them into what is known as the "smash hit" class, thus achieving a financial parallel with their artistic status.

The serious play to which I refer is, of course, Eugene O'Neill's *Mourning Becomes Electra.* It is not part of my present purpose to go into a discussion of this now famous trilogy. Nor is it important that O'Neill's trio of plays, fashioned after a Greek model, is not in my opinion a perfect masterpiece. Even O'Neill's failures are more important than the mean successes of lesser men. The nobility of his aims confers upon him something of that same tragic nobility which he would get into his characters. The light piece of which I wish mainly to speak is, from my point of view, just as important to the American stage and to American culture as O'Neill's trilogy—perhaps, indeed, even more important than this tale of Greek doom transplanted to the austere atmosphere of Civil War New England, since O'Neill has already shown his characteristic qualities in plays essentially better than his *Electra.* It is the work of four remarkable young gentlemen—a satiric operetta entitled *Of Thee I Sing.*

Political satire set to music is not new in the history of the world. It goes back as far as Aristophanes, one of the Greeks whom O'Neill overlooked; it comes as far forward as Gilbert and Sullivan and that high-spirited, infectiously jolly French Jew, Jacques Offenbach. It is really a pity that Offenbach is known in this country only for his *Tales of Hoffman.* This is a most melodious score; we do not know, however, his comic operas, with their Gallic gaiety that not even Sullivan could often capture. And now, almost out of the blue, in *Of Thee I Sing* comes a satire of politics and love that combines the spirit of a Gilbert and Sullivan with the spirit of an Offenbach. We have had nothing like it in the history of our stage; after this event in our theater, musical comedy can never be the same. Overnight, as it were, our musical stage, so long burdened by sentimental inanities, by childish plots, by hollow jingles, has come of age.

Ladies and gentlemen, meet Messrs. George S. Kaufman, Morrie Ryskind, Ira Gershwin and his brother George. All of these fellows, for some years past, have been converging toward the production

of just such a hilarious piece as is now drawing regiments of radiant spectators and auditors to the Music Box Theatre, New York. In my book on George Gershwin, recently published, I finished by saying that if George Gershwin ever found a librettist who was worthy of his own high gifts, we should have at last a national comic opera. Hardly was the book off the press when along came *Of Thee I Sing* to fulfill, in great part, my prediction.

There had been a sort of preparation for this satirical salvo. Some of you may have attended a musical comedy entitled *Strike Up the Band.* Kaufman had a hand in this libretto, too, but with the obstinate integrity that characterizes this remarkable stage director, one of the foremost wits of our day, he withdrew from the piece when the managers began to transform it into just another musical comedy. At that, it remains one of the best satirical pieces that preceded *Of Thee I Sing.* In the preparation of the latter production Kaufman was given, by Sam H. Harris, the producer, an absolutely free hand. There was no one now to tell him, "We need another hot number in this scene or else our customers will begin to be bored," or "Better bring the girls on at this juncture, for the tired businessmen will be getting tired again around 10:15."

Kaufman has already done long and valiant service to our lighter stage, which some solemn persons mistakenly consider beneath our serious stage in importance. He has brought the healing of intelligent laughter, directed not in poisoned malice against individuals but rather in sharp but good-natured fun against personal and social foibles. You will remember his essential share as collaborator in such pronounced successes as *Beggar on Horseback, The Royal Family, Dulcy,* and *Once in a Lifetime.* What O'Neill is to our drama of the tears of things, Kaufman is to our drama of laughter. The one is our tragic mask; the other, our comic. It is not the first time that the Irish and the Jews have been paired in boldness of conception, originality of execution, and a dedication to intellectual freedom.

Kaufman has a high esteem for his present collaborator, Ryskind. Ryskind came to prominence during the late war when he was expelled from Columbia University for his pacifist notions. The other day, by an irony that Ryskind was the first to appreciate, Nicholas Murray Butler of Columbia University shared with Jane Addams the award of the Nobel Peace Prize. Ryskind has collaborated with Kaufman before, particularly in providing vehicles for the Marx Brothers.

In *Of Thee I Sing* there are three elements which fuse admirably into one: the libretto, the verses, and the music. Let us consider these in turn. The book of the action deals with the refusal of the candidate for the presidency of the United States to marry Miss White House, who has been chosen for the distinction by a nationwide contest that assembles the most successful beauties at Atlantic City for the final choice. Instead, he falls in love at first sight with Mary Turner, a maiden of beautiful simplicity who can bake the best corn muffins in the land. Suddenly it appears that the rejected winner of the contest, Diana Devereaux, is of French descent; through the French ambassador France demands justice, under threat of severing diplomatic relations. This is averted when the vice president, one of the most original roles that has ever been devised for the modern comic stage, discovers that it is his duty to assume any obligations which the president is unable to fulfill. Not only does Mr. V.P. get a beauty—the poor fellow has been yearning for one all

through the piece—but France's honor is satisfied.

So told, the plot sounds ordinary. For it is the detail that not only lends surprising unity to the action, but provides it with so many laughable incidents that one departs from the spectacle almost weak with too much enjoyment. Two of the scenes—that of the Madison Square election rally in Act I, and the meeting of the United States Senate in Act II—stand for their peculiar excellency alone. With several strokes of well-aimed travesty, the Madison Square scene simply debunks the pretenses of our political life; the Senate scene is likewise a howlingly sardonic treatment of the congressional record. Truth mingled with absurdity forms an irresistible combination.

Bold rhymes and a skillful music that underscores the narrative provide likewise a sanative commingling of radiant lunacy with home truths. Ira Gershwin was never happier with his conceits and jingles, to which brother George has written a score that travesties music in terms of music itself. It is a delightful shock when, for the first time, the presidential candidate, who is touring the country with his sweetheart on a platform of "Love in the White House," sings the theme song of the campaign: "Of thee I sing, *ba-by*! . . ." It begins as a national anthem; the sudden twist, with that *"ba-by,"* turns it

The writers of **Of Thee I Sing** *were George S. Kaufman and Morrie Ryskind, who here fine-tuned the political satire of their previous operetta,* **Strike Up the Band***; the production was directed by Kaufman himself. The authors closely collaborated with the brothers Gershwin to produce a seamless play whose music is integral to the action. From the Boston tryouts to the New York premiere, the critical and popular response to* **Of Thee I Sing** *was extraordinary. One of Broadway's revolutionary works, for both its satirical content and musical structure, this operetta boasts complete musical scenes, much musical underpinning of the action, choral pieces, and "songs" of irregular lengths that significantly advance the narrative.* **Of Thee I Sing** *was George Gershwin's biggest musical-comedy success, running for 441 performances and then generating two national road tours.*

into a parody of Tin Pan Alley. Ira's verses are not only clever in themselves; they fulfill what should be the function of all operatic verse, whether grand or light—they elucidate and advance the story. Consider a couple of examples: the girls, for instance, singing of their chances at the Atlantic City finals: "If a girl is sexy, / She may be Mrs. Prexy. . . ."

Let me, out of long experience with librettos, assure you that this is by no means as easy as it looks. In the Senate scene we have really an operetta by itself in which the collaborators ride at the top of their bent. There has been nothing like this in comic opera since that glorious evening in 1875 when Gilbert and Sullivan disclosed *Trial by Jury* to a delighted London public. The gaiety of this selfsame scene is to be matched only by certain scenes in Offenbach or in Gilbert and Sullivan's *Iolanthe*.

The score abounds in felicitous touches. There is, in Act I, the finaletto in which the candidate for president glorifies his American girl for her culinary skill. Not only is this well-aimed satire (in this scene the lyricist achieves the feat of rhyming "quinces" with good old-fashioned "blintzes"); it is excellent seriocomic music—a sort of audible eye-winking at which George Gershwin is expert. Gershwin, even in his music for the symphony orchestra, is a wit. It was Beaumarchais who wrote that what cannot be said can be sung. The wit and melody and sound musicianship of Gershwin's score lie like a salve over the pertinent jibes that Kaufman and Ryskind have provided.

Of Thee I Sing has one of the finest openings that I can remember in a play of like appeal. It is, on the part of all concerned, a masterstroke, representing a political torchlight procession. It takes about five minutes, with its illuminated signs, its appeal for votes to the Irish and the Jews, its musical mélange of election slogans. At once it establishes, almost dangerously, the mood of what is to follow. Yet, unbelievably enough, the action is a steady crescendo to the final curtain, when we are treated to a glorification of American motherhood (twins: a boy and a girl) such as should bring tears of envy to the originator of Mother's Day.

I must revert to the role of Alexander Throttlebottom, the vice president, who provides such a marked contrast to President John P. Wintergreen. Throughout the play nobody can remember him or his name, not even the man who nominated him at the convention. In order to gain admission into the White House he is compelled to patronize a special tour of the premises. In the end he himself all but forgets his name. This conception is really an inspiration. Quickly, before you can ransack your memory, try to name a few vice presidents of your country or a few lieutenant governors of your state. Need I say more?

Of Thee I Sing suggests a new art form for a new, a sophisticated, a courageous, a laughing America. Kaufman and Ryskind could have made it, with many necessary alterations, into a straight play.

*For **Of Thee I Sing**, Gershwin orchestrated one choral number, "Hello, Good Morning," and conducted on opening night. His overtures—this one preeminent—are not snippets of a show's big songs strung together by the musical director or orchestrator, but are thoroughly composed (though not composer-orchestrated) tone poems setting moods, reworking thematic material, and linking selected songs with creative passages. **Of Thee I Sing**'s complete piano-vocal score was published.*

But they were wise to conceive it as a musical extravaganza; music is excellent for holding such tonic absurdity in solution. Time and again Gershwin's music points, heightens, and sustains this absurdity. Consider again the opening political procession. Not only does it strike the right note at once, with its parodies and its spirit; at the same time it is musicianly to the very last sound. It is excellent musical humor, moreover. Recall the line "Loves the Irish and the Jews." Well, the music has a spirit both Irish and Jewish. ("Wintergreen for President" is almost Hassidic in its minor appeal.) The shifting of keys, with the vocal emphasis landing on a note announcing a new modulation, is fine fun and fine writing . . . This is but one of a whole group of felicities . . . Take the finaletto about the corn muffins; this, like the Senate scene, is a comic operetta in miniature; the melodic line is soft, with a mock-heroic reference; the use of three melodies, contrapuntally, adds humor to the situation by treating the absurdity to sober musical development . . . Take the entrance of the nine Supreme Court judges: George has them count themselves out to a whole-tone scale; at the end, when this counting-line is repeated, the tempo is doubled with excellent effect . . . This is humor *in tones* . . . His use of recitative, brief as it is, could well be tried by composers of "serious" opera. That snatch about "the most beautiful blossom in all the Southland," with the Debussyan chords that speak of her castles coming tumbling down, is again fun *in tones* . . . The "vamp till ready" chords with which the Senate scene begins—again this type of essentially musical humor . . . The street-corner-quartet "Whereases," ditto. I maintain that no other American composer has yet displayed this feeling for comicality in the tones themselves.

You will notice that, thus far, I have made no mention of melodies or songs. I have been emphasizing the tonal values purely. The rest of the operetta abounds in happy touches. Let me recall a few: the theme song is firmly constructed—real composing, not the vaporings of an idle troubadour. If you examine even the printed sheets you will discover that the harmonization is very careful, with a definite musical reason for every note; it is, indeed, most careful in the inner voices. And this, to me, is the least interesting song in the score . . . "Who Cares?"—to name now the printed selections—has a beautiful melodic contour, alternating the gentle line that Gershwin learned from Kern with a subtle syncopation. Notice, in the verse, not only the injection of the Charleston rhythm into the accompaniment, but the changes to unrelated keys . . . "Because, Because": fine rhythms, and a charming gaiety that only Kern and Gershwin can give us today. Herbert—who wrote some fine tunes in his day—never had this soft subtlety. George's accompaniments, in these tunes, are well worthy of close attention. There is nothing perfunctory . . . "Love Is Sweeping the Country": one peach of a tune, harmonized with enviable skill; the shifting from major to minor (not to speak of the sturdy rhythms) at the words "Feels that passion'll / Soon be national" is a typical Gershwin "find" . . . As for the unprinted music, it teems with happy touches. The entire Senate scene gathers effect from the music . . . The swing of the "illegitimate" French tune . . . The two waltzes, in succession: first, the "Jilted" number, with its sentimental line, and then the quasi-Viennese "I'm About to Be a Mother," with its descents of a minor or major octave at the important words . . . The Salvation Army takeoff in the posterity number. Is there, in American musical comedy, a scene that equals it for gusto, for tonal eye-winking and nose-thumbing? . . . The finale of the second act has some exquisite modal harmonies in the Irish fashion (remember that Wintergreen loves the Irish and the Jews) . . . Time and again the composer—and I include Ira for rhymes that can't be dug out of dictionaries—is as felicitous as Sullivan and Offenbach. Not only does this sound good; it bears scrutiny in the study.

Of thee we sing, *Of Thee I Sing*!

'OF THEE I SING' DELIGHTS A CROWDED HOUSE AT THE MAJESTIC

Brooklyn Daily Eagle, April 17, 1933

John P. Wintergreen has been elected president of the United States. There is no particular news in the statement, for John P. Wintergreen had been elected president of the United States every night, except Sunday, during the past two years and more across the East River in Manhattan. Last night, however, John P. Wintergreen and his ticket mate, Alexander Throttlebottom, together with the beautiful Mary Turner, moved into the White House, on their platform of love, at the Brooklyn Majestic Theatre to the great enjoyment of an audience that occupied practically every seat.

Of course, all this took place in the musical comedy *Of Thee I Sing,* which was the winner of the Pulitzer Prize a year ago. So much has been written about this piece that its story hardly needs to be retold. Suffice it to say that everything that has been written and said of *Of Thee I Sing* proved to be true last night. There was not a single person in the Majestic Theatre who did not say that the political satire by George S. Kaufman and Morrie Ryskind, to which the brothers Gershwin added lyrics and music, was a splendid entertainment.

It is interesting to note that Sam H. Harris, who produced the prize-winning piece, has moved the entire company from Manhattan to Brooklyn. William Gaxton, looking like a certain metropolitan political figure no longer in the limelight, was John P. Wintergreen. Victor Moore, also funny in his droll way, was Alexander Throttlebottom, his running mate, who finally was elected vice president.

Lois Moran was Mary Turner, demure and sweet as another Mary, well-beloved of the moving picture audiences. Grace Brinkley was "the illegitimate daughter, etc.," who won the Atlantic City beauty contest but finally lost out to the demure Mary, because the latter could make corn muffins. Incidentally, Miss Brinkley sang delightfully; in fact, she appeared to be the only real singer in the cast. Of course, Miss Moran sings sweetly, but last night her voice seemed lost in the big Majestic Theatre. Of the men, Florenz Ames sang best as the French ambassador. To him fell the "Illegitimate Daughter" song, a splendid bit of composition that showed George Gershwin far away from jazz.

Of course, *Of Thee I Sing* is full of jazz. The opening number, "Wintergreen for President," sets the pace. That opening scene is enough to make any play. It is too bad it arrives so early. It is hard to remember a better ensemble number since the "March of the Vagabonds" made another musical piece famous. But the best parts of the score are little bits that continually crop up in big ensemble numbers, such as the few bars sung by the Supreme Court justices in the final minutes of the piece. That is one of the best of the Gilbert and Sullivan touches that continually crop up.

Knowing that the American people are different from the English and that 1932 is not 1880, Kaufman has made his humor decidedly more slapstick than anything ever written by Gilbert. Not that Kaufman cannot write nicely and politely when he feels so inclined. In *Of Thee I Sing* he has let himself go, burlesquing his subject. It is all great fun. It creates plenty of laughter. And it is undoubtedly the best evening's entertainment that has come to Brooklyn so far this winter. It simply must be seen.

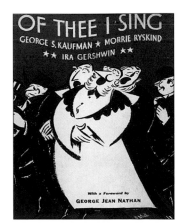

Of Thee I Sing, *which won the 1932 Pulitzer Prize for drama (though the music was not eligible), was published in book form in 1932, presenting the complete play as well as Ira Gershwin's lyrics, which are integral to the action.*

GEORGE GERSHWIN PLAYS HIS 'SECOND RHAPSODY' FOR FIRST TIME HERE

New York Times, February 6, 1932

OLIN DOWNES

The program offered by Serge Koussevitzky and the Boston Symphony Orchestra last night in Carnegie Hall was refreshing for its catholicity and interest. Mr. Koussevitzky is one of the very few conductors today who appear to realize that music was not made exclusively in Germany, Italy, or France, either; who examines scores of all kinds

The Boston Symphony's conductor, Serge Koussevitzky, was an admirer of Gershwin and a champion of new music. Gershwin took his short **New York Rhapsody** *from the movie* **Delicious** *and expanded it into a large serious composition, renaming it simply* **Second Rhapsody.** *He had finished the whole sketch before leaving Hollywood, by late February 1931, and the orchestration exactly three months later. Koussevitzky and his orchestra unveiled the work in Boston on January 29, 1932—with Gershwin at the piano—and in New York on February 5. Most reviewers were impressed with Gershwin's technical strides but thought the piece a pale and uninspired imitation of the* **Rhapsody in Blue.**

and schools with curiosity and a singular appreciation, whatever their contents may be; who can be relied upon to supplement the routine sort of program which, in the main, New York City still receives.

The novelty of last night's concert was George Gershwin's *Second Rhapsody,* scored for piano and large modern orchestra, with the composer as solo pianist. The originality of the Gershwin *Rhapsody in Blue,* first heard in this city February 12, 1924, was the cause of Mr. Gershwin's later adventures in the symphonic field, with his Concerto in F (1925) for piano and orchestra and *An American in Paris,* a score which will probably remain the best constructed and most effective of Mr. Gershwin's present "period"—this though certain of the ideas of the *Rhapsody in Blue* are more original.

The score performed last night is the expansion of a five-minute [*sic*] sequence inserted into the picture *Delicious,* a screen comedy-drama, based on a story by Guy Bolton, with lyrics by Ira Gershwin and music by George, produced in 1931. The rhapsody was written in California in the spring of the same year and later somewhat revised. Some of the comedy scenes showed the streets of New York, and for the five-minute orchestral sequence Gershwin conceived a "rivet theme" to echo the tattoo of the skyscrapers. The *Second Rhapsody* had originally the title of *Rhapsody in Rivets.*

This rhapsody has more orchestration and more development than the *Rhapsody in Blue.* Its main motive is reasonably suggestive of rivets and racket in streets of this metropolis; also, if you like, of the bonhomie of inhabitants. There is a second theme, built into a contrasting section. Thus, jazz dance rhythm and sentimental song are opposed and juxtaposed in this score. The conception is wholly orchestral. The piano is not so prominent as in the *Rhapsody in Blue*; it is, in fact, merely one of the instruments of the ensemble.

But with all its immaturities, the *Rhapsody in Blue* is more individual and originative than the piece heard last night. In fact, the *Second Rhapsody* is imitative in many ways of the *Rhapsody in Blue*. One of the figures of the first part, and certain harmonic cadences, and the song theme of the middle part, have all quite direct derivations from the earlier work. Furthermore, the *Second Rhapsody* is too long for its material.

The work was superbly performed. Mr. Koussevitzky, who conducts it for the second time this afternoon, led the orchestra as earnestly as if he had been introducing a new symphony by a Roussel or a Miaskovsky, and patiently labored to obtain from the players the last ounce of their energy. It was a virtuoso performance. Mr. Gershwin played a modest piano part simply but

with the composer's authority. There was royal welcome for the composer, the performers, the music. Nevertheless, we have had better things from Mr. Gershwin, and we expect better in time to come.

Mr. Koussevitzky also figured on this occasion as the one conductor who has seen fit to honor in New York the memory of a great French composer, the late Vincent d'Indy, with a performance of one of his representative works. The second item of the program was the *Istar Variations*. . . . Mr. Koussevitzky read the music with realization of its poetical and sensuous quality. . . .

Throughout the evening the glorious orchestra responded with the utmost bravura and sensitiveness to every wish of the leader, and Mr. Koussevitzky was on particularly favorable ground. He played not only d'Indy and Gershwin for the middle of his program, but Prokofiev of the *Classic*[al] Symphony for a beginning and Scriabin of the *Poème de l'Extase* for an end. . . .

A refreshing program and a brilliant concert, which caused the audience to admire anew the conductor and the band, and to applaud all participants with an enthusiasm deserved by their achievements.

Among the featured players in the 1932 film version of **Girl Crazy** *(RKO) are* **Robert Woolsey, Arlene Judge,** *and* **Stanley Fields.** *The Gershwins' second Hollywood musical, unlike* **Delicious,** *was based on an already existing show; like* **Delicious,** *it was not a success. While many of the original* **Girl Crazy's** *numbers were discarded, the brothers did provide a new song for the movie version, "You've Got What Gets Me."*

GEBRUDER GERSHWIN

Vanity Fair, June 1932

ISAAC GOLDBERG

Lyrics by Isidore Gershovitz. Music by Jacob Gershovitz.

Which is the way the credits to the words and music men, respectively, would read on the program of New York's reigning musico-political satire at the Music Box Theatre, if the process of Americanization had not early begun to get in its work with the parents of the gebrüder Gershwin, Ira and George. Jacob was early transformed into George. As recently as 1914, however, in his eighteenth year, Ira, the firstborn of the quartet of Gershwin children, was still Isidore, and even the altered patronymic was printed with a *v* instead of a *w* on the first program to which George was contributing his amateur talents.

A few years ago an ardent columnist of Gotham divulged the news that the real name of the Gershwins was Bruskin. He had got his cues slightly mixed, for Bruskin is the maiden name of Mama Gershwin. A columnist of far greater renown, for that matter, not so long ago informed his gossipivorous readers that the true name of the Astaires was Oesterreicher. He was almost right; the patronymic of the dancers is Austerlitz, and if you slice off that last syllable—in college they call it apocopation—you get the stage name of the brother-sister act without too much trouble. But that is a step from another dance.

There was not always harmony between the Gershwin brothers. Neither was a smash hit as a scholar, and one of Ira's chief duties as a youngster—after settling his own score with his teachers in Public School No. 20, at Rivington and Forsyth Streets—was to explain to them the whys and wherefores of George's scholastic deficiencies. Meantime, Ira himself was consuming dime novels at the rate of seven or more per week. Pop Gershwin freely predicted that George would grow up to be a bum, but he had high hopes for Ira. And then Ira, after ineffectual attempts to make the grade at college, suddenly informed his parents that

he was going to take a job with a minor circus outfit. Mama Gershwin wanted Ira—oh, irony!—to be a teacher. As for George, when his awakened musical nature carried him into the cubicles of the Remick pluggers, his mother frowned upon the move. A son of hers must be something more than a thumper at twenty-five dollars a week!

To understand the parental qualities and their divergences is the better to understand Ira and George. The brothers are separated by almost twenty-two months, by a penthouse wall (their apartments adjoin one another on an eyrie atop Riverside Drive) and by temperaments that mirror, across the family resemblances, the traits that distinguish mother from father.

Ira, appreciably, takes after his father. He is, beneath his lyrical flights, and above them, too, a rather hard-headed fellow. One cannot imagine his ambition misleading him, and he is more likely than any of his critics to underestimate his peculiar gifts. The nearer he comes to providing an American parallel to the dexterities of Gilbert, the more he depreciates any effort to institute a comparison. He is generally, except under pressure, a slow and even a phlegmatic worker.

George, though often outwardly the calmer man, is the other face of this medallion—very much the son of his mother. He has the nervousness of the spirited racehorse—an eagerness that, after the first disorganizing attack of uneasiness, flows into channels of invigorating control.

Ira, as the senior child, was the first to take up the study of the piano in the Gershwin household. George quickly crowded him off the revolving stool.

George, after his phenomenal start in the musical-show business, did not at first smile upon Ira's ventures into verse. And Ira, bent upon hoeing his own row, refused to take advantage of the reputation that was beginning to crystallize around the name of his brother. For a long time he experimented upon lyrics with a number of other composers. His earliest pseudonym, Bruskin Gershwin, was patently derived from his mother and father and was signed to his prelyrical writings. His next, Arthur Francis, signed to his first lyrics, was as patently derived from his younger brother and still younger sister, and was employed to conceal his relationship to George. It wasn't until *Be Yourself* came along—a musical comedy fashioned by Kaufman and Connelly—that Ira decided to emerge into the full glare of Broadway as Ira Gershwin.

There he has been ever since. And by happy coincidence, just as it had been Alex Aarons who gave George his first big musical-comedy opportunity with *La La Lucille,* so it was this same Aarons, newly linked in partnership with Vinton Freedley, who gave Ira his first important commission as lyricist for a full production, *Lady, Be Good!*

Outwardly, the brothers' musical collaboration appears all but effortless. Between shows they manage to do a few songs of a general nature, such as can be fitted into almost any sort of "book." The music, in all but a very few instances, is written first; usually it is of a nature to suggest the type of words suited to it. Though musical chiefly from association and not by training, Ira quickly learns the contours of a melody and works, if need be, by himself.

George as a party pianist is already a Gotham byword. His friend and collaborator George Kaufman was hearing the tunes from *Of Thee I Sing* whistled and sung about town before he knew what show they came from and at one time set about devising an Ed-Wynnian invention to keep composers from granting these prepremiere auditions. He gave it up, he recently told me in Boston, when he found that he would require at least eight sturdies to man the contraption. Later it occurred to him that perhaps these prehearings served a subtly useful purpose; on the first night the audience would contain some fifty persons who were familiar with the music, and who thus formed a sort of wedge into popularity.

Those who have heard George at the piano alone, gradually possessed by the demonic spirit of his own brand of jazz, launching off into variations upon the choruses of his hits, know what a rare treat is. It is even a rarer one to listen to George and Ira perform one of their songs together. George sings as he plays. It used to be through the aroma of a long, black cigar, but he doesn't smoke at all as he once did. (Ira still chants through expensive clouds; the cigar bill of this sybarite runs to something like a thousand dollars yearly.) At need, George takes the part of the various orchestral instruments and even interpolates enough of the dialogue to give point to the entrance of the song. At an actual production, if he could he would divide himself into half a dozen Georges, conduct-

For a sumptuous 1932 collection of his music called **George Gershwin's Song Book,** *Gershwin finally set down on paper the piano variations based upon some of his favorite tunes, which he often played at parties. These have come to be called in performance the* **Piano Transcriptions of Eighteen Songs,** *and they form a suite of harmonically and rhythmically captivating piano etudes. Each of these "piano solos" was published adjacent to the more traditional piano-vocal music, the whole accompanied by stylized comic illustrations by magazine artist Constantin Alajalov. Among the songs included in the book are "Swanee," "Do It Again," "I Got Rhythm," "Strike Up the Band," "Fascinating Rhythm," "Sweet and Low-Down," and "Somebody Loves Me."*

ing the orchestra, dancing with the chorus, singing the solos, setting up the scenery, holding the prompter's book, and handing out water between the acts.

Ira, on the other hand, to those who don't know him might sometimes give the impression of glumness. He stands beside the piano, fills his chest with air—even in stature his short, fleshy figure forms an instructive contrast to George's height and athletic spareness—and gazes ceilingward out of closed eyes. He sings with the same self-depreciation that I have already mentioned, every once in so often surprising his hearers—and perhaps himself—with a quasi-operatic outburst. For his brother's rhymes George has an ever-fresh appreciation; it is he, rather than Ira, who underscores the points with a lilt of his eyebrow, an upward curl of his lower jaw (à la Maurice Chevalier), or a commentative glance from the corner of his eye. Ira owns six rhyming dictionaries, but lines like . . . "The prize is consequential, / Presidential" come from the thesaurus of his own imagination, not from a catalogue of consonance. And when Ira sets down such couplets as . . . "Feel that passion'll / Soon be national" he is rhyming like a true poet, by ear, and not remaining in slavery to the eye and mere print. . . . George is a queer combination of the showman and the artist. He once had a secret yearning to be an actor, and frequently, even in his most ambitious scores, you

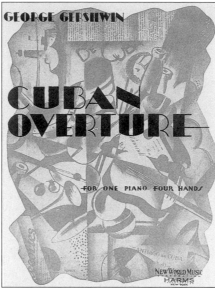

The premiere performance of the Cuban Overture was on August 16, 1932, at the first all-Gershwin concert at Manhattan's Lewisohn Stadium. From his 1932 Havana vacation Gershwin derived a flashy orchestral piece that he called Rumba. As with the taxi horns in An American in Paris, Gershwin strove to add authenticity to his work by incorporating several Cuban percussion instruments into the score—these, he instructed, were to be displayed and played prominently during a performance. This exciting and unique work is one of his finest serious compositions, structurally simple yet internally sophisticated—contrapuntal, polytonal, even dissonant. It shows the influence of the methods of Joseph Schillinger, with whom Gershwin was just beginning to study at the time. The piece's name was changed to Cuban Overture in its second performance at the Metropolitan Opera on November 1; the 1933 published version was an arrangement by Gershwin for one piano, four hands.

can detect the actor in his music instead of on the stage. For that matter, Ira was something of a cartoonist in his days of physical and spiritual Wanderlust. Just to prove that he's kept his hand in practice, Ira makes little drawings on his presentation copies.

Recent reports from the penthouse, indeed, indicate that the Gershwins have gone in rather heavily for art with a capital *A*. George, for many years a collector with independent tastes and with a strong leaning toward American talents, has made many pen and pencil sketches of his family and friends, not to speak of a self-portrait that indulges in no flattery. Of late, between the premieres of *Of Thee I Sing* and of his *Second Rhapsody*, he has gone in for oil painting, and his very first attempt, a portrait of his sister-in-law, Emily Paley, won the admiration of no less a professional than Maurice Sterne. Not to be outdone, Ira, with his brother doing quick life, turned to stills, and for once conversation on the roof bristles not with scenes-in-one, finalettos, reprises, and the argot of the showhouse, but with oils, tempera, wash, pigment, and the jargon of the studio.

This will probably last until the next operetta, when Ira with his rhymes and unreason, and George with his chords, lost and found, will leap *con amore e con fuoco* into the fray, to put our national operetta another milestone ahead on its path to gay independence.

THE RELATION OF JAZZ TO AMERICAN MUSIC

from *American Composers on American Music* (1933),
edited by Henry Cowell

GEORGE GERSHWIN

All the great music of the past in other countries has always been built on folk music. This is the strongest source of musical fecundity. America is no exception among the countries. The best music being written today is music which comes from folk sources. It is not always recognized that America has folk music; yet it really has not only one but many different folk musics. It is a vast land, and different sorts of folk music have sprung up in different parts, all having validity, and all being a possible foundation for development into an art music. For this reason, I believe that it is possible for a number of distinctive styles to develop in America, all legitimately born of folksong from different localities. Jazz, ragtime, Negro spirituals and blues, Southern mountain songs, country fiddling, and cowboy songs can all be employed in the creation of American art music, and are actually used by many composers now. These composers are certain to produce something worthwhile if they have the innate feeling and talent to develop the rich material offered to them. There are also other composers who can be classed as legitimately American who do not make use of folk music as a base, but who have personally, working in America, developed highly individualized styles and methods. Their newfound materials should be called American, just as an invention is called American if it is made by an American!

Jazz I regard as an American folk music; not the only one, but a very powerful one which is probably in the blood and feeling of the American people more than any other style of folk music. I believe that it can be made the basis of serious symphonic works of lasting value, in the hands of a composer with talent for both jazz and symphonic music.

Pardon My English opened on January 20, 1933; it was the last effort by the team of Aarons and Freedley, which had produced so many of the Gershwins' hit musicals. In financial trouble, and having lost their theater, the Alvin, in May 1932, the partners turned to the Gershwin brothers to provide another big hit. Unfortunately, the story of Pardon My English is a confused mess; the critics were unkind, and it suffered through the shortest run of any Gershwin musical, forty-six performances. Nevertheless, its score has sophisticated and interesting music by the Gershwins, particularly the songs parodying psychologists and a lengthy choral-dance number, "Dancing in the Streets."

'LET 'EM EAT CAKE': SURPASSES AS SEQUEL

New York *Morning Telegraph,* October 24, 1933

WHITNEY BOLTON

The curse which harries any sequel pays only a flitting visit to *Let 'Em Eat Cake,* the musical satire which Mr. Sam H. Harris offers as the logical series of mad events to follow the capers of *Of Thee I Sing.* Now that the hallowed work has been buried—with reverence and bronze plaques, I trust—let's forget about it and look upon the new work in its own strength.

We are not concerned here with the merits of *Of Thee I Sing* as compared with the merits of *Let 'Em Eat Cake.* Beyond the fact that it is a sequel and employs the same cast of wonder workers in the same roles they had in the first production, there is no reason to make comparisons. You will be buying seats to *Let 'Em Eat Cake,* and so long as that is the fact, the thing to do is report the condition of *Let 'Em Eat Cake.*

It must be taken into consideration that when you go to *Let 'Em Eat Cake,* fond and stirring memories of *Of Thee I Sing* will be dancing in your mind. That's natural enough, so natural indeed that your first impulse will be to sit there and, in effect, grumble: "All right, you just had to write a sequel; now show me." It goes beyond that: you may even arrive at the intermission convinced that *Let 'Em Eat Cake* hasn't the gusto and fine tornadic nonsense of *Of Thee I Sing.* Plenty of bright young measure-uppers did just that at the opening and lived to arrive at the finale convinced that they had measured up too quickly.

The truth is that *Let 'Em Eat Cake* starts out more patiently and definitely, takes its time to establish its story, and then plays out that story logically and sensibly. Such a course inevitably must seem, on the surface, to slow up the proceedings, and that's why the boys grumbled at the intermission. They expected great speed, insane gags, and mad situations. Instead, they got a look at the exact and deplorable situation which might have come to us as a city and even as a nation at any time last winter and, if you believe the economists, still could come to us. That in itself is sobering.

The Messrs. Kaufman and Ryskind set before you the sad night of election when President Wintergreen finds himself snowed under by John P. Tweedledee. He and Mary are out of work, the senators are out of work; it looks bad for the Wintergreen party. They decide to go into the shirt business with five thousand dollars' capital furnished by that addled little man Alexander Throttlebottom, and the experience in business of Master Lippman, the secretary of agriculture.

The business is set up on Union Square and is about to fade into bankruptcy when a wild-eyed radical, foaming at the mouth with outrage, weeps from his soapbox for a revolution. Wintergreen is struck with a magnificent idea: start a revolution and clothe everybody in blue shirts. The boys catch the idea and a few weeks later they are wealthy, the country demands them back in the White House, and they lead the revolutionists on to Washington. President Tweedledee is seized and ejected from Washington.

Wintergreen becomes dictator and manages things skillfully until the League of Nations accepts his challenge to play the Supreme Court a game of baseball: double or nothing on the war debts for the winner. Throttlebottom is made umpire, calls a safe ball safe by inches in the ninth inning, and the League wins the game. He is tried for treason and sentenced to be guillotined. Wintergreen, Lyons, Carver Jones, and all the rest of them are deposed by the army, creating a revolution within a revolution, and Kruger, the little Union Square radical who started it all, himself becomes dictator.

The boys are saved at the last minute by Mary.

You remember Mary saved Wintergreen from impeachment in *Of Thee I Sing* by confessing herself about to become a mother. She tries it again and Kruger laughs at her. Then, hurriedly, she thinks up another scheme. She has a lot of smart, beautiful gowns made up to sell at $15.95 retail and gives a fashion parade of them in front of the guillotine.

The women of America are so entranced, and so bored with wearing revolutionary blue dresses day in and out, that they rush to her support and their executions arc canceled.

The same team that created Of Thee I Sing *was responsible for its 1933 sequel,* Let 'Em Eat Cake; *even the earlier musical's producer, Sam H. Harris, and the lead actors returned. The essential spirit of the work—and its main problem—can be summed up by one of its songs: "Down with Ev'rything That's Up!" Recalling the bad timing for 1927's* Strike Up the Band, *this political musical full of biting satire, with its anarchists and revolutionaries and counterrevolutionaries and executions, did not arouse much laughter from Depression audiences getting their first glimpse of hope from a new president, Franklin Delano Roosevelt. The music, however, is inspired, building brilliantly on the operetta-style structure of* Of Thee I Sing, *with lots of choral numbers, completely musical scenes that advance the story, and few stand-alone songs (except for the hit tune, "Mine"). By the end of the musical,* Of Thee I Sing's *jovial heroes, Alexander Throttlebottom and John P. Wintergreen, are prisoners in jail awaiting execution—the dreadful doings accompanied by a wonderful bluesy spiritual, "They're Hanging Throttlebottom in the Morning." Most critics branded the Gershwins' last Broadway show as sorely lacking in humor, and* Let 'Em Eat Cake *closed after ninety performances.*

To this viciously satiric plot Mr. George Gershwin has added a score which cannot be as bathtub-whistling popular as the score for *Of Thee I Sing,* but which is a more musicianly work. And in spite of its beauty as a classic score it still gives you at least four numbers for bathtub singing and whistling: "Mine," "Comes the Revolution," "Let 'Em Eat Cake," and a doleful but unforgettable threnody called "They're Hanging Throttlebottom in the Morning." You'll like all of them and you won't forget in a hurry the opening scene which repeats the marching song "Wintergreen for President" counterpointed against the new "Tweedledee for President," a magnificently stirring and effective piece of staging.

Mr. Ira Gershwin, that grand lyricist, has accomplished miracles this time, forging couplets and rhymes which never let down the satiric implications of the story.

The cast is that of *Of Thee I Sing,* with Mr. William Gaxton,

Miss Lois Moran, Mr. Victor Moore, and the rest of the boys carrying on. There is a new secretary of agriculture, this one being Mr. Abe Reynolds, a convulser from the burlesque wheels, who comes into legitimate nicely. The other new player, and what a brilliant piece of casting it was, is Mr. Philip Loeb, who makes of Kruger a portrait of searching rightness, and you need only to hear the last line he speaks in the production to know the profound psychology of his mad role.

Maybe you'll feel disappointment. I know I did. I felt disappointed up to the intermission and still, but in less quantity, disappointed when it was over, but that faded away in a Sunday of studying the program and remembering the scenes and numbers. The more you think about *Let 'Em Eat Cake,* the more certain you become that it is a stalwart, able, and completely acceptable sequel. The thing grows on you and grows and grows and grows.

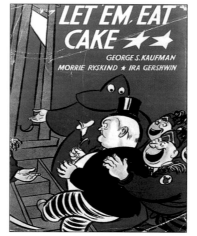

A companion to the 1932 edition of **Of Thee I Sing,** *the* **Let 'Em Eat Cake** *book was published in 1933.*

A COMPOSER'S PICTURES

Arts & Decoration, January 1934

America knows Mr. Gershwin as a musician, as the man who, with a touch of his wand, transformed lowly jazz into the coach and four of symphony. Because he is a pretty thorough master of the musical medium, we are properly astonished at his interest in another art. When we put a hero in a cubbyhole we want to keep him there.

But that the composer should take to painting or collecting paintings, or that the painter should take to composing is not unusual. For the artists the passage from one medium to another is not a dark, circuitous route.

Alfred [*sic*] Schoenberg has had an exhibition of his own paintings. Rousseau used to give violin lessons.

As Mr. Gershwin points out, music is design—melody is line; harmony is color; contrapuntal music is three or four times forming an abstraction or sometimes a definite shape; dissonance in music is like distortion in a painting, and as Alice Toklas adds, like the eggshell in the coffee.

Scriabin has written tone poems based on color, and one opus to be played with the color organ. Werner Jostin wrote a score stimulated by the sight of a triptych. Music's connection with the plastic arts is a deeper one than that of analogy.

It is still a moot question in Mr. Gershwin's mind whether he collects the moderns because he wants to learn to paint; or whether he wants to learn to paint in order better to understand the modern masters. But he buys paintings for a fairly simple reason—because he gets pleasure out of them. And he can study them during the interludes from composing, not in brief tours to the art galleries, but at leisure. He surrounds himself with the works of men whom he admires because they say something to him through a technique which he wants to master. A collector, like a critic, is often a disappointed creator. But Mr. Gershwin has made some humble beginnings in painting. And just as he is studying music all the time—he has three lessons a week—so he is studying painting when the moment allows. His collection consists of examples of Derain, Utrillo, Rouault, a Gauguin, Modigliani, a Rousseau, Picasso, Pascin, and among the Americans, Weber, Brook, Benton, Eilshemius, Sterne, Coleman, and many of the younger men. Knowing the scarcity of buyers in this day and age, he makes every effort to assist the struggling painter.

The walls of his living room are hung with paintings. Over the mantel is a Utrillo, to the right of this the beautiful *Absinthe Drinker* by Picasso.

Gershwin's penthouse on Riverside Drive (and subsequently his apartment on 72nd Street, to which he moved in 1933) was filled with paintings and art objects, including the famous bronze portrait bust of the composer by noted sculptor Isamu Noguchi.

On the opposite wall the little Rousseau. In the dining room is hung a large Derain still life. A Thomas Benton decorates the barroom. In the library are Rouault and Pascin. The upstairs hallway is thick with fine paintings, but to come out into Mr. Gershwin's working room is to come out on stark simplicity and a piano—with one small figure of a woman done by Matisse (from the collection of the late Arthur Davies) and two African wood images.

Of [a] Modigliani . . . , Mr. Gershwin said as we stood before [his] canvas, "Those who like the art of the moderns like this painting especially. If they heartily dislike the moderns, they hate this particularly." Of his whole collection Mr. Gershwin gets the most pleasure out of his big Weber. The painting hangs in the place of honor in his living room, in an arched niche. It is about five by seven feet, called *Invocation.* Mr. Gershwin sees in it a deeply wrought picture, tremendously felt. To him the distortion increases its feeling and adds to the design. Technically, he points out, it is a composition of triangles, and in it there is strict absence of line, only color against color. And in the whole there is great movement.

Mr. Gershwin is now so interested in painters and in painting himself that he is sure if his family had presented him with an easel and some paints when he was a child, instead of with a piano, he would be a professional painter today rather than a musician. But today his first love still has the upper hand. His avocation, his interest in the visual arts, is in the last analysis an inspiration for new musical compositions.

And if Mr. Gershwin feels it is too late to become a painter of distinction, he has, nevertheless, considerably enriched his musical background by his more than superficial knowledge of the effects the painter is attempting to achieve.

Four years ago Mr. Gershwin started to paint; three years ago he bought the first canvas in his collection. He has recently shown several of his canvases in Chicago, and loaned individual pieces many times.

In 1926 Gershwin began to purchase art with the help of a cousin, Henry Botkin, who, while studying in Europe in 1926, bought works by the leading modernists for the composer. In 1927 Gershwin himself started to do watercolors and pen-and-ink sketches, and by 1932 he was creating portraits in oil. He frequently visited art galleries and museums and admired, above all, the French expressionist master Georges Rouault.

PORGY AND BESS RETURN ON WINGS OF SONG

Stage, October 1935

DuBOSE HEYWARD

Nothing could be more ill-advised than the writing of this article. It exhibits all too clearly the decay of a human will, and it is strewn with the debris of broken resolutions. Out of a limited but illuminating Broadway experience, I have grasped the simple fact that a play does not exist until the critics and the public have looked upon it and found it good. Could there then be a more perfect example of artless, parental exhibitionism than the spectacle of a playwright prattling about his expected brainchild a full month before the hazardous accouchement?

How did it happen? I will tell you. I can at least expose the system of which I am a victim.

You leave the first rehearsal, hypnotized by the music of your own words. You are beguiled into the sanctum of an editor. Your fingers close of their own volition about a cocktail glass. You are told things about your work which, in your state of initial intoxication, you are fatuous enough to believe. You conclude that the editor is also a discriminating critic and altogether an excellent fellow. And then, since in any event it is against nature for an author to say no to an editor, you find yourself committed. It is not until later that you realize your deadline for a monthly periodical is a month in advance of publication, and that your story may burst from the presses, not as a bright paean for the living, but a sad and ironical epitaph for the dead.

But the story of *Porgy* has a def-

Gershwin first read the novel **Porgy** *during rehearsals of* **Oh, Kay!** *in 1926. He immediately contacted its author, DuBose Heyward, about the future possibility of turning the book into an opera. He learned that the Theatre Guild had Heyward under contract to adapt the novel for the dramatic stage; at the same time, he acknowledged that he was not yet ready to write grand opera.*

inite past, as well as a projected reincarnation, and the production of the opera is the materialization of an idea suggested by George Gershwin in a letter written to me nine years ago. The drama had not yet been produced, but was being written by my wife, Dorothy Heyward, and myself for the Theatre Guild, when George read the novel and suggested a meeting.

My first impression of my collaborator remains with me and is singularly vivid: a young man of enormous physical and emotional vitality, who possessed the faculty of seeing himself quite impersonally and realistically, and who knew exactly what he wanted and where he was going. This characteristic put him beyond both modesty and conceit. About himself he would merely mention certain facts, aspirations, failings. They were usually right.

We discussed *Porgy*. He said that it would not matter about the dramatic production, as it would be a number of years before he would be prepared technically to compose an opera. At the time he had numerous Broadway successes to his credit, and his *Rhapsody in Blue*, published three years before, had placed him in the front rank of American composers. It was extraordinary, I thought, that in view of a success that might well have dazzled any man, he could appraise his talent with such complete detachment. And so we decided then that someday when we were both prepared we would do an operatic version of my simple Negro beggar of the Charleston streets.

In the meantime, the play went into rehearsal at the Guild Theatre. Rouben Mamoulian, in his first appearance on Broadway, was entrusted with its direction. A cast was assembled from Negro night-clubs and Harlem theaters. Then for six weeks, what we all believed to be Broadway's most highly speculative venture dragged its personnel through the extremes of hope and despair toward the opening night.

I suppose it is sheer physical exhaustion, plus the emotional bludgeoning an author undergoes during rehearsals, that reduces him to pessimistic witlessness on the night of the premiere. Out of that night, I remember only vaguely a few moments of startling beauty: Mamoulian's fantastic shadows, the heartbreaking quality of the funeral spiritual, Porgy's pathetic leave-taking. But never to be forgotten was that awful moment when

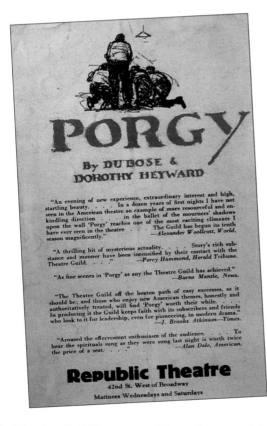

The Theatre Guild's memorable and successful production of **Porgy,** *adapted by DuBose and Dorothy Heyward from the 1925 novel, was imaginatively directed by Rouben Mamoulian.*

Crown shouted to the silent heavens, "Gawd laugh and Crown laugh back." Then, after an aching interval, came the belated clap of thunder that was supposed to be the laugh of God. The scene shifts seemed interminable. And lastly, and most crushing as we cowered at the back of the house under the protective wing of Philip Moeller, came the exit of Woollcott before the last scene of the play.

I have never seen him since, but I could point him out immediately in any crowd, so vivid is my impression of him. He stands about forty feet in his stockings, is about thirty feet broad; and when he rises to his full height from the second row in the orchestra, he can blot out an entire proscenium arch. His mouth is that of a medieval executioner, and when he strides down a theater aisle and past a terror-stricken playwright, his footsteps shake the building with the tread of doom.

Somebody might have warned us that he had an early deadline, and had to get his copy in, but nobody did. To us it was a walkout. He gave us a fine review. He proved that dramatic critics really are omniscient by knowing how the show ended. But the mischief had been done. Thirty months later, when the play closed after a run in America and a successful journey across the Atlantic, the authors were still more or less nervous wrecks.

Time passed and Porgy and the goat lay comfortably dossed down in Cain's warehouse. But every year, between novels with me, and Broadway productions with George, I would journey North and we would meet and discuss our opera. I remember George saying once—it was, I think, when he was planning to stage *An American in Paris*—that he would stay abroad and put in some intensive study in counterpoint. As always, he knew just where he was going. The success of his symphonic poem in Paris was flattering, but the main idea was to build toward the opera.

Later he worked with Joseph Schillinger, the musicologist, who carried him from Bach to Schoenberg, concentrating his attention on polytonality, modern harmony, and counterpoint.

And then in October, exactly two years ago, our impatience got the better of what may prove to have been our better judgment, and the actual adventure of composing began.

It is the fashion in America to lament the prostitution of art by the big magazine, the radio, the moving pictures. With this I have little patience. Properly utilized, the radio and the pictures may be to the present-day writer what his prince was to Villon, the king of Bavaria was to Wagner.

At no other time has it been possible for a writer to earn by hiring himself out as a skilled technician for, say, two months, sufficient income to sustain him for a year. And yet the moving pictures have made it possible. I decided that the silver screen should be my Maecenas, and George elected to serve the radio [with *Music by Gershwin*].

During my first year I wrote the screen version of *The Emperor Jones.* For this I may have lost the friendship of Eugene O'Neill. I haven't dared to look him up since. And to finance my second year I made a pilgrimage to Hollywood to tinker at Pearl Buck's *Good Earth.* My selection for this assignment presented a perfect example of motion picture logic. When I arrived on the lot and asked why I had been offered the job, it was made perfectly plain to me. Negroes were not a Caucasian people. . . . I wrote understandingly of Negroes. It was obvious then that I would understand the Chinese. I suspect that before my engagement closed, their faith in their reasoning power was shaken. But I gave them my best, and when I left for the East I was free to complete my work on the opera.

Statistics record the fact that there are 25 million radios in America. Their contribution to the opera was indirect but important. Out of them for half an hour each week poured the glad tidings that Feenamint could be wheedled away from virtually any drug clerk in America for one dime—the tenth part of a dollar. And with the authentic medicine-man flair, the manufacturer distributed his information in an irresistible wrapper of Gershwin hits, with the composer at the piano.

There is, I imagine, a worse fate than that which derives from the use of a laxative gum. And, anyhow, we felt that the end justified the means, and that they also served who only sat and waited.

At the outset we were faced by a difficult problem. I was firm in my refusal to leave the South and live in New York. Gershwin was bound for the duration of his contract to the microphone at Radio City. The matter of effecting a happy union

between words and music across a thousand miles of Atlantic seaboard baffled us for a moment. The solution came quite naturally when we associated Ira Gershwin with us. Presently we evolved a system by which, between my visits North, or George's dash to Charleston, I could send scenes and lyrics. Then the brothers Gershwin, after their extraordinary fashion, would get at the piano, pound, wrangle, swear, burst into weird snatches of song, and eventually emerge with a polished lyric. Then too, Ira's gift for the more sophisticated lyric was exactly suited to the task of writing the songs for Sportin' Life, the Harlem gambler who had drifted into Catfish Row.

I imagine that in after years when George looks back upon this time, he will feel that the summer of 1934 furnished him with one of the most satisfying as well as exciting experiences of his career. Under the baking suns of July and August we established ourselves on Folly Island, a small barrier island ten miles from Charleston. James Island, with its large population of primitive Gullah Negroes, lay adjacent and furnished us with a laboratory in which to test our theories, as well as an inexhaustible source of folk material. But the most interesting discovery to me, as we sat listening to their spirituals, or watched a group . . . [standing] before a cabin or country store, was that to George it was more like a homecoming than an exploration. The quality in him which had produced the *Rhapsody in Blue* in the most sophisticated city in America found its counterpart in the impulse behind the music and bodily rhythms of the simple Negro peasant of the South.

The Gullah Negro prides himself on what he calls "shouting." This is a complicated rhythmic pattern beaten out by feet and hands as an accompaniment to the spirituals, and is indubitably an African survival. I shall never forget the night when, at a Negro meeting on a remote sea-island, George started "shouting" with them. And eventually to their huge delight stole the show from their champion "shouter." I think that he is probably the only white man in America who could have done it.

Another night, as we were about to enter a dilapidated cabin that had been taken as a meeting house by a group of Negro Holy Rollers, George caught my arm and held me. The sound that had arrested him was one to which, through long familiarity, I attached no special importance. But now, listening to it with him, and noticing his excitement, I began to catch its extraordinary quality. It consisted of perhaps a dozen voices raised in loud rhythmic prayer. The odd thing about it was that while each had started at a different time, upon a different theme, they formed a clearly defined rhythmic pattern, and that this, with the actual words lost, and the inevitable pounding of the rhythm, produced an effect almost terrifying in its primitive intensity. Inspired by the extraordinary effect, George wrote six simultaneous prayers producing a terrifying primitive invocation to God in the face of the hurricane.

We had hoped, and it was logical, that the Theatre Guild would produce the opera. An excursion into that field of the theater was a new idea to the directors. But then they had gambled once on *Porgy* and won. There was a sort of indulgent affection for the cripple and his goat on Fifty-second Street. Most certainly they did not want anybody else to do it, and so contracts were signed.

Having committed themselves, the Guild proceeded to deprive us of all alibis in the event of failure by giving us a free hand in the casting and a star producing staff.

Mamoulian returned from Hollywood to assume the direction. Alexander Smallens, who had conducted the Philharmonic Stadium Concerts and the Philadelphia Symphony, and who, in spite of having conducted the orchestra of [the 1934 Virgil Thomson–Gertrude Stein opera] *Four Saints in Three Acts,* still made his wants known in comprehensible English, was made conductor.

Alexander Steinert, pianist and composer, with a Prix de Rome to his credit, was entrusted with the coaching of the principals.

For a year George had been cast-hunting. It had been an exciting, if at times a strenuous, sport. But last April, when I journeyed North to hear the aspirants and advise on the final decisions, I was

While he was still reviewing Heyward's first pages of the libretto for Porgy and Bess, *Gershwin composed* Variations on "I Got Rhythm." *This flashy orchestral trifle was unveiled early in 1934 during a concert tour the composer undertook with the expanded Leo Reisman band. As he worked on the opera, he also served as host of his own radio program,* Music by Gershwin, *for two seasons in 1934.*

amazed at the amount of promising talent exhibited. The cast was assembled. Steinert took them in hand, and at the first rehearsal he had them ready to read the difficult score from beginning to end.

We were in rather a dither about the name. The composer and author both felt that the opera should be called simply *Porgy*. But there was a feeling in the publicity department that this would lead to a confusion in that amorphous region known as the public mind, and that *Porgy* in lights might be construed as a revival of the original play, rather than as the Gershwin opus.

There had of course been Pelléas and Mélisande, Samson and Delilah, Tristan and Isolde.

"And so," said Heyward, with the humility characteristic of those who draw their sustenance from the theater, "why not *Porgy and Bess*?"

To which Gershwin replied, with the detachment to which I have referred and which could not possibly be mistaken for conceit, "Of course, it's right in the operatic tradition."

Two years! It doesn't seem that long. There has been so much to do. The published version of the piano and vocal score, fresh from the press, runs to 560 pages. And when that was finished, George tackled the orchestration single-handed. The resulting manuscript is impressive. It contains 700 pages of closely written music, and it is the fruit of nine months of unremitting labor.

For my own part, I had a play which needed to be cut 40 percent for the libretto; yet nothing of dramatic value could be sacrificed. The dialogue had to follow that of the drama, but it had to be arranged to form a new pattern, to escape monotony and adapt itself to the music. And then there were the spirituals, and the lyrics upon which Ira and I worked.

In the theater every production is a gamble. In some, naturally, the odds are greater than in others. *Porgy and Bess* has, I believe, a fair chance of scoring. But whether it does or not, we who have written and composed the opera cannot lose. We have spent two years doing exactly what we wanted to. It has been a very especial sort of adventure. That, at any rate, is in the bag.

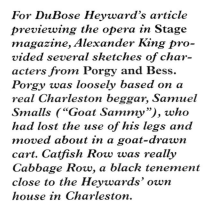

For DuBose Heyward's article previewing the opera in **Stage** *magazine, Alexander King provided several sketches of characters from* **Porgy and Bess.** *Porgy was loosely based on a real Charleston beggar, Samuel Smalls ("Goat Sammy"), who had lost the use of his legs and moved about in a goat-drawn cart. Catfish Row was really Cabbage Row, a black tenement close to the Heywards' own house in Charleston.*

'PORGY AND BESS,' NATIVE OPERA, OPENS AT THE ALVIN

New York Times, **October 11, 1935**

BROOKS ATKINSON AND OLIN DOWNES

Dramatic Values of Community Legend Gloriously Transposed in New Form with Fine Regard for Its Verities

After eight years of savory memories, *Porgy* has acquired a score, a band, a choir of singers, and a new title, *Porgy and Bess,* which the Theatre Guild put on at the Alvin last evening. DuBose and Dorothy Heyward wrote the original lithograph of Catfish Row, which Rouben Mamoulian translated into a memorable work of theater dynamics. But *Porgy and Bess* represents George Gershwin's longing to compose an American folk opera on a suitable theme. Although Mr. Heyward is the author of the libretto and shares with Ira Gershwin the credit for the lyrics, and although Mr. Mamoulian has again mounted the director's box, the evening is unmistakably George Gershwin's personal holiday. In fact, the volume of music he has written during the last two years on the ebony fable of a Charleston rookery has called out a whole brigade of Times Square music critics, who are quite properly the masters of this occasion. Mr. Downes, soothsayer of the diatonic scale, is now beetling his brow in the adjoining cubicle. There is an authoritative ring to his typewriter clatter tonight.

In these circumstances, the province of a drama critic is to report on the transmutation of *Porgy* out of drama into music theater. Let it be said at once that Mr. Gershwin has contributed something glorious to the spirit of the Heywards' community legend. If memory serves, it always lacked glow of personal feeling. Being a fairly objective narrative of a neighborhood of Negroes who lived a private racial life in the midst of a white civilization, *Porgy* was a natural subject for theater showmanship. The groupings, the mad fantasy of leaping shadows, the panic-stricken singing over a corpse, the evil bulk of the buzzard's flight, the screaming hurricane—these large audible and visible items of showmanship took precedence over the episode of Porgy's romance with Crown's high-steppin' gal.

Whether or not Mr. Gershwin's score measures up to its intentions as American folk opera lies in Mr. Downes's bailiwick. But to the ears of a theater critic Mr. Gershwin's music gives a personal voice to Porgy's loneliness when, in a crowd of pitying neighbors, he learns that Bess has vanished into the capacious and remote North. The pathetic apprehension of the "Where's My Bess" trio and the manly conviction of "I'm on My Way" add something vital to the story that was missing before.

These comments are written by a reviewer so inured to the theater that he regards operatic form as cumbersome. Why commonplace remarks that carry no emotion have to be made in a chanting monotone is a problem in art he cannot fathom. Even the hermit thrush drops into conversational tones when he is not singing from the topmost spray in a tree. Turning *Porgy* into opera has resulted in a deluge of casual remarks that have to be thoughtfully intoned and that amazingly impede the action. Why do composers vex it so? "Sister, you goin' to the picnic?" "No, I guess not." Now, why in Heaven's name must two characters in an opera clear their throats before they can exchange that sort of information? What a theater critic probably wants is a musical show with songs that evoke the emotion of situations and make no further pretensions. Part of the emotion of a drama comes from the pace of the performance.

And what of the amusing little device of sounds and rhythms, of sweeping, sawing, hammering, and dusting, that opens the last scene early one morning? In the program it is solemnly described as "Occupational Humoresque." But any music hall would be glad to have it without its tuppence-colored label. Mr. Mamoulian is an excellent director for dramas of ample proportions. He is not subtle, which is a virtue in showmanship. His crowds are arranged in masses that look as solid as a victory at the polls; they move with simple unanimity, and the rhythm is comfortably obvious.

Mr. Gershwin knows that. He has written the scores for innumerable musical shows. After one of them he was presented with the robes of Arthur Sullivan, who also was consumed with a desire to write grand. To the ears of a theater critic there are intimations in *Porgy and Bess* that Mr. Gershwin is still easiest in mind when he is writing songs with choruses. He, and his present reviewer, are on familiar ground when he is writing a droll tune like "A Woman Is a Sometime Thing" or a lazy . . . solo like "I Got Plenty o' Nuttin'," or made-to-order spirituals like "Oh, de Lawd Shake de Heavens," or Sportin' Life's hot-time number entitled "There's a Boat Dat's Leavin' Soon for New York." If Mr. Gershwin does not enjoy his task most in moments like this, his audience does. In sheer quality of character they are worth an hour of formal music transitions.

For the current folk opera Sergei Soudeikine has prepared Catfish Row settings that follow the general design of the originals but have more grace, humor, and color. In the world of sound that Mr. Gershwin has created, the tattered children of a Charleston byway are still racy and congenial. Promoting *Porgy* to opera involves considerable incidental drudgery for theatergoers who agree with Mark Twain that "classical music is better than it sounds." But Mr. Gershwin has found a personal voice that was inarticulate in the original play. The fear and the pain go deeper in *Porgy and Bess* than they did in penny-plain *Porgy*.

Brooks Atkinson

Exotic Richness of Negro Music and Color of Charleston, S.C., Admirably Conveyed in Score of Catfish Row Tragedy

George Gershwin, long conspicuous as an American composer with a true lyrical gift and with original and racy things to say, has turned with his score of *Porgy and Bess* to the more pretentious ways of the musical theater. The result, which vastly entertained last night's audience, has much to commend it from the musical standpoint, even if the work does not utilize all the resources of the operatic composer, or pierce very often to the depths of the simple and pathetic drama.

It is in the lyrical moments that Mr. Gershwin is most completely felicitous. With an instinctive appreciation of the melodic glides and nuances of Negro song, and an equally personal tendency to

Standard Weekly Guide to the World's Greatest City

THIS WEEK IN NEW YORK

ANITA LOUISE
Appearing in the motion picture "Here's to Romance," at the Center Theatre.

ANNE BROWN
In "Porgy and Bess," the Guild musical, opening Thursday at the Alvin.

WEEK OF OCTOBER 6 to 12, 1935

• WHERE TO GO AND WHAT TO DO

Porgy and Bess *premiered in Boston on September 30, 1935, to critical acclaim. By the time it opened in New York, at the Alvin Theatre on October 10, 1935, Gershwin had agreed to some cuts to reduce the excessive length and tighten the dramatic flow. Anne Brown, who played Bess, was featured on the cover of a New York events magazine the week of the opera's Manhattan opening.*

rich and exotic harmony, he writes a melody which is idiomatic and wholly appropriate to the subject. He also knows the voices. He is experienced in many phases of the theater, and his work shows it. His ultimate destiny as an opera composer is yet to be seen. His native gifts won him success last night, but it appears in the light of the production that as yet he has not completely formed his style as an opera composer.

The style is at one moment of opera and another of operetta or sheer Broadway entertainment. It goes without saying that many of the songs in the score of *Porgy and Bess* will reap a quick popularity. Many of them are excellent, as we have a right to expect of Mr. Gershwin. But that is the least important thing about this work. There are elements of a more organic kind in it. Here and there flashes of real contrapuntal ingenuity combine

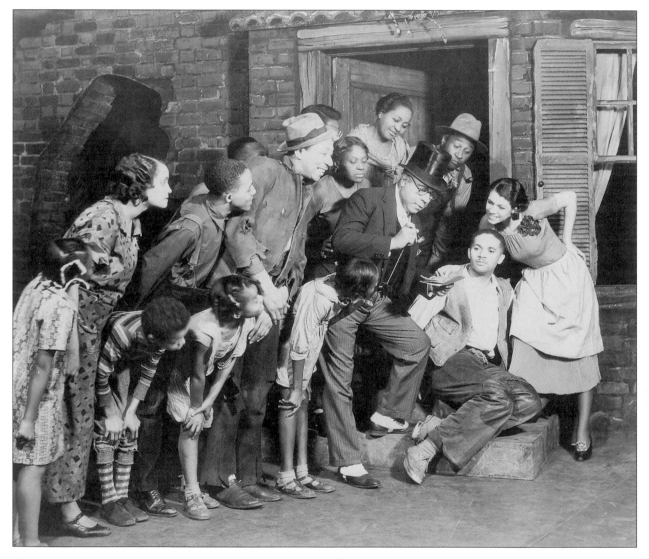

One of the lighter scenes in **Porgy** *and* **Bess** *involves a "lawyer" who fraudulently claims Bess must have a proper divorce from Crown, for which Porgy must pay. Played by the distinguished composer/arranger/musicologist J. Rosamond Johnson in the 1935 production, lawyer Frazier tries to sell a divorce to Porgy (Todd Duncan) and Bess (Anne Brown).*

themes in a manner apposite to the grouping and action of the characters on the stage. In ensemble pieces rhythmic and contrapuntal devices work well. Harmonic admixtures of Stravinsky and Puccini are obvious but not particularly disconcerting. Sometimes the spicy harmonies heighten felicitously the color of the music. There is effective treatment of the "spirituals." No one of the "spiritual" melodies is actually Negro in origin. They are all Mr. Gershwin's invention. He makes effective use of them, not only by harmony sometimes "modal" but by the dramatic combination of the massed voices and the wild exhortations of individual singers.

It must be admitted that in spite of cuts there are still too many set songs and "numbers" which hold back the dramatic development, and the treatment of passages of recitative is seldom significant. The songs were welcomed. Porgy's "I Got Plenty o' Nuttin'" held up the show, while all the inhabitants of Catfish Row beat time for it. Clara's lullaby, "Summertime," sets early a melodic pace that is fairly maintained in the lyrical moments of the score. The prayer of Serena for Bess is eloquent, original, and the most poetical passage in the whole work. The duets of Porgy and Bess are more obvious and savorous of Puccini.

The performance had much that was uncommonly interesting, particularly to a reviewer accustomed to the methods of the opera stage. These methods are usually as out of date as the dodo. Operatic acting and stage management have too often been fit subjects for ridicule. When it comes to sheer acting, last night certain operatic functionaries should have been present. If the Metropolitan chorus could ever put one-half the action into the riot scene in the second act of *Meistersinger* that the Negro cast put into the fight that followed the crap game, it would be not merely refreshing but miraculous. And when did Isolde

wave a scarf more rhythmically from the tower than those who shook feather dusters and sheets from the windows to accompany Porgy's song? Or Hans Sachs cobble more rhythmically to Beckmesser's Serenade than the shoemaker on the doorstep? What could excel the beautiful precision of the tremolo of the shoeshiner?

As individual and collective acting, these and many other things were admirable. There were magnificent effects of choral song and action. Other groupings were often astonishingly conventional in the operatic manner, and thus contrary to dramatic purpose. This was probably due to the sectional character of the score, but why should the pathetic and tragically helpless Porgy be given the position and the air of the strutting opera baritone? . . .

Did the inhabitants of Catfish Row set themselves in centrifugal patterns along the floor and wiggle hands and toes like the ladies who are auxiliary to a soloist's performance in a revue? Of course this was amusing. So was the capital clogging of Sportin' Life in the forest scene. He was a rare fellow, with magnificent clothes. There were a hundred diverting details in this spectacle. What had become of the essential simplicity of the drama of *Porgy*? Let Mr. Atkinson answer.

The cast provided some excellent singing. None of the vocalists fell short of musicianship and expressiveness. The Porgy, Todd Duncan, has a manly and resonant voice, which he uses with eloquent effect. The fresh tone, admirably competent technique, and dramatic delivery of Anne Brown as Bess was a high point of interpretation. Miss Elzy's Serena was equally in key with her part, and distinguished by truly pathetic expression. Musically this was a very eloquent interpretation by soloists and chorus. Smallens conducted with superb authority and spirit.

Olin Downes

RHAPSODY IN CATFISH ROW

New York Times, **October 20, 1935**

GEORGE GERSHWIN

Since the opening of *Porgy and Bess* I have been asked frequently why it is called a folk opera. The explanation is a simple one. *Porgy and Bess* is a folk tale. Its people naturally would sing folk music. When I first began work on the music I decided against the use of original folk material because I wanted the music to be all of one piece. Therefore I wrote my own spirituals and folksongs. But they are still folk music—and therefore, being in operatic form, *Porgy and Bess* becomes a folk opera.

However, because *Porgy and Bess* deals with Negro life in America, it brings to the operatic form elements that have never before appeared in opera, and I have adapted my method to utilize the drama, the humor, the superstition, the religious fervor, the dancing, and the irrepressible high spirits of the race. If, in doing this, I have created a new form, which combines opera with theater, this new form has come quite naturally out of the material.

The reason I did not submit this work to the usual sponsors of opera in America was that I hoped to have developed something in American music that would appeal to the many rather than to the cultured few.

It was my idea that opera should be entertaining—that it should contain all the elements of entertainment. Therefore, when I chose *Porgy and Bess,* a tale of Charleston Negroes, for a subject, I made sure that it would enable me to write light as well as serious music and that it would enable me to include humor as well as tragedy—in fact, all of the elements of entertainment for the eye as well as the ear, because the Negroes, as a race, have all these qualities inherent in them. They are ideal for my purpose because they express themselves not only by the spoken word but quite naturally by song and dance.

Humor is an important part of American life, and an American opera without humor could not possibly run the gamut of American expression. In *Porgy and Bess* there are ample opportunities for humorous songs and dances. This humor is natural humor—not "gags" superimposed upon the story but humor flowing from the story itself.

For instance, the character of Sportin' Life, instead of being a sinister dope peddler, is a humorous, dancing villain, who is likable and believable and at the same time evil. We were fortunate in finding for that role a young man whose abilities suit it perfectly, John W. Bubbles, or, as he is known to followers of vaudeville, just plain Bubbles, of Buck and Bubbles. We were equally fortunate in finding Todd Duncan for the role of Porgy and Anne Brown for the role of Bess, both of whom give to the score intense dramatic value. We were able to find these people because what we wanted from them lies in their race. And thus it lies in our story of their race. Many people questioned my choice of a vaudeville performer for an operatic role but on the opening night they cheered Bubbles.

We were fortunate, too, in being able to lure Rouben Mamoulian, a great director, back from Hollywood to stage the production. It was Mr. Mamoulian who staged the original production of *Porgy* as a play. He knew all of its value. What was even more valuable, he knew opera as well as he knew the theater, and he was able to bring his knowledge of both to this new form. In my opinion, he has left nothing to be desired in the direction. To match the stage in the pit we obtained Alexander Smallens, who has directed the Philadelphia and Philharmonic Symphony Orchestras and who has conducted more than 150 operas and who has been invaluable to us.

I chose the form I have used for *Porgy and Bess* because I believe that music lives only when it is in serious form. When I wrote the *Rhapsody in Blue* I took "blues" and put them in a larger and more serious form. That was twelve years ago and the *Rhapsody in Blue* is still very much alive, whereas if I had taken the same themes and put them in songs they would have been gone years ago.

No story could have been more ideal for the serious form I needed than *Porgy and Bess.* First of all, it is American, and I believe that American music should be based on American material. I felt when I read *Porgy* in novel form that it had 100 percent dramatic intensity in addition to humor. It was then that I wrote to DuBose Heyward suggesting that we make an opera of it.

My feelings about it, gained from that first reading of the novel, were confirmed when it was produced as a play, for audiences crowded the theater where it played for two years. Mr. Heyward and I, in our collaboration on *Porgy and Bess,* have

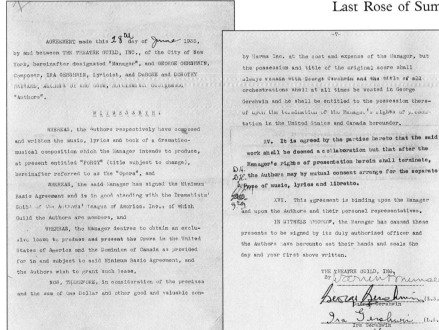

George Gershwin's first opera contract was with the Metropolitan Opera in 1929 for **The Dybbuk;** *the proposed 1931 completion never materialized due to rights issues over S. A. Ansky's Yiddish play of Jewish mysticism. In 1933 Gershwin was offered a contract for* **Porgy** *by the Met's Otto Kahn; instead, the composer chose the Theatre Guild because of its previous experience with the play (and with its black cast) and the greater exposure and number of performances a Broadway production would generate. Gershwin and Heyward signed contracts for* **Porgy** *with the Theatre Guild in 1933 and 1935.*

attempted to heighten the emotional values of the story without losing any of its original quality. I have written my music to be an integral part of that story.

It is true that I have written songs for *Porgy and Bess.* I am not ashamed of writing songs at any time so long as they are good songs. In *Porgy and Bess* I realized I was writing an opera for the theater and without songs it could be neither of the theater nor entertaining, from my viewpoint.

But songs are entirely within the operatic tradition. Many of the most successful operas of the past have had songs. Nearly all of Verdi's operas contain what are known as "song hits." *Carmen* is almost a collection of hits. And what about "The Last Rose of Summer," perhaps one of the most widely known songs of the generation? How many of those who sing it know that it is from an opera?

Of course, the songs in *Porgy and Bess* are only a part of the whole. The recitative I have tried to make as close to the Negro inflection in speech as possible, and I believe my songwriting apprenticeship has served invaluably in this respect, because the songwriters of America have the best conception of how to set words to music so that the music gives added expression to the words. I have used sustained symphonic music to unify entire scenes, and I prepared myself for that task by further study in counterpoint and modern harmony.

In the lyrics for *Porgy and Bess* I believe that Mr. Heyward and my brother Ira have achieved a fine synchronization of diversified moods—Heyward writing most of the native material and Ira doing most of the sophisticated songs. To demonstrate the range of mood their task covers, let me cite a few examples.

There is the prayer in the storm scene written

by Mr. Heyward: "Oh, de Lawd shake de Heavens an' de Lawd rock de groun' . . ." And in contrast there is Ira's song for Sportin' Life in the picnic scene, "It Ain't Necessarily So." . . . Then there is Mr. Heyward's lullaby that opens the opera: "Summertime, an' the livin' is easy . . ." And, again, Ira's song for Sportin' Life in the last act,

"There's a Boat Dat's Leavin' Soon for New York." . . .

All of these are, I believe, lines that come naturally from the Negro. They make for folk music. Thus *Porgy and Bess* becomes a folk opera—opera for the theater, with drama, humor, song, and dance.

A dramatic photograph of **Porgy and Bess's** *creators, George Gershwin, DuBose Heyward, and Ira Gershwin, was used on the cover of* **Musical America** *magazine in 1935.*

GERSHWIN'S 'PORGY AND BESS' HAILED IN NEW YORK

Musical America, October 25, 1935

A. WALTER KRAMER

Departing from its custom of devoting itself to the drama . . . the Theatre Guild produced George Gershwin's opera, *Porgy and Bess,* at the Alvin Theatre on the evening of October 10. . . . *Porgy and Bess* is a very fine achievement. That, because it is a splendid evening's entertainment, an evening in the theater during which your interest and attention are held from curtain rise to final curtain fall. The program lists *Porgy and Bess* as "an American folk opera." I don't know just what a "folk opera" is, but I imagine it is called that to suggest something of the type of *The Bartered Bride* rather than *Götterdammerung.* So far the program is right. But his work requires no classification by conventional titles. . . . There is a listing of the songs and ensembles after the record of the act and scenes, . . . recalling musical comedy.

And why not? Mr. Gershwin has made his reputation, a very important one, too, in musical comedy, and I for one doubt whether he is ashamed of it. . . . I applaud the frankness in setting down the names of these songs. For they should be remembered. I want to remember them myself, as I expect to be playing them on my piano many times this winter, for my own delectation and that of my friends. . . .

Let me first make clear that Mr. Gershwin has written a musical version of the play *Porgy* that is one of the most exciting things that has come before my eyes and ears in years. . . . Mr. Gershwin has written a score of amazing fluency, in an idiom readily recognizable as his own, filled with melodic, harmonic, and rhythmic interest, rising at times to strong emotional climaxes and quite free, at all points, from dullness. Call it "folk opera," if you will. I find it a natural development of the music this composer has written for years for his musical comedies, in which he has more than once attained to passages of distinction. The music of *Porgy and*

Bess goes further, to be sure, but it stems from the same vocabulary, perhaps with greater technical skill and certainly with more intense application. Mr. Gershwin has doubtless wished to gain new honors with this work. As is the custom, he allows others to orchestrate his musical comedies; but *Porgy and Bess* he has orchestrated himself. And his instrumentation is worthy of high praise for its suppleness, its appropriateness, and its unusual variety. He mixes his colors and his shades today more than skillfully.

The solos are tremendously effective, as are the ensembles, sung by a Negro chorus that, by its fidelity to the pitch and its emotional simplicity, puts many a white chorus to shame. In Scene 1, there is a lullaby, "Summertime," sung beautifully by Abbie Mitchell, which is a happy melodic fancy, and in the same scene, Edward Matthews, the admirable baritone, remembered from *Four Saints in Three Acts,* sings a fascinating song, "A Woman Is a Sometime Thing," that will be heard everywhere before many days have passed. For sheer intensity of expression, the arioso "My Man's Gone Now," sung by Ruby Elzy, the Serena of the opera, in the "saucer burial" scene of Act I, is one of the score's highest achievements. Miss Elzy's delivery of this music is a masterpiece of its kind.

But the hit of the work will doubtless be "I Got Plenty o' Nuttin'," which Porgy sings in Act II, well matched by "It Ain't Necessarily So," sung by Sportin' Life in the following scene, and "There's a Boat Dat's Leavin' Soon for New York," sung by the same character in the last act. These are the infectious, spontaneous songs that captivate you by their genuineness and lack of pose. Like the songs in Gershwin musical comedies, they are perfect expressions of their texts. "I Got Plenty o' Nuttin'" literally stopped the show; the audience kept on applauding and would have been delighted with a repetition, which conductor Smallens wisely refused.

Some of the more serious moments fared slightly less well, for example, the duet between Porgy and Bess in Act II called "Bess, You Is My Woman Now." Here Mr. Gershwin, desiring to write love music of expansive warmth, suffered a bit from having the Puccini blues, if I may so term it, and again in the trio in the final scene, "[Oh, Bess, Oh] Where's My Bess?" he remembers too well the trio

The Victor label released a recording of **Porgy** *and Bess high-lights (with white opera stars Lawrence Tibbett and Helen Jepson) soon after the opera's opening.*

in *Madama Butterfly,* "Io so che alle sue pene," sung by Sharpless, Suzuki, and Pinkerton. But his sense of the fitting is acute, and in this scene he brings back the duet music at the moment when Porgy realizes that Bess has left him. The effect of rehearing this music is truly poignant, as Porgy sings his final song with the ensemble, "[Oh, Lawd,] I'm on My Way," a stirring thing.

That Mr. Gershwin has succeeded in finding natural musical expression for the more conversational part of his libretto I cannot grant. The ease with which opera composers of other lands have

done this is something that practically every American composer has yet to acquire. Some of his text Mr. Gershwin handles fairly awkwardly. He errs, we think, in having part of it sung, and part of it spoken. . . .

No praise is too great for the men and women who sang and acted the Gershwin opera. They were everything that could be desired, in song, action, and speech. It is no exaggeration to say that they lived their roles so completely that the listener was not conscious even for a moment that they were acting. . . .

Todd Duncan's Porgy, in action and singing, was as eloquent a portrayal as we can imagine, illumined by a touching humility. As Bess, Anne Brown revealed herself an artist of unlimited resources. From her first entrance, she was the personification of that strange mixture of good and evil, which the author called for in the role.

Rouben Mamoulian's direction was truly brilliant, as were the settings designed by Sergei Soudeikine. Alexander Smallens's musical direction of both orchestra and chorus was sure and authoritative, with the result that the score was heard to advantage in even its minute details. The chorus was Eva Jessye's famed Negro choir, trained by her for this production with the same skill she has exhibited in the past. It sang so beautifully as to defy description. In the "saucer burial" scene, in "Oh, Doctor Jesus" and "Clara, [Clara,] Don't You Be Downhearted," its performance was the acme of moving choral singing.

Mr. Gershwin has reason to rejoice that his *Porgy and Bess* has been given by the Theatre Guild. It is a work that our Metropolitan Opera, for instance, would have done far less convincingly. For its place is extraterritorial, as far as opera houses are concerned. . . . But I do feel that it is a successful achievement in clothing an appealing, dramatic story with music. For doing that Mr. Gershwin has the gratitude and approval of all who have been awaiting just such an effort by an American composer.

With *Porgy and Bess* he has expressed himself in the terms of a story taken from the life of his own times, in a section of his country, and has pointed the way for other composers to follow. American opera must not be legendary, it must not be anything but illustrative of American life. *Porgy and Bess* meets that requirement in its libretto. George Gershwin has fulfilled it superbly in his music.

Will Cotton created an entertaining series of full-color celebrity portraits for **Vanity Fair** *in the 1930s. His deco-ish caricature of George Gershwin during the run of* **Porgy** **and Bess** *depicts a confident composer and the stylized gestures of the singers. Gershwin had been personally involved in all aspects of the opera's production. Notably, he insisted on well-trained black singers for the roles and personally auditioned and handpicked much of the cast. Todd Duncan, who played Porgy, was a classically trained baritone who disliked jazz. Gershwin traveled with Duncan—a problematical arrangement for a trip through the South at the time—to librettist Heyward's Charleston, so that the singer could absorb the authentic songs and dialect of the indigenous people.*

RHAPSODY IN BLACK

Stage, November 1935

MARCIA DAVENPORT AND RUTH WOODBURY SEDGWICK

As an Opera

A few minutes after the curtain rises on *Porgy and Bess* the secure realization overtakes the listener that he is hearing an opera. Never mind at the moment whether it is American, Negro, folk, or otherwise catalogued. It is an opera. It has a chemical quality of conviction and genuineness and importance, a strong underlying security in its creation by a composer of genius and honesty and skill. Some thoughtful people have been predicting this since Gershwin's first musical comedy. They shrug their shoulders now, not in the spirit of "I told you so," but meaning simply, "Of course."

An indication of the failure of contemporary composers to produce a true opera is that any of the so-called operas of the past twenty years would make about the same impression without music as they make with the music they have. They could as well be spoken, or read. Strauss was the last composer to produce true opera—drama in musical form realizing itself in an indissoluble integration of music, emotion, and thought. Now there is *Porgy and Bess,* such a work, and therefore an honest-to-God opera.

One thing it has is tunes. Melodies, of course; but such a plain word as tunes is the essence of its direct, natural, and spontaneous beauty. Furthermore, the tunes are song—the ecstatic and physical element that differentiates opera from other music and the thing that escapes all of Mr. Gershwin's contemporaries. Many of them have no song within them. Gershwin has it utterly, a wellspring. Also he has pulsating emotion, rushing and fearless expression, and now through his own peculiar efforts, the equipment of a conscientious and commanding composer. When he chooses to "paint" in choral voices he does so with all the subtlety of the resource, and he gives his chorus something to paint with, a palette laden with unlimited nuances of melody.

Then after one scene of dazzling virtuosity, ranging from Clara's lullaby to the hard-boiled business of the crap game and the astounding reality of Robbins's murder, there comes the wake, the "saucer burial." This is a scene to glorify any opera. Quite aside from the tension built up by inspired grouping, lighting, acting, and direction, the music pours out a wail of mourning, a torrent of despair. It mounts vitally and tensely, its rhythms Negroid, its soaring, minor cadences yearningly Hebraic, to the point where Serena begins to sing "My Man's Gone Now." And that is the point where this opera can stand comparison with anything written in many, many years. Forbiddingly difficult, Miss Ruby Elzy sings this dirge in a high, piercing soprano voice that embodies every shade of difference between the black throat and white. The burden is a wail, a minor arpeggio for which the composer's direction is *glissando*—something that demands a violin rather than a voice. The singer has it. She distills heartbreak from this extraordinary piece of music.

The variety of the work is deeply satisfying and a variety necessarily held within the frame of the simple story. But everything there—the thumping strut of the picnic song, the delicious and tantalizing sinuousness of two of the best humorous numbers Gershwin ever wrote—"I Got Plenty o' Nuttin'" and "It Ain't Necessarily So."

The music is so well balanced and naturally developed that one reacts alike to a solo, a duet, a chorus, or the orchestra. All flow together, strung on recitative that never lags, never turns stagy and phony. Gershwin has not feared to lay down his work on the general lines of the soundest operas ever conceived; plot borne out by natural and realistic dialogue in music, songs that rise from the foundation and illuminate it. The simple plot unfolds to the ear directly as to the eye. Porgy and Bess held together by love and fear, torn apart by the animal lust of the primitive Crown; his murder by Porgy; the hurricane that piles up the burden of atmosphere and color and climaxes in the amazing prayer meeting; the seduction of Bess by Sportin' Life's dope and vicious promises; Porgy's return from jail to find her gone, and his gallant departure on the crest of the closing chorus—"Oh, Lawd, I'm on My Way"—which does everything that might be done with basic jazz rhythms and harmonies. One does not and will not forget them.

In the orchestration, every note of which is his own work, Gershwin has made perhaps the most spectacular stride of all. He reveals here fully matured and certain musicianship. His work is a riot of imagination and richness. He shows restraint, with which, in his brasses and woodwinds, he tells a saga. Probably the most remarkable instance of this is his hurricane music, where instead of the melee of the full-voiced orchestra, the whole scene is painted with timpani and sinister melody for the tuba solo. A great deal is added to this score by the playing of a good orchestra and the splendid conducting of Alexander Smallens. No more ideal conductor could have been chosen—a man whose beat is masterful, whose ability to mold and direct an opera is almost unsurpassed. Here the spontaneous reality of the Negro actors and the magnificent choral work are the finest elements of the performance. Most of the soloists are excellent. Todd Duncan, making his first appearance on any stage, as Porgy, gives a vital performance and sings with real beauty and great feeling. Miss Elzy is a notable artist. Miss Anne Wiggins Brown, also a novice, offers the only disappointment in the cast, as Bess. Her voice lacks the warm characteristic racial quality of the others and sounds commonplace.

There are two duets for Porgy and Bess, "Bess, You Is My Woman Now" and "I Loves You, Porgy,"

which are the points of the score that tend to pull it to the level of routine opera and away from its realistic inspiration. Only during them is there a sense of staginess, and that may well come from the singing, which at these places turns self-conscious, at least on the part of Miss Brown. On the other hand, in the wilderness of the palmetto island, the duet "What You Want with Bess?"—magnificently sung and acted by Miss Brown and Mr. Coleman as Crown—is a stunning specimen

Dramatic shadows and massing of figures marked Rouben Mamoulian's direction of both the 1927 and 1935 Theatre Guild productions of DuBose Heyward's tale of Catfish Row.

of high dramatic excitement. From the original *Porgy* production, the symphony of tenement noises, now called "Occupational Humoresque," has been retained and built into the score with finesse and wit. Its mounting cacophony of rhythm and sound is swept into a sudden rush of music as the orchestra tumbles into the din with the high conversational cackle that Gershwin has used before.

Because this work was written for Negro singers, within the framework of racial atmosphere, it goes down on record as the first American folk opera. It is indeed that. It abounds in color, it retains the quality of the Negro chant, the spiritual, the wail, the jazz, and the blues. It is derivative only so far as it should be derivative for authenticity. It is a folk opera rich in suggestions of native tunes, like Smetana's *Bartered Bride*; and like that masterpiece it is the work of a man who could compose within a fixed milieu, yet lead the imagination on to believe in the wider intrinsic importance of his music. *Porgy and Bess* must be sung by a Negro cast, and derives much stature from the Theatre Guild's scrupulous and beautiful production. It is limited, ranged alongside other opera. But it has two qualities, aside from its technical virtues, that no new opera has enjoyed for a long time: melody, abundant and consistent; and honesty. There is not one phony or attitudinous or posing thing about the opera, no moment when you can whisper "Hooey!" to the person beside you. Its melodies carry the hearer along like a ride on a ferris wheel. They stay in the head and go on singing and pop out in unexpected phrases days and weeks later, even after one hearing. This is what makes people love *Carmen* and *Rigoletto*. It is the quality that makes an opera—and George Gershwin is about the only living composer who has it.

Marcia Davenport

As a Play

Perhaps even more notable than the music of *Porgy and Bess,* certainly more exceptional (for the world *has* seen important folk opera before), is the fact that it brings lyric drama to life with all of the authenticity and completeness of great theater presentation. In it, singing becomes a casual and easy medium for the exchange of human ideas and emotions—not a difficult art on a remote pedestal, scattering ecstasy. Wagner can introduce your soul to the spacious courts of Heaven and Hell, but he does not involve you emotionally in the home life of Nuremberg, the endearing domesticities of Valhalla. Strauss creates the symbols, not the actualities, of existence.

Only twice in *Porgy and Bess,* however, do you remember that you are hearing two people on a stage singing a duet. For the rest of the time you are hardly conscious that tragedy and joy, laughter and tears, as they ebb and flow through the crowded alleyways of a Southern slum, come to you through the medium of song.

That illusion of reality, of course, has its roots buried deep in the artistic veracity and unpretentious beauty of DuBose and Dorothy Heyward's story of a crippled Negro beggar of the Charleston streets. Through the years, Porgy has been slowly creeping up that ladder of fame which leads to the shrines of those great American legends: Uncle Tom, Huck Finn, Jo March. As a novel, as a play, as an opera, this warm chronicle, which is as fundamental, as rich in color, as the red soil of South Carolina itself, has become a proud part of our folk literature. Mr. Heyward has written the libretto for *Porgy and Bess* himself, making it almost an exact transcription of the play, produced by the Guild in 1927. The lyrics, too, which he wrote with Ira Gershwin, slip with the easy vigor of primitive speech from the lips of these Negro singers. Opera lyrics do not often come as these do with the simplicity and beauty of authentic poetry.

In major part, however, the great theatric vitality and veracity of *Porgy and Bess* is due to its director—that same director who, then completely unknown, made theater history and fame for himself overnight with the first *Porgy* eight years ago. Then, working with an untrained group of Negroes, picked up mostly from the nightclubs and streets of Harlem; and a rhythmic interpretation of gesture, speech, slum noises; combined with interesting arrangements of Negro spirituals—he produced a cadenced drama which was almost a folk opera. Now, building on an operatic score, he has simply heightened and advanced his earlier concept. Here Smallens, in the pit, gives the beat which Mamoulian has transmuted into the veritable pulse of life. As Gershwin has made an opera for the ears, using all the techniques of the musician's art, Mamoulian has made one for the eye, with lights, gesture, grouping, body movement, acting, all the pictorial and imitative skills of the theater.

His actors are this time a group of well-trained singers, most of whom have not been on stage before. After five weeks of rehearsals they are able to contribute that rarest of all the theater's fine gifts: a wholly spontaneous and almost subconscious integration of player and story. These people, even to the littlest [child] tossed on stage like a cinnamon cookie and the least important chorus

After **Porgy and Bess** *closed in New York, the Theatre Guild took the opera on a multicity tour. Before its opening in Philadelphia in late January 1936, Gershwin appeared there in concert, playing his Concerto in F with Alexander Smallens conducting. For this occasion he prepared his Suite from* **Porgy and Bess** *(later called* **Catfish Row***), which contains much of the music that had to be cut for the opera's New York production.*

boy in the back row (there isn't even any back row, by the way), are citizens of Catfish Row, living its sprawling, colorful existence, mourning its sudden and casual deaths.

That sweet-voiced veteran Abbie Mitchell is Clara, crooning tenderly to her baby; vaguely uneasy when her Jake starts off for The Banks in hurricane season; a desperate woman (she has only to stride across the stage to send you into a "cauld grue") while the storm outside thunders against the tenement windows. Georgette Harvey, with her pipe and baritone voice, is again Maria. John W. Bubbles, who dances like an arrow shot from the high gods' laughter, stylizes Sportin' Life into the finest black Puck ever strayed from the realm of classic mischief, and yet remains Charleston's own. Warren Coleman, who is Crown, and Anne Wiggins Brown, who is Bess, strapped in self-consciousness, stand only on the threshold of their parts.

The most notable characterizations, however, are the work of novices. Todd Duncan, a singer and teacher from Howard University, who has, except for a single opera performance, never been on the stage before, creates the new Porgy with sensitivity and sustained power. His crippled legs, his love for Bess, his faith in God, the light which continuously floods his face blend into an important stage portrait. Before Ruby Elzy, however, a young graduate of the Juilliard School and another amateur player, one pauses with awe. This girl plays Serena, that gentle woman of God immortalized once by Rose McClendon. Always exactly right, at times her acting takes on real stature. At Robbins's wake, as she crouches before his bier, the shadows across her tired face, her hands stretched out to Maria on one side and Clara on the other, her angelic voice lifted, she becomes for a stabbing moment a symbol of all the patient sorrow in the world. As she sings "Oh, Doctor Jesus" while Bess is lying ill, she almost makes visible her rapt vision.

It is, however, in the group work, the complete stage picture, that Mamoulian's most distinguished contribution lies. One has only to glance back shudderingly across the opera choruses seen in one lifetime to estimate its importance. Each of the seventy people almost continuously on stage during the three acts of *Porgy and Bess* not only has a plausible and reasonable appearance and behavior but is an individual, with a life of his own and a purpose in living it. Whether these Negroes are sweeping, or shooting craps, or blowing soap bubbles, or dancing, or shaking rugs out of upper windows, or bending over washtubs, or snoring, or simply sitting in doorways in the sun, they do it convincingly. You might see the opera a dozen times and still not grasp all the nuances of expression and movement—the amusing suggestions of what is going on behind the doors and windows of Catfish Row.

Like the brushwork of Gauguin, it all looks casual but is painstakingly accurate to the last fraction of detail. There is not even the turn of a head which has not been calculated. The architecture of the groupings, constantly changing, always beautiful, is as true as though the medium were marble. You remember particularly the fantastic and exciting compositions of arms and legs and bodies, either moving with or breaking across the beat of the music. Gesture is constantly used in counterpoint. The women sew, and their needles flash against the cadence of the fishermen's song. The hands of the mourners lift and fall in rotation, not unison, at the wake. A woman, with arms extended to form a cross, rises slowly like an organ peal, through the frantic beat of the hurricane motif. Astutely, Mamoulian has gauged the pictorial and dramatic effectiveness of the pale palms of Negro hands. Arranged in spectacular designs, they are constantly used to help tell the story, emphasize the mood of the music. Sometimes they are the Holy Ghost descending; sometimes dark pilgrims supplicating; sometimes little quivering devils celebrating the joyous lusts of the flesh. Feet alternately dance and drag. Bodies sway in abandon and prayer.

The light plot is a libretto in itself. Mamoulian has used small spots like a paintbrush, daubing on colors in patterns which are now enchanting, now terrifying. Of a dozen superb effects, perhaps the most haunting is the wake. At first the lights pick up fingers, transform them into tongues of black flame darting through the air. Then faces, raised, and beautiful with quiet resignation, take on the flat quality of Italian primitives. Finally the lamp goes out, the white spots in the footlights come on, and voodoo shadows begin their dance of death along the wall. At the end, Lord Jesus has entirely gone, and the sultry soul of Africa broods over the room. The sets of Sergei Soudeikine, satisfactorily and happily, if a little too neatly, recreate Catfish Row. His costumes blaze appropriately, humorously, at times vindictively, through the warm and lovable windings of the story.

When it is all over and you pause to look back to that first *Porgy,* you realize that you have lost only a little in terms of naiveté, of simplicity—a small price to pay for such reinforcements of exaltation and power. *Porgy and Bess* is still great folk theater, with the added lift and inspiration of song.

Ruth Woodbury Sedgwick

'SHALL WE DANCE': ASTAIRE, ROGERS, AND THE GERSHWINS

New York World-Telegram, **May 8, 1937**

Fred Astaire and Ginger Rogers Start a Film by Rehearsing the Most Difficult Dances First

Fred Astaire and Ginger Rogers believe in getting off to a difficult start in their musical pictures. Instead of beginning a production with easy scenes and working up gradually to the intricate dance routines, they select one of their hardest terpsichorean numbers as the shooting-schedule takeoff.

"Once we get a hard dance filmed, the ice is broken," Astaire explained on the set of *Shall We Dance* at the RKO Radio studio. "I never feel we are really in the show until that is accomplished. After the first routine is finished, the others are spaced at regular intervals throughout the production."

For the launching of *Shall We Dance,* booked for the Radio City Music Hall next Thursday, Astaire and Miss Rogers chose their roller-skat-

ing dance, certainly one of the most difficult of the picture's routines, although not the most lavish or spectacular. When that dance was stepped—or "rollered" is the right word, perhaps—into celluloid, all hands heaved a sigh of relief that there were no disastrous spills with resultant injuries.

Shall We Dance's exciting skating-dance scene in New York's Central Park, set to orchestral variations on "Let's Call the Whole Thing Off," is among the most memorable Fred Astaire and Ginger Rogers movie duets. Fred plays Peter P. Peters (a.k.a. Petrov), a ballet dancer with one foot on Broadway, and Ginger is Linda Keene, a musical-comedy star.

The finale of Shall We Dance *(RKO, 1937) begins as a purposely pretentious ballet with Harriet Hoctor (as herself). Showing off one of the film's sleek art deco settings, the ballet turns jazzy when Petrov dances with an evening-gowned ensemble of masked "Linda Keenes." In addition to a wealth of unforgettable songs—highlighted by the poignant "They Can't Take That Away from Me"— Gershwin supplied the instrumental accompaniments for several nonsong musical sequences. Especially effective is the sprightly "Walking the Dog" (a.k.a. "Promenade"), subtly scored by the composer for a chamber ensemble.*

The setting for the unique routine represented a section of New York's Central Park and occupied the entire interior of one of the larger sound stages. Trees and shrubbery surrounded a circular cement floor, embracing approximately sixteen hundred square feet of skating space.

As usual, Astaire was one of the first persons on the set on opening morning, although he was not to go into action for at least two hours. Skates

under arm, he took a sideline seat to watch thirty atmosphere skaters whirl about the floor. These youngsters, ranging in age from ten to twenty, had been picked from a local roller rink upon instructions from director Mark Sandrich.

Soon Harry Cornbleth and Marie Osborne (former Baby Marie of silent-film fame) skated onto the set. Cornbleth is Astaire's stand-in, and Miss Osborne has the same job for Miss Rogers. Both wore large pillows strapped to their backs to protect them in case of a spill on the cement floor.

The camera, mounted on a huge steel crane, was finally lined up for the first shot and the vast setting was properly lighted. At the command of director Sandrich, the atmosphere skaters commenced to tear along at high speed while the camera performed acrobatic feats to match, thanks to the mobile crane.

This "establishing shot" was finished to the director's satisfaction when Miss Rogers, natty in chic short skirt and near-fitting blouse, skated onto the stage. Ten minutes were consumed in lining the camera for the next shot.

Then came "the works." Again the atmosphere skaters whirled about the floor. Starting slowly, Astaire and Miss Rogers rollered their way through the group and across the floor, to drop to a bench which flanked the arena.

The morning was consumed in "washing up" the introductory scenes. Then the atmosphere players were dismissed. The stars' dance number was ready to get under way.

Afternoon found Fred and Ginger singing one of the George and Ira Gershwin songs.

In the evening of the first day the heavy roller work was just beginning. But a dent in the routine had been made and fortunately there were no dents in the stars.

Gershwin Film Tunes in New Recordings Among His Best

The new George Gershwin score for the picture *Shall We Dance* is among the best things he's done in a long while, and especially when sung (and danced) by Fred Astaire on the Brunswick records. Though not strong vocally, he does a very pleasant job with "They Can't Take That Away from Me" and its companion piece, "[I've Got] Beginner's Luck"; furnishes a superb arrangement of tap dancing and bass fiddling on "Slap That Bass," which has on the reverse side "They All Laughed"; and shows off to excellent advantage the clever lyrics of "Let's Call the Whole Thing Off" and the dancing possibilities of "Shall We Dance." Johnny Green and his orchestra do the skillful accompanying.

If you are interested in swing arrangements of some of these numbers, Vocalion has released "They Can't Take That Away from Me" and "Let's Call the Whole Thing Off," as sung and played by Billie Holiday and her orchestra, or "Slap That Bass," for which Ike Ragon and his orchestra "go to town." . . .

EPILOGUE

THE LAST FILMS

The Gershwins worked on their final Fred Astaire RKO film, A Damsel in Distress, *in March and April 1937. Although it does not feature Ginger Rogers (Astaire's love interest is played by Joan Fontaine), the movie, set in England, boasts perhaps Astaire's most literate and wittiest script, cowritten by P. G. Wodehouse (based on his novel of the same name). Gershwin provided eight songs, including two unusual madrigal-type pieces—"The Jolly Tar and the Milk Maid" and "Sing of Spring"—and three exceptional melodies, "A Foggy Day," "Nice Work If You Can Get It," and "Things Are Looking Up." "Stiff Upper Lip" and variations thereon by orchestrator Robert Russell Bennett are used in a long and memorable comic funhouse scene, which highlights the considerable talents of the film's supporting team, George Burns and Gracie Allen.* A Damsel in Distress, *released in November 1937, was George Gershwin's last complete musical score.*

Between RKO films George Gershwin concertized, appearing in a series of all-Gershwin programs in Los Angeles in
February. It was at one of these that the composer experienced his first indication of the seriousness of the brain
tumor that would soon end his life, when he momentarily
blacked out during a solo piano passage of the Concerto
in F. In late May 1937, Gershwin started work on The
Goldwyn Follies, which was to feature a new ballet with his
music, tentatively entitled Swing Symphony. His alarming
symptoms worsened, with frequent headaches and dizzi-
ness, accompanied by inconclusive medical tests and
diagnoses of stress and psychological problems. Gershwin
completed five songs for Samuel Goldwyn before Ira
Gershwin requested, on July 8, that the studio release his
brother from his contract (leaving Ira and Vernon Duke to
complete the score). On July 9 George Gershwin lapsed into
a coma and was rushed to Cedars of Lebanon Hospital; a five-hour operation
concluded that he had an inoperable brain tumor. George Gershwin died Sunday
morning, July 11, 1937, at the age of thirty-eight. Among the last songs he wrote
with his brother Ira for The Goldwyn Follies (released in February 1938) are two
of the finest he or any American songwriter ever created: "Love Walked In" and
"Love Is Here to Stay."

GEORGE GERSHWIN: IN MEMORIAM

The Etude, **September 1937**

George Gershwin, one of the most versatile of American composers, died on July 11, at Hollywood, California, from an operation for a cerebral tumor. Born in Brooklyn, September 26, 1898, he gave no indication of musical talent until at the age of twelve his interest was accidentally aroused. While coming up through the musical life of Tin Pan Alley, New York, he found time for serious study of counterpoint and composition; and by mixing this knowledge with his fertile genius for ear-tickling rhythms and melody, he in February 1924 sprang into international renown by the performance of his *Rhapsody in Blue* at a Paul Whiteman concert in Aeolian Hall, New York. Gershwin was a prodigious worker, having created many successful songs and musical comedies, as well as the widely produced more serious operatic work *Porgy and Bess.*

Many photographs of George Gershwin, particularly publicity shots, date from his "Hollywood year" and were taken at the RKO studios. An informal one of him alone, playing the piano exuberantly at an RKO convention in June 1937, is believed to be the last one taken of the composer.

THE WORKS OF GEORGE GERSHWIN

The musical shows are listed chronologically with dates of premieres (and places, if other than New York City); lyricists and book authors are included (Arthur Francis was the pseudonym of Ira Gershwin); shows for which George Gershwin did not write the entire score are listed separately. Films listed are those for which Gershwin wrote original music; release dates and directors, as well as lyricists, are included. Dates of concert works and operas are for their first performances. Individual songs include those published without a relation to a musical show and ones interpolated into shows featuring other composers.

Musical Shows

Half Past Eight (Syracuse, New York, December 9, 1918). Lyrics by Ira Gershwin and Edward B. Perkins.

La La Lucille (May 26, 1919). Lyrics by Arthur Jackson and B. G. DeSylva; book by Fred Jackson.

Morris Gest Midnight Whirl (December 27, 1919). Lyrics and book by B. G. DeSylva and John Henry Mears.

George White's Scandals of 1920 (June 7, 1920). Lyrics by Arthur Jackson; book by Andy Rice and George White.

A Dangerous Maid (Atlantic City, March 21, 1921). Lyrics by Arthur Francis; book by Charles W. Bell.

George White's Scandals of 1921 (July 11, 1921). Lyrics by Arthur Jackson; book by Arthur Baer and George White.

George White's Scandals of 1922 (August 28, 1922). Lyrics by B. G. DeSylva, E. Ray Goetz, and Arthur Francis; book by Andy Rice, George White, and W. C. Fields.

Our Nell (December 4, 1922). Lyrics by Brian Hooker; book by Brian Hooker and A. E. Thomas; additional music by George Gershwin and William Daly.

The Rainbow Revue (London, April 3, 1923). Lyrics by Clifford Grey; book by Albert de Courville, Edgar Wallace, and Noel Scott.

George White's Scandals of 1923 (June 18, 1923). Lyrics by B. G. DeSylva, E. Ray Goetz, and Ballard MacDonald; book by George White and William K. Wells.

Sweet Little Devil (January 21, 1924). Lyrics by B. G. DeSylva; book by Frank Mandel and Laurence Schwab.

George White's Scandals of 1924 (June 30, 1924). Lyrics by B. G. DeSylva; book by George White and William K. Wells.

Primrose (London, September 11, 1924). Lyrics by Desmond Carter and Ira Gershwin; book by George Grossmith and Guy Bolton.

Lady, Be Good! (December 1, 1924). Lyrics by Ira Gershwin; book by Guy Bolton and Fred Thompson.

Tell Me More (April 13, 1925). Lyrics by B. G. DeSylva and Ira Gershwin; book by Fred Thompson and William K. Wells.

Tip-Toes (December 28, 1925). Lyrics by Ira Gershwin; book by Guy Bolton and Fred Thompson.

Song of the Flame (December 30, 1925). Lyrics and book by Oscar Hammerstein II and Otto Harbach; additional music by George Gershwin and Herbert Stothart.

Oh, Kay! (November 8, 1926). Lyrics by Ira Gershwin; book by P. G. Wodehouse and Guy Bolton.

Strike Up the Band (Long Branch, N.J., September 2, 1927). Lyrics by Ira Gershwin; book by George S. Kaufman.

Funny Face (November 22, 1927). Lyrics by Ira Gershwin; book by Fred Thompson and Paul Gerard Smith.

Rosalie (January 10, 1928). Lyrics by Ira Gershwin and P. G. Wodehouse; book by Guy Bolton and William Anthony McGuire; additional music by Sigmund Romberg.

Treasure Girl (November 8, 1928). Lyrics by Ira Gershwin; book by Fred Thompson and Vincent Lawrence.

Show Girl (July 2, 1929). Lyrics by Ira Gershwin and Gus Kahn; book by William Anthony McGuire and J. P. McEvoy.

Strike Up the Band (revised version; January 14, 1930). Lyrics by Ira Gershwin; book by George S. Kaufman and Morrie Ryskind.

Girl Crazy (October 14, 1930). Lyrics by Ira Gershwin; book by Guy Bolton and Jack McGowan.

Of Thee I Sing (December 26, 1931). Lyrics by Ira Gershwin; book by George S. Kaufman and Morrie Ryskind.

Pardon My English (January 20, 1933). Lyrics by Ira Gershwin; book by Herbert Fields.

Let 'Em Eat Cake (October 21, 1933). Lyrics by Ira Gershwin; book by George S. Kaufman and Morrie Ryskind.

The following shows had Gershwin songs (see "Individual Songs") interpolated: **The Passing Show of 1916, Hitchy-Koo of 1918, Ladies First** *(1918),* **Good Morning, Judge** *(1919),* **Lady in Red** *(1919),* **The Capitol Revue** *(1919),* **Dere Mabel** *(1920),* **Ed Wynn's Carnival** *(1920),* **The Sweetheart Shop** *(1920),* **Sinbad** *(1920),* **Broadway Brevities of 1920, Piccadilly to Broadway** *(1920),* **Blue Eyes** *(1921),* **Selwyn's Snapshots of 1921, The Perfect Fool** *(1921),* **The French Doll** *(1922),* **For Goodness Sake** *(1922),* **The Dancing Girl** *(1923),* **Little Miss Bluebeard** *(1923),* **Nifties of 1923, Americana** *(1926),* **9:15 Revue** *(1930),* **The Show Is On** *(1936).*

Films

The Sunshine Trail (Associated First National; April 1923; silent film; one theme song of same title). Lyric by Arthur Francis; directed by Thomas Ince.

Delicious (Fox; December 1931). Lyrics by Ira Gershwin; screenplay by Guy Bolton and Sonya Levien; directed by David Butler.

Shall We Dance (RKO; May 1937). Lyrics by Ira Gershwin; screenplay by Allan Scott and Ernest Pagano; directed by Mark Sandrich.

A Damsel in Distress (RKO; November 1937). Lyrics by Ira Gershwin; screenplay by P. G. Wodehouse, Ernest Pagano, and S. K. Lauren; directed by George Stevens.

The Goldwyn Follies (Samuel Goldwyn; February 1938). Lyrics by Ira Gershwin; screenplay by Ben Hecht; directed by George Marshall; additional music by Vernon Duke.

Concert Works/Operas

Lullaby (for string quartet; 1919; published in 1968).

Blue Monday ("opera à la Afro-American"; presented for one night only, August 28, 1922, in *George White's Scandals of 1922*). Libretto/lyrics by B. G. DeSylva; orchestration by Will Vodery; reorchestrated by Ferde Grofé and retitled *135th Street* (1925).

Rhapsody in Blue (for jazz band and piano; February 12, 1924; orchestration by Ferde Grofé).

Short Story (for violin and piano; February 8, 1925; arranged by Samuel Dushkin).

Concerto in F (for piano and orchestra; December 3, 1925).

Preludes for Piano (five performed on December 4, 1926; six, on January 15, 1927; three published in 1927).

An American in Paris (tone poem for orchestra; December 13, 1928).

Second Rhapsody (for orchestra with piano; January 29, 1932).

Cuban Overture (for orchestra; August 16, 1932).

Piano Transcriptions of Eighteen Songs (published in *George Gershwin's Song Book*, 1932).

Variations on I Got Rhythm (for piano and orchestra; January 14, 1934).

Porgy and Bess (folk opera in three acts; October 10, 1935). Libretto by DuBose Heyward; lyrics by Ira Gershwin and DuBose Heyward.

Suite from Porgy and Bess (for orchestra; January 21, 1936; retitled *Catfish Row* in 1958).

Individual Songs

When You Want 'Em You Can't Get 'Em, When You've Got 'Em You Don't Want 'Em (1916). Lyric by Murray Roth.

Making of a Girl (1916). Lyric by Harold Atteridge; music with Sigmund Romberg.

Rialto Ripples (for piano; 1917). Music with Will Donaldson.

You-oo, Just You (1918). Lyric by Irving Caesar.

The Real American Folk Song (Is a Rag) (1918). Lyric by Ira Gershwin.

Some Wonderful Sort of Someone (1918). Lyric by Schuyler Greene.

I Was So Young (You Were So Beautiful) (1919). Lyric by Irving Caesar and Al Bryan.

There's More to the Kiss Than the X-X-X (1919). Lyric by Irving Caesar.

O Land of Mine, America (1919). Lyric by Michael E. Rourke.

Something About Love (1918). Lyric by Lou Paley.

Swanee (1919). Lyric by Irving Caesar.

Come to the Moon (1919). Lyric by Ned Wayburn and Lou Paley.

Yan-Kee (1920). Lyric by Irving Caesar.

We're Pals (1920). Lyric by Irving Caesar.

Back Home (1920). Lyric by Arthur Francis.

I Don't Know Why (When I Dance with You) (1920). Lyric by Irving Caesar.

Oo, How I Love to Be Loved by You (1920). Lyric by Lou Paley.

Waiting for the Sun to Come Out (1920). Lyric by Arthur Francis.

Spanish Love (1920). Lyric by Irving Caesar.

Lu Lu (1920). Lyric by Arthur Jackson.

Snow Flakes (1920). Lyric by Arthur Jackson.

On the Brim of Her Old-Fashioned Bonnet (1920). Lyric by E. Ray Goetz.

The Baby Blues (1920). Lyric by E. Ray Goetz.

Futuristic Melody (1921). Lyric by E. Ray Goetz.

My Log-Cabin Home (1921). Lyric by Irving Caesar and B. G. DeSylva.

No One Else but That Girl of Mine (1921). Lyric by Irving Caesar.

Tomale (I'm Hot for You) (1921). Lyric by B. G. DeSylva.

Dixie Rose (a.k.a. **Swanee Rose**; 1921). Lyric by Irving Caesar and B. G. DeSylva.

In the Heart of a Geisha (1921). Lyric by Fred Fisher.

Wanting You (1921). Lyric by Irving Caesar.

Do It Again! (1922). Lyric by B. G. DeSylva.

Someone (1922). Lyric by Arthur Francis.

Tra-La-La (1922). Lyric by Arthur Francis.

The Yankee Doodle Blues (1922). Lyric by Irving Caesar and B. G. DeSylva.

That American Boy of Mine (1923). Lyric by Irving Caesar.

I Won't Say I Will but I Won't Say I Won't (1923). Lyric by B. G. DeSylva and Arthur Francis.

At Half Past Seven (1923). Lyric by B. G. DeSylva.

Nashville Nightingale (1923). Lyric by Irving Caesar.

That Lost Barbershop Chord (1926). Lyric by Ira Gershwin.

Toddlin' Along (1930). Lyric (revised from "The World is Mine," for *Funny Face*) by Ira Gershwin.

Mischa, Jascha, Toscha, Sascha (1922/1932). Lyric by Arthur Francis.

Till Then (1933). Lyric by Ira Gershwin.

King of Swing (1936). Lyric by Albert Stillman.

Strike Up the Band for UCLA (1936). Lyric (revised from "Strike Up the Band") by Ira Gershwin.

By Strauss (1936). Lyric by Ira Gershwin.

The above list omits songs that were written for, but not used in, the musical comedies. Unused but published songs from these shows: **The Love of a Wife** *(1919, lyric by Irving Caesar and B. G. DeSylva);* **Sunday in London Town** *(1923, lyric by Clifford Grey);* **Pepita** *(1924, lyric by B. G. DeSylva);* **Show Me the Town** *(1926, lyric by Ira Gershwin);* **Feeling Sentimental** *(1929, lyric by Ira Gershwin and Gus Kahn);* **Dance Alone with You** *(1927, lyric by Ira Gershwin, revised as "Ev'rybody Knows I Love Somebody" for* Rosalie, *1928);* **Wake Up, Brother, and Dance** *(1937, lyric by Ira Gershwin). The following songs were added to the London productions of various New York Gershwin musicals:* Lady, Be Good! *(1926)—***Something About Love** *(lyric by Lou Paley);* **I'd Rather Charleston** *(lyric by Desmond Carter);* **Buy a Little Button** *(lyric by Desmond Carter).* Tell Me More *(1925)—***Murderous Monty (and Light-Fingered Jane)** *(lyric by Desmond Carter);* **Love, I Never Knew** *(lyric by Desmond Carter);* **Have You Heard** *(lyric by Claude Hulbert).* Funny Face *(1928)—***Look at the Damn Thing Now** *(lyric by Ira Gershwin). The first film version of* Girl Crazy *(1932) added a song to the (abbreviated) Broadway score,* **You've Got What Gets Me** *(lyric by Ira Gershwin). The following songs were written for the unproduced Ziegfeld show* Ming Toy *(a.k.a.* East Is West; *1929, lyrics by Ira Gershwin):* **Sing Song Girl; Embraceable You; We Are Visitors; In the Mandarin's Orchid Garden; Yellow Blues** *(a.k.a.* **Blues in Two Keys,** *a.k.a.* **Impromptu in Two Keys,** *for piano);* **China Girl; Lady of the Moon** *(revised as "Blah, Blah, Blah" for* Delicious*);* **Under the Cinnamon Tree.**

PERMISSIONS AND PHOTO CREDITS

The following essays appear by permission.

"The Composer in the Machine Age" by George Gershwin: from *Revolt in the Arts* by Oliver M. Sayler; copyright © 1930 by Brentano's, renewed © 1958 by Oliver M. Sayler; reprinted by permission of The Putnam Publishing Group.

"A Concert of Jazz," "George Gershwin Plays His *Second Rhapsody,*" and "Exotic Richness of Negro Music" by Olin Downes; "Dramatic Values of Community Legend" by Brooks Atkinson; "Rhapsody in Catfish Row" by George Gershwin; "Words and Music" by Ira Gershwin: copyright © 1924, 1930, 1932, 1935 by The New York Times Co.; reprinted by permission.

"George Gershwin: An American Composer Who Is Writing Notable Music in the Jazz Idiom" by Carl Van Vechten: courtesy *Vanity Fair*; copyright © 1925 (renewed 1952, 1980) by The Condé Nast Publications, Inc. "Gebrüder Gershwin" by Isaac Goldberg: courtesy *Vanity Fair*; copyright © 1932 (renewed 1960, 1988) by The Condé Nast Publications, Inc.

"George Gershwin; or, A Drunken Schubert" by Beverley Nichols: originally published in *Are They the Same at Home?* (1927); reprinted by permission of the estate of Beverley Nichols.

"Troubadour" by S. N. Behrman: originally published in *The New Yorker,* May 25, 1929; copyright © 1929 by S. N. Behrman; reprinted by permission of Brandt & Brandt Literary Agents, Inc.

For the use of photos and art the following sources are gratefully acknowledged.

Archive Photos: page 125.

Billy Rose Theatre Collection, New York Public Library for the Performing Arts, Astor, Lenox, and Tilden Foundations: pages 7, 21, 35, 68 (White Studio), 76, 78 (White Studio), 86 (White Studio), 110 (Vandamm Collection), 114 (Vandamm Collection).

Division of Prints and Photographs, Library of Congress: pages ii, xiii, xv, xx (gift of Carl Van Vechten estate), 1 (gift of Carl Van Vechten estate), 53, 101, 102.

Sandy Marrone Collection: pages 3 (left), 14, 20.

Museum of the City of New York: pages 42 (DeBarron Studios, gift of Harold Friedlander), 51 (bottom right; gift of Ira Gershwin), 79 (bottom; set design by Donald Oenslager), 96, 113 (left, right).

Museum of Modern Art Film Stills Archive: pages 11 (top left), 85 (top), 93, 123, 124, 126 (bottom), 128.

Private Collection: pages iii, ix, x, xi, xii, xiv (top, bottom), xv, xvi, xvii, xix, 3 (right), 4, 5 (top, bottom), 6, 8 (top left, top right, bottom), 9, 10 (left, right), 11 (top right, bottom), 12, 13, 15 (left, right), 17, 22, 25, 29, 30, 32, 33, 36, 38, 40, 43 (top, bottom), 45, 47, 48 (top, bottom), 51 (top, bottom left), 55, 56, 59, 61, 65, 66, 71, 74 (top, bottom left, bottom right), 77, 79 (top), 82, 83, 85 (bottom), 88, 89, 91, 92, 95, 97, 99 (top, bottom), 100, 103, 104, 106, 107, 109, 116, 119, 121 (top, bottom), 126 (top), 127 (top, bottom).

Time, Inc.: page 27; copyright © 1925 Time, Inc.; reprinted by permission.

Vanity Fair: page 117; copyright © 1935 (renewed 1962, 1990) by The Condé Nast Publications, Inc.

Chappell published the music and lyrics in the song sheets illustrated on pages 126 (top), 127 (bottom).

Chappell/Harms published the music and lyrics in the song sheets illustrated on pages 15, 20, 22.

Chappell/New World Music/Harms published the music and lyric in the song sheet illustrated on page 51 (bottom left).

Leo Feist published the music and lyric in the song sheet illustrated on page 74 (bottom left).

Harms published the music and lyrics in the song sheets illustrated on pages ix, xii, xiv (top, bottom), 3 (right), 6, 8 (top right, bottom), 10 (left, right), 11 (top right, bottom), 14, 25, 30, 36, 43 (bottom).

New World Music/Harms published the music and lyrics in the song sheets illustrated on pages iii, 56, 59, 66, 71, 79 (top), 83, 85, 89, 96, 97, 99 (bottom).

Jerome H. Remick published the music and lyrics in the song sheets illustrated on pages 3 (left), 5 (top; Remick/Harms).

Brentano's published the book *Revolt in the Arts* (Oliver M. Sayler, 1930): illustration on page 82.

John Day published the book *Tin Pan Alley* (Isaac Goldberg, 1930): illustrations on pages xvii, 77.

George H. Doran published the book *Porgy* (DuBose Heyward, 1925): illustration (Grosset & Dunlap edition) on page 103.

Harms distributed the book *George Gershwin's Song Book* (and published its music and lyrics), whose cover is illustrated on page 95; the 1932 first printings were published by Random House (deluxe) and Simon and Schuster (trade); the *Piano Transcriptions* are copyright © 1932 by George Gershwin.

Alfred A. Knopf published the books *Of Thee I Sing* and *Let 'Em Eat Cake* (George S. Kaufman and Morrie Ryskind, 1932 and 1933): illustrations on pages 91, 100.

Little, Brown published the book *So This Is Jazz* (Henry O. Osgood, 1926): illustrations on pages xv, 17, 32.

Brunswick issued the record whose label is illustrated on page 33; Columbia, the labels on pages x, 43; Perfect, the label on page xvi; Victor, the labels on pages 9, 15 (left), 61, and album cover on page 116.

Associated First National released the movie whose images are illustrated on page 11 (top left, top right); Fox, the images on page 85 (top, bottom); Samuel Goldwyn, the images on pages xix, 127 (bottom); RKO, the images on pages x, 123, 124, 125, 126 (top, bottom), 127 (top).

INDEX